Healing

the Adult Children of

Narcissists

Essays on The Invisible War Zone
and Exercises for Recovery and Reflection

By Shahida Arabi, M.A.
www.shahidaarabi.com

"Do narcissistic parents ever do good in this world? Sure. They give birth to children who seek to heal the world they sought to destroy."

-Shahida Arabi

Author's Note

This book is a collection of essays and recovery exercises for the empathic adult children of narcissistic parents. It is broken down into five major parts designed to help the reader learn more about childhood narcissistic abuse and incorporate that information in practical ways for their recovery and healing journey. Be sure to bookmark this page to come back to it whenever you need to refer to a particular section.

INTRODUCTION

The **introduction** of this book provides an in-depth and extensive overview of narcissistic parents, their traits and their tactics. It also explores the effects of this type of parenting. It includes the survey results of 733 adult children of narcissists who graciously offered their stories, insights and input for the purpose of this book.

PART ONE: THE EFFECTS OF CHILDHOOD TRAUMA

Part 1 includes essays about the effects of this childhood trauma on the brain, and how children of narcissists navigate relationships in adulthood. A large focus of this section is trauma reenactment: how our early childhood wounds make us susceptible to predators in adulthood and how we can break this cycle. At the end of this section, you will also get insights from both therapists and survivors about the symptoms and aftermath of an abusive childhood.

PART TWO: LOVE AND RELATIONSHIPS

Part 2 of this collection features essays I have written about adult children of narcissists navigating love and relationships. It is clear that adult children of narcissists "love differently" in that they can struggle with a myriad of issues in relationships, including getting involved with partners very much like their parents, trust issues, and exhibiting certain attachment styles.

PART THREE: NARCISSISTIC FATHERS VS. NARCISSISTIC MOTHERS

Part 3 of this collection offers insights about the unique experiences of having a narcissistic mother and narcissistic father. It includes my popular "Daddy Issues" series which specifically focuses on daughters of narcissistic fathers, an underexplored topic in the existing literature.

PARTS FOUR AND FIVE:
- **HEALING AND RE-PARENTING THE INNER CHILD**
- **DIVERSE HEALING MODALITIES FOR ADULT CHILDREN OF NARCISSISTS**
- **PRACTICAL EXERCISES FOR RECOVERY**

Parts 4 and 5 focus on healing and re-parenting the inner child. They provide an extensive look into the specific healing modalities (both traditional and alternative) available for children of narcissists. These sections offer practical exercises for adult children of narcissists to connect with their inner child.

The practical exercises in Part 5 are designed to help with common struggles adult children of narcissists face such as people-pleasing, inner child work, grief work, overcoming self-isolation, dating after narcissistic abuse, connecting with anger, emotional regulation skills, and much more.

These chapters also discuss how to go No Contact with a toxic parent, offering communication tips for those who must maintain contact. They also expound upon the life skills we need on the recovery journey as well as the "superpowers" adult children of narcissists already possess and can tap into resourcefully to live their best lives. These traits often get used by toxic people against adult children of narcissists, yet these are the same strengths they can use to break free of toxic people and lead lives of freedom, success and peace.

Throughout the book, you will also find insights interspersed from the 733 adult children of narcissists who I surveyed, as well as some insights by therapists I surveyed. I have also included exploratory questions at the end of certain essays to help you better synthesize the major takeaways of each chapter.

While the collection as a whole is best read from beginning to end, you may use this book however you like, jumping to sections you deem most relevant to you, or reading from the very beginning. However, I do recommend ensuring that you read the introduction and leave time to read these last few chapters as they are probably some of the most important sections of this book.

It is my hope that this collection helps to inform, inspire, and empower you. Empathic adult children of narcissists have an enormous amount of strength and resilience, and so much to offer this world.

Contents

Part Three: Narcissistic Mothers and Fathers

Part Four: Healing and Re-Parenting the Inner Child

Part Five: Exercises for Adult Children of Narcissists

Introduction

Chronic feelings of emptiness and loneliness. A pervasive sense of never being quite safe, good enough, or worthy. Rarely feeling heard, understood, or validated in childhood. Neglected, abused, scapegoated, and compared unfavorably to others. Engaging in people-pleasing and negative self-talk. Overachieving or self-sabotaging to either excessively prove yourself or subconsciously prove your parent "right." Turning to destructive behaviors to fill the void. A pattern of toxic relationships, friendships or situations where you feel taken advantage of in adulthood. Self-harm, addiction and compulsive behavior. A sense of learned hopelessness for the future. If these sound familiar to you, you may have been the child of a narcissistic parent.

Adult children of narcissists grow up feeling like they don't quite belong anywhere. They internalize the belief that something is wrong with them. They seek an external "savior" to come rescue them from their intense pain. As a result, perpetrators can swoop in easily into their lives with their love-bombing, temporarily morphing into their knights in shining armor. These deep core wounds of unworthiness, of feeling defective, can lead children of narcissists to become further entangled in the web of complex trauma.

Time and time again, adult children of narcissists find themselves in situations where their traumas are reenacted – with friendships, relationships, and business partners who bear a striking resemblance to their toxic childhood caretakers. They feel held captive by constant chaos and dysfunction, self-sabotage and self-destruction throughout their adult lives, without knowing why. Many suffer a lifetime's worth of bullying which reinforces and cements the unhealthy belief systems they learned as children.

The identities of adult children of narcissists become fragmented and much of their healing journey consists of finding a way back to wholeness. It takes a great deal of inner work and healing on the level of both their bodies and their psyches to recover their "true selves" – the self which has been hidden and buried beneath the many core wounds caused by the violations of childhood.

What is Childhood Narcissistic Abuse?

Childhood abuse is one of the most devastating health issues affecting us today, yet very few acknowledge or recognize its widespread impact. Early traumas which occur at a crucial developmental stage of life have the power to shape our identities, belief systems, and life-course trajectories. Research indicates that the brains of abused children are literally rewired and that even their physical growth is stunted. The infamous studies from Romanian orphanages tell us that neglected and abandoned children demonstrate a variety of behavioral and socioemotional problems as they develop into adults (Nelson, Fox & Zeanah, 2014; Nelson, et al. 2007).

Yet it is not just physical abandonment which leaves scars; emotional wounding can also leave invisible battle wounds that last a lifetime. The Adverse Childhood Experiences Study confirms that early childhood experiences such as emotional abuse, emotional neglect, witnessing domestic violence and the mental illness of a parent are all associated with a wide range of psychological and chronic health problems throughout a person's lifespan – including placing victims at high risk for suicidal ideation (Felitti et al., 1998).

The effects of verbal abuse cannot be underestimated; Dr. Martin Teicher (2006) has pointed out the growing evidence that verbal abuse in childhood can also shape the brain, increasing the risk for anxiety, suicidal ideation, and dissociative symptoms in adulthood. Studies have confirmed that parental verbal aggression has an impact on key areas of the brain related to learning, memory, decision-making and emotional regulation (Choi et al., 2009; Teicher, 2003).

As trauma expert Bessel van Der Kolk, author of *The Body Keeps the Score* notes, childhood trauma rewires the brain for fear. Childhood trauma can affect our impulse control, increase our likelihood of substance abuse, heighten our hypervigilance, and destroy our self-esteem (Bremner, 2006; Shin et al., 2006).

Childhood abuse is *lethal*, yet it is overlooked and minimized.

All forms of abuse are horrific, including psychological and emotional abuse. Narcissistic abuse is a form of psychological abuse inflicted by a parent who meets the criteria for Narcissistic Personality Disorder (NPD) or has strong narcissistic traits. These traits disable narcissistic parents from seeing their children as anything other than extensions of themselves. Parents who are narcissistic lack the core empathy which would enable them to be caring and compassionate caretakers and to meet the emotional needs of their children.

Some adult children of narcissists had a parent who also had antisocial tendencies. These tendencies can include a complete lack of remorse, pathological deception, and in some cases, criminal activity.

What Is Narcissistic Personality Disorder?

The Diagnostic and Statistical Manual of Mental Disorders defines a narcissist as someone who has a pervasive pattern of grandiosity (in fantasy or behavior), an excessive need for admiration, and lack of empathy. This is indicated by five (or more) of the following:

- Has a grandiose sense of self-importance (e.g., exaggerates achievements and talents, expects to be recognized as superior without commensurate achievements).
- Is preoccupied with fantasies of unlimited success, power, brilliance, beauty, or ideal love.
- Believes that he or she is "special" and unique and can only be understood by, or should associate with, other special or high-status people (or institutions).
- Requires excessive admiration.
- Has a sense of entitlement (i.e., unreasonable expectations of especially favorable treatment or automatic compliance with his or her expectations).
- Is interpersonally exploitative (i.e., takes advantage of others to achieve his or her own ends).
- Lacks empathy: is unwilling to recognize or identify with the feelings and needs of others.
- Is often envious of others or believes that others are envious of him or her.
- Shows arrogant, haughty behaviors or attitudes.

If you have a parent with Antisocial Personality Disorder, this is someone who has usually engaged in some form of criminal activity, fraud, or emotional con artistry.

Someone with Antisocial Personality Disorder would display the following characteristics:

- Failure to conform to social norms.
- Failure to obey laws by engaging in behavior which results in criminal arrest or would warrant criminal arrest.
- A pattern of disregard and violation for the rights of others.
- Lying, deception, and manipulation, for profit or personal pleasure.
- Impulsive behavior.
- Irritability and aggression, usually shown by instigating fights with others.

- A blatant and reckless disregard for the safety of self and others.
- A pattern of irresponsibility.
- A lack of remorse for actions.

According to Dr. Robert Hare's psychopathy checklist, psychopaths also exhibit the following traits:

- Glibness and superficial charm.
- Pathological lying.
- Parasitic lifestyle.
- Cunning and manipulative.
- Impulsivity.
- Callousness and lack of empathy.
- Shallow emotions.
- Need for stimulation.
- Shallow affect.
- Irresponsibility.
- Failure to take responsibility for their behavior.
- Lack of realistic long-term goals.
- Sexual promiscuity.
- Prone to boredom.
- Early behavioral problems or juvenile delinquency.
- A number of short-term, marital relationships.
- Criminal versatility.
- Grandiose sense of self.

Narcissistic or Antisocial Parent? The Spectrum of Narcissism

Under the umbrella term of ASPD are the more colloquially termed "sociopaths" and "psychopaths." While there is much overlap between the two, sociopaths are considered to be "made" by their environment while psychopaths are said to be born with no conscience. There are also those who meet the criteria of the Dark Tetrad. They possess characteristics such as narcissism, sadism, psychopathy, and Machiavellianism (Međedović & Petrovic, 2015). These individuals are far more amoral than your garden-variety pathological narcissist, and their abuse is inflicted with sadistic pleasure. Then, there are what psychiatrist Dr. Otto Kernbeg (1984) has coined as "malignant narcissists." Malignant narcissists have traits comprised of narcissism, antisocial tendencies, aggression, sadism, *and* paranoia – quite the dangerous mix!

There are actual brain differences between empathic individuals and narcissists on the higher end of the spectrum. Research has uncovered that there are structural abnormalities related to compassion and empathy in the brains of narcissistic individuals. While narcissists have deficiencies in empathy, psychopaths demonstrate brain abnormalities when it comes to empathy *and* in the processing of pro-social emotions such as guilt and moral reasoning (Schulze et al., 2013; Sethi et al., 2015).

However, it's important to realize that these brain abnormalities do not take away the accountability of abusive narcissists or sociopaths. These individuals are not in a state of psychosis; they can intellectually distinguish between right and wrong. As studies have shown, they still have cognitive empathy, which allows them to assess and target the vulnerabilities of their victims (Wai & Tiliopoulos, 2012). They just lack the affective empathy which would enable them to care about the harm they cause.

While these labels are fascinating, it's important to remember that they all fall under the spectrum of narcissism. For the purpose of simplicity, we must recognize that chronically abusive parents fall on the higher end of the spectrum. The more extreme of a narcissist someone is, the more likely he or she will inflict harm on their targets with a lack of remorse and empathy. No parent is perfect, but narcissistic parents go beyond garden-variety imperfection; they step over into the realm of pathological self-interest and entitlement. Some narcissistic parents lack not only empathy but also a conscience if they possess these antisocial traits, making them all the more dangerous, unpredictable, sadistic, volatile, and potentially violent.

Since these are such hardwired behaviors, narcissistic parents rarely see the error of their ways. They are not motivated to change their behaviors, and these behaviors are what make them irreparably toxic. You will not benefit from explaining to them why their behavior is toxic – nor will you be able to appeal to their empathy because they *have no empathy to appeal to*. Many narcissists on the higher end of the spectrum do not have the capacity or the willingness to change.

The Traits of Narcissistic Parents

For this book, I surveyed 733 adult children of narcissistic parents who had eerily similar experiences across the board. The family structures of these adult children ranged from having a primary narcissist in the family to the whole family unit being narcissistic. 36% of these adult children had only a narcissistic mother, 22% had only a narcissistic father, 14% had both parents who were narcissists, 17% reported having a situation where one parent was a narcissist, and the other parent had a different disorder. Finally, 11% of those surveyed had a whole family comprised of narcissists, including siblings.

The survey results confirmed what we already know to be true: these types of toxic parents have a long-lasting, destructive effect on the lives and well-being of their children.

A narcissistic parent usually displays the following traits:

LACK OF EMPATHY

86% of adult children of narcissists surveyed had a parent who showed a lack of empathy.

Empathy is the ability to understand someone else's point of view, thoughts, and feelings. Narcissistic parents are unable and unwilling to empathize with their children. They discount and invalidate the emotions of their children. This leads their children to feel as if their pain is unseen and unheard. Extreme emotional invalidation in childhood such as this can even lead to the development of disorders such as Borderline Personality Disorder. Highly empathic people can see someone else in pain and feel this pain themselves, which often causes them to be restrained in the pain they inflict on others. Empathic individuals are conscientious about how they make others feel.

Empathy-deficient people, on the other hand, show a callous disregard for the pain of others. They are far less concerned about the harm they may cause and do not feel as much guilt when they inflict pain. The toxic mother who perpetually scolds her daughter for crying over the insults she doles out teaches her to be numb to verbal assaults in adulthood. The narcissistic father who tells his son to "man up" after violently beating him makes him believe that his pain does not matter – that abuse has to be tolerated in order to prove one's masculinity. A lack of empathy allows the narcissistic parent to inflict more and more violence without constraint. There is nothing to hold the abusive parent back from lashing out verbally, sexually violating the child, or physically injuring him or her. When one cannot take another's perspective, one feels "free" to violate the basic rights and needs of others without as many emotional consequences.

SELF-CENTEREDNESS.

84% of adult children of narcissists surveyed had a parent who exhibited self-centeredness.

In the early years of life, children depend on their parents for emotional and physical nourishment. Narcissistic parents who are overly preoccupied with themselves or self-centered show little to no regard for the welfare of their children. Even if they provide physically for their children, they emotionally abandon them and their needs. Self-centered individuals believe the world revolves around them, their needs, their belief systems, and *their* desires. Narcissists are pathologically self-centered – they go beyond normal self-absorption. They are genuinely not interested in the lives or the desires of their children.

Children of self-centered narcissists are not asked about themselves, their days, their inner world – and if they are, it is usually done for an agenda or in a shallow way. As a result, children of narcissists often feel emotionally starved, ignored, neglected and they may seek out attention in other ways by engaging in self-destructive behavior or by using various addictions to fill the void. Adult children of narcissists often develop a sense of perceived burdensomeness, feeling as if they are "burdens" to anyone they enter into a relationship or friendship with. They may hesitate to ask for help or to ask to have their needs met from others. This is because their toxic parent taught them that they were not important enough to be considered, treating them like hindrances any time they dared to speak about their needs or concerns.

EXCESSIVE SENSE OF ENTITLEMENT.

76% of adult children of narcissists surveyed had a parent who showed an excessive sense of entitlement.

Those who have an excessive sense of entitlement believe that the world, and the people in it, owe them something. Narcissistic parents feel entitled to special treatment they have not earned, and they expect complete obedience from their children. It is not uncommon, for example, for a narcissistic parent to expect for their adult children to continue to obey them even as adults, to marry and have children on *their*timetable, or to feel entitled to their hard-earned money. They demand the compliance, the time, the energy and the efforts of the very children they abuse. In some cases, narcissistic parents can pass on their sense of entitlement to the "golden child," children who they dote upon and overvalue. They may teach these children to believe that they are entitled to everything even if it comes at the expense of violating the rights of others. However, their empathic, scapegoated children may not develop this same sense of entitlement. These children fall on the other end of the spectrum – their sense of entitlement is severely skewed towards self-deprivation. Empathic adult children of narcissists lack a sense of "deservingness," causing them to believe they are not owed anything – not even basic respect or decency.

CHRONIC AND EXCESSIVE RAGE IN RESPONSE TO PERCEIVED CRITICISM OR SLIGHTS.

74% of adult children of narcissists surveyed had a parent who showed chronic and excessive rage in response to perceived criticism or slights.

+

HOSTILITY TOWARDS OTHERS

70% of adult children of narcissists surveyed had a parent who showed hostility toward anyone who threatened their entitlement in any way.

Narcissists are prone to what is known as "narcissistic injury" and subsequent rage when they feel slighted in any way. When narcissistic parents feel that their children are not complying with their wishes, they serve their demands and pressure with an extra heaping of shaming and hostility. They react with extreme animosity when their adult children finally establish their independence, stand up to them, or show disagreement or disobedience in any way. Lashing out brutally, sometimes even violently, conditions their children to walk on eggshells around their abusive parents and to silence their own needs. Narcissistic parents perceive any threat to their sense of entitlement and superiority as an attack – and they must punish the offenders, each and every time.

In the stories of adult children of narcissists, it's very common to find accounts of rage attacks and of unpredictable, emotionally volatile behavior. Being on the receiving end of such unpredictable attacks leads adult children of narcissists to minimize or rationalize horrific acts of psychological violence in adulthood. Since rage as a reaction to boundaries is normalized in childhood, children of narcissists have a difficult time maintaining boundaries or handling conflict in adulthood. They may actively try to avoid conflict by attempting to please those they suspect to be toxic. They might avoid standing up for themselves because they are so accustomed to being punished for doing so.

HAUGHTY, CONDESCENDING ATTITUDE.

69% of adult children of narcissists surveyed had a parent who had a haughty and condescending attitude.

Narcissistic parents look down on their children and treat their children with contempt. They may infantilize them, put their abilities down repeatedly, sarcastically invalidate their emotions and make light of their pain. Children of narcissists can internalize the contempt of their parents as evidence of their own inferiority. They may develop low feelings of self-worth and an unstable self-image. The lack of respect they are given as children can also condition them to become desensitized to or highly sensitive to verbal abuse when they become adults. Adult children of narcissists might overlook verbal abuse while navigating friendships and relationships or be highly sensitive and reactive to anything that feels like bullying behavior.

GRANDIOSE SENSE OF SUPERIORITY.

69% of adult children of narcissists surveyed had a parent who had a grandiose sense of superiority.

Narcissistic parents believe they are God. This superiority complex enables them to wield their power and control over their children, causing fear rather than genuine respect. Grandiose fantasies of unlimited fame, wealth, status, and power are not uncommon among narcissistic parents, and in extreme cases, some narcissists do in fact create large followings.

Infamous cult leader Jim Jones[1] convinced 900 of his followers in Jonestown to participate in mass-murder suicide. Although Jim Jones was the head of his own ministry, the Peoples Temple, his aims were less spiritual and far more superficial. His position of authority in any community was always more about power, grandiosity, and control. For a recent ABC interview, Jones' biological son, Stephan, speaks about the experience of having Jones as a father.

He says, "Dad, like any good demagogue, would conjure up fear…what I'm hearing in the audience is all the gloom and doom: the pending nuclear war. 'We're all going to be ushered into, or put into, concentration camps if we're not exterminated some other way. There are racists around every corner that want to take us out.' The immediate community that we were in, in Redwood Valley, they all hated us, as far as my father was concerned. His message was incredibly violent as time went on. And it was erratic. If we weren't having an open meeting where he was trying to bring in new members, we were having closed meetings where he was trying to control the members."

Isolation, fear-mongering, and a narcissistic personality make for a dangerous mix. Narcissistic parents can create miniature "cults" and harems out of their families, instilling in them rigid belief systems and a "us versus them" mentality. Creating this atmosphere of fearing "the other," whoever that may be, keeps the family unit insulated from outside influences which would threaten to take away the narcissistic parent's power and control.

CONSTANT NEED FOR ATTENTION – LOVES TO BE THE CENTER OF ATTENTION

70% of adult children of narcissists surveyed had a parent who had a constant need for attention.

Narcissistic parents require that they be the center of attention at all times. They perceive anything that takes the attention off of them as a threat. It's not uncommon for narcissistic parents to compete with their own children. If they feel "upstaged" in any way, they will retaliate against their innocent children.

As Maggie, a survivor from Maryland tells me, "I remember feeling like my mom competed against me for my father's attention when I was a teenager. I also felt like when my mother and I fought that it was like fighting with a sibling." Another survivor, Linda, writes, "She is unsatisfiable, she craves attention, approval and admiration. She boasts all the time. She ignores, downplays or denies my accomplishments."

Cealie, a survivor from New York, writes vividly about the moment in her childhood when she realized something was terribly wrong with her mother. "The shopkeeper said to my mom, "What a beautiful little girl! She has your eyes." So, I was thrilled, thinking that maybe my mom would like that. I looked at her, and she was scowling like a beast! The man actually made a shocked groan when he saw my mother's face. I am grateful for that because even though I didn't understand it completely, I knew there was something wrong with how my mother treated me there. As crushed as I was, I understood that there was something wrong with her."

VANITY AND SELF-ABSORPTION

67% of adult children of narcissists surveyed had a parent who was vain and self-absorbed.

When parents focus outwardly on external appearances at the expense of modeling a healthy self-image and self-esteem, it teaches their children that they, too, are objects and should seek validation from the outside world. The daughter who witnesses her narcissistic mother constantly primping in front of the mirror rather than spending time with her may learn to rely on her looks as a source of attention and approval. A narcissistic mother may even go so far as to compare her looks to her daughter's, teaching her daughter to compete with other women in adulthood. Her daughter is then taught that she is an object to be "seen" rather than heard. As a result, she may develop an excessive focus on her own appearance, body image, and weight. The narcissistic father who spends hours each day at the gym teaches his son to associate hypermasculinity with strength and force, of "looking" a certain way rather than acting in an honorable manner.

SUPERFICIAL AND GLIB CHARM.

64% of adult children of narcissists surveyed had a parent who had superficial and glib charm.

Narcissistic parents know how to turn on the charm if they believe it will get them what they want. Their false image and persona are quite different from their true, callous selves. They can maintain these personas for quite some time. For example, sociopathic CEO Elizabeth Holmes defrauded investors out of billions of dollars for a famous blood-testing startup, Theranos, whose technology delivered none of what it promised. She was able to cultivate relationships with some of the world's wealthiest and influential people using her charisma and charm, leading some investors to hand over millions of dollars to a company that placed the health of others at stake.

A narcissistic parent may commit emotional fraud rather than engage in financial schemes, but they use their charm to gain approval from the outside world nonetheless, and to build relationships with those they deem "unique and special" to benefit them. They can use their charisma to fool the public. When they appear to be the perfect doting parents to society, their children suffer the invalidation and pain of being terrorized behind closed doors, feeling as if no one would believe them.

SUPERFICIAL FRIENDSHIPS AND RELATIONSHIPS

63% of adult children of narcissists surveyed had a parent who had superficial friendships and relationships.

Since narcissistic parents operate in the world with their "false self" rather than their true self, they make a habit of showboating to gain praise from their local communities. To them, it is all about appearances and social status rather than genuine fulfillment. It's not uncommon for dysfunctional families with a primary narcissist to have an "enabler" parent or "helper," someone who looks the other way, excuses the narcissist's horrific and abusive behavior or even helps with carrying out the abuse due to the pathological need to maintain a public image.

As one survivor from Wisconsin, Anastasia, writes, "My father would not take active measures to protect me from the psychological abuse of my mother. At one point, I was forcibly hospitalized in a mental institution. My father was a prominent businessman, and he told me in later years that he could not have had my mother arrested, or committed, or treated for her alcohol abuse and physical abuse of me, because it would have reflected poorly in "the public eye." She once beat me until I had a concussion and contusions on my face; he would not take me to the hospital for treatment, because of his desire to protect her. Or because he was terrified of her. Which is crazy, because my father was this very large man, and a business mogul." The harmful effects of narcissistic parenting can be exacerbated by other family members who participate in the bullying or who look the other way in the interest of maintaining a certain reputation.

These superficial and shallow friendships are doubly dangerous not only because they place the onus on children to behave a certain way in public but also because the children of narcissistic parents are forced to serve the parent's emotional needs since other people cannot fill these needs. The narcissistic mother may "enmesh" herself with her children and micromanage their lives because she has no authentic social life of her own aside from these superficial alliances. The narcissistic father may demand that his children provide for his egotistical needs and provide an adoring audience.

SHALLOW, FLEETING EMOTIONS

58% of adult children of narcissists surveyed had a parent who exhibited shallow, fleeting emotions.

Rage, envy, and contempt: these are the emotions narcissistic individuals feel strongly. Otherwise, emotions are quite surface-level and fleeting for them. While narcissistic parents can lash out in unprecedented fury and humiliate their children with an astounding level of emotion, they can rarely show love or affection towards their children with the same level of commitment. Many adult children of narcissists describe their parents as being "emotionally cold," unable to provide them with or convey any kind of depth or warmth in their communication. This lack of healthy modeling of emotions can lead adult children of narcissists to feel a chronic sense of emptiness; rather than the nurturing of their parents, they were shown a superficial display of emotions which neither comforted or validated them. In adulthood, children of narcissists may flee from their own emotions or have difficulty connecting with them. Adult children of narcissists may also gravitate towards emotionally unavailable partners and friends who are emotionally cold like their parents.

EXPLOITING OTHERS FOR THEIR OWN GAIN

59% of adult children of narcissists surveyed had a parent who exploited others for their own gain.

Narcissistic parents who actively exploit others do so without considering the emotions or rights of others. They may exploit their children to gain financial resources, social status and approval from others, use their children for excessive domestic labor or even exploit their children to gain sympathy and emotional gratification from others. They may even go so far as to injure their children to garner sympathy from others as the concerned, caretaking and doting parent.

Survivor Cealie writes regarding her narcissistic mother, "She pushed me down the stairs when I was a toddler, but I don't think it was to kill me. I think she wanted to swoop down the stairs and act all concerned and tragic. She grabbed me up and started wiping my face with a washcloth, and to this day I wonder why she thought that was going to save me from any damage I sustained in the fall. I was fine and was trying to wriggle away from her. The whole thing has always puzzled me."

In the horrifying case of Gypsy Blanchard, her mother faked Gypsy's illnesses and made her believe she had to be wheelchair-bound even though she could walk. She made Gypsy depend on her and abused her violently behind closed doors. It was only after Gypsy murdered her mother after years of chronic abuse, deception, and exploitation, that the truth about Gypsy being healthy came out.

Although Gypsy's mother likely had Munchausen by Proxy, the issues of narcissistic entitlement and exploitation still come into play. Experts claim that those with tendencies like Gypsy's mother are fully aware of what they're doing, even if they deny it when presented with evidence. They just believe their needs are above the needs of others. MBP expert Louisa Lasher says, "They're using the child as an object to get a need met—whether it's getting attention in general, or jealousy or revenge."

This type of exploitation is not unlike the way a narcissist exploits their children. Rather than just making them physically ill, however, they can cause dependency in their children in other ways such as financially or emotionally and use their children as objects in other nefarious affairs or scams.

A number of the adult children of narcissists surveyed also had parents with certain antisocial traits like the following:

PATHOLOGICAL LYING AND DECEIT

56% of adult children of narcissists surveyed had a parent who engaged in pathological lying and deceit.

Antisocial parents have a track record of pathological lying and deception. In the infamous case of Mary Jo Buttafuoco, her sociopathic husband was able to hide his chronic deception and affair even after his mistress decided to physically show up on Mary's doorstep and shoot her in the head.

Mary thankfully survived, and as she writes in her book, *Getting It Through My Thick Skull: Why I Stayed, What I Learned, And What Millions of People Involved With Sociopaths Need to Know*, her sociopathic husband was quite skilled in lying. She writes:

"To the rest of the world, it might have looked obvious, but no one close to us believed for a minute that Joe had had an affair with her. His denials were extremely convincing; his arguments completely justifiable...Joey was absolutely hysterical in his denials. It was a very persuasive portrayal of a wrongly accused man. "Show me a statement! Play me a tape where I said that! They won't because they don't have one! They are making this up."

One of the most prominent and telling traits of many sociopaths is their fantastic ability to manipulate others and lie for profit, to avoid punishment, or seemingly just for fun. As someone who faced a firestorm of public anger, disapproval, and just plain incomprehension over the years from those who asked, "How could she stay with him after that?" all I can say is that if you haven't ever been under a sociopath's spell, be grateful. They can charm the birds out of the trees and tell you black is white, and have you believing it."

CALLOUSNESS AND SADISM

45% of adult children of narcissists surveyed had a parent who exhibited callousness and sadism.

There is a cold indifference with which narcissists operate in the world. They do not view others around them as human beings. Narcissistic parents are cruel and insensitive to the plight of their children, ignoring them in times of distress. Narcissists with antisocial traits are often sadistic: they enjoy seeing others in pain and use the most intimate details of their loved ones against them to hurt and taunt them. While empathic humans rush to the aid of those they perceive to be hurting, narcissistic and sociopathic individuals abandon their loved ones in times of great need. Their level of callousness is startling and inhumane.

Survivor Leslie from Australia, who has encountered narcissists not only in her family of origin but also her friendships and relationships, describes to me the callous attitude of the narcissists in her life during a life-threatening illness. She says, "After my second brother's suicide last year, I was quite a mess, and that's when narcissists have their most fun and I witnessed it. The interesting thing was the narcissist's abusive actions happened right around the time the death of my other brother, Brad. I now have rheumatoid arthritis and factor V Leiden blood clotting disorder which makes you more prone to getting blood clots - that's when I learned how much my partner John cared about me. *He could not have cared less - the same as my family of origin. I was told I could die from it.* My children came in to visit me but not my mother or siblings. I had a tough time seeing the very things that I was in denial about."

IMPULSIVITY AND IRRESPONSIBILITY.

43% of adult children of narcissists surveyed had a parent who was impulsive and irresponsible.

The inability to keep up with day to day responsibilities is a trademark of sociopaths. They live impulsively moment to moment, never thinking or caring about the consequences of their actions. It's not uncommon for a sociopath to move from city to city to escape accountability for their heinous crimes, or to hide an enormous amount of debt from their spouses and children, and to live parasitic lifestyles leeching off of others. Their impulsivity and irresponsibility can be dangerous, placing the lives of their children at risk. As survivor Bambi recalls, "My father was a self-indulgent Peter Pan type living close to danger his entire adult life. He hid money and assets, forgot about me when he was lost in the desert for 10 days, then expected me to care for him when he became disabled from diabetes."

LEADING DOUBLE LIVES.

36% of adult children of narcissists surveyed had a parent who led double lives.

+

INFIDELITY AND NUMEROUS AFFAIRS.

32% of adult children of narcissists surveyed had a parent who engaged in infidelity and had numerous affairs.

Those with antisocial traits are notorious for leading double lives and infidelity. It's not uncommon for sociopathic parents to be duplicitous to the extent of carrying on long-term affairs, having secret addictions, having other children in different states, or committing criminal acts like fraud or even physical violence.

One terrifying example is that of Emile Cilliers who attempted to murder his wife *twice* – first by causing a gas leak which also endangered the lives of his two children, then by tampering with her parachute before a skydive. Although his wife miraculously survived the 4,000 feet fall, what the police discovered about her husband's double life was nothing short of appalling. They uncovered 30,000 texts which detailed his ongoing deception. He had been having numerous affairs, including one with a girlfriend he planned to start a new life with after his wife's death. He was also having unprotected sex with prostitutes.

Due to their ability to lie without remorse, sociopaths can keep these double lives under wraps for quite some time before they are exposed. This type of exposure can threaten to dismantle the false image of the "perfect family" and have long-term consequences on all family members involved.

DANGEROUS RISK-TAKING, CONSTANT NEED FOR STIMULATION, PRONE TO BOREDOM.

21% of adult children of narcissists surveyed had a parent who exhibited dangerous risk-taking, a constant need for stimulation and a propensity for boredom.

Psychopathic parents are prone to boredom and have a need for constant stimulation. Like Emile Cilliers who had unprotected sex with prostitutes, thereby risking the health of his wife, they will jump from affair to affair with a callous disregard for anyone else's feelings or wellbeing. This constant need for stimulation can lead them to engage in dangerous activities that place their own welfare as well as the welfare of others at risk.

SEXUAL DEVIANCE AND SADISM.

18% of adult children of narcissists surveyed had a parent or narcissistic family member who exhibited sexual deviance and sadism.

Narcissists, sociopaths, and psychopaths are notorious for trespassing the boundaries of others – this can sometimes include sexual boundaries. Those who exhibit sexual deviance and sadism can engage in pedophilia, voyeurism, child sexual exploitation rings, rape, assault, or even the enabling of other sexual predators.

Survivor Kim described to me the horrific way her mother enabled her grandfather's predatory behavior: "When I was a young child and she was bathing me in the tub, I told her my grandfather was molesting me. She held me underwater by the throat and nearly drowned me in order to shut me up. I did not remember anything until I was 36 years old." This level of violence to silence a young child, especially a child victimized by sexual violence, is nothing short of sadistic and appalling.

Another survivor, Isabella from California, writes that her mother was able to overlook the molestation of her children to stay married to her second husband, who was a sociopath. Her mother even went as far as to do couples therapy with him.

In these harrowing stories, we see how narcissistic enablers not only look the other way, they help to perpetuate the violence of sociopathic sexual predators in the family. Dysfunctional family units thrive in secrecy, enabling, and the exploitation of their children. They uphold the sexual sadism and deviance of the perpetrators, and further gaslight, silence and shame the innocent victims of these atrocities.

PROPENSITY FOR VIOLENCE.

36% of adult children of narcissists surveyed had a parent who exhibited a propensity for violence.

Although not all narcissists are violent, escalation to violent acts given what the narcissist deems the "right" circumstances is not uncommon. Psychopathic husbands Chris Watts and Scott Peterson both murdered their wives and their unborn children. Chris Watts killed his two living children in addition to his unborn child and buried them in oil wells without any signs of remorse, even going so far as to initially blaming his wife for the murders before confessing. Both men had mistresses lined up to start new lives with and believed they would get away with these murders. Other psychopathic individuals can also recruit their family members to help them with their violent sprees. Psychopathic mother Sante Kimes enlisted the help of her son to commit mortgage fraud and to later kill the co-worker who threatened to expose them. They killed a total of three people together.

Abusive Tactics Used by Narcissistic Parents

The children of narcissistic parents often bear witness to and are on the receiving end of the following abusive behaviors, which we'll be discussing more in-depth later in this book:

EMOTIONAL NEGLECT. A staggering 91% of adult children of narcissists experienced emotional neglect.

Narcissistic parents refuse to validate your emotions, rarely comfort you when you're upset, fail to follow up with questions about your life, schoolwork, or any other issues you may be struggling with. They do not provide a safe or secure base for the child to come to them for help in times of distress or need. Childhood emotional neglect like this teaches children that their feelings don't matter and burdens them with a sense of invisibility, low self-worth and attachment issues in adulthood.

GASLIGHTING. An overwhelming 81% of adult children of narcissists had experienced gaslighting by their narcissistic parent.

Narcissistic parents deny the abuse ever happened, causing you to question your reality and sanity. This is known as gaslighting[2]. They might minimize the harm they've done when you call them out, pretend they did not say or do something that was abusive, or even call into question your mental health if you dare to set boundaries or speak out against their mistreatment. Chronic gaslighting in childhood leads to perpetual self-doubt in adulthood. Children of narcissists are not given the emotional tools to validate their perceptions or experiences; instead, they are taught to silence their inner voice. This can make them highly vulnerable to being gaslighted and invalidated by predators in relationships, friendships, and the workplace as adults. When we do not trust our own instincts, we are far more likely to subscribe to an abuser's falsehoods.

STONEWALLING AND THE SILENT TREATMENT. 73% of adult children of narcissists experienced stonewalling and the silent treatment.

Stonewalling is when a person withdraws from a conversation or discussion and refuses to address your concerns. The person may choose to outright ignore your requests, respond with dismissive, invalidating replies or evade responding appropriately altogether by giving vague responses that refuse to answer your original questions. Narcissistic parents shut down conversations before they begin and refuse to answer your questions or pleas to discuss their behavior.

Narcissistic parents may also give you the silent treatment when they perceive you've "disobeyed" them or threatened their sense of entitlement in some way. The silent treatment is a form of social rejection which has an actual impact on the brain; it activates the same part of the brain which detects physical injury. Being ignored like this can be painful – literally.

Licensed mental health counselor Richard Zwolinski (2014) asserts that this tactic is a favorite of narcissists. He says, "The silent treatment is an abusive method of control, punishment, avoidance, or disempowerment (sometimes these four types overlap, sometimes not) that is a favorite tactic of narcissists, and especially those who have a hard time with impulse control, that is, those with more infantile tendencies. The silent treatment can be used as an abusive tactic that is the adult narcissist's version of a child's "holding my breath until you give in and give me what I want."

As Vicky, a survivor, describes, "My mom was the queen of the silent treatment. If we had a disagreement, she wouldn't talk to me for days - and then suddenly, one day she would talk to me again as if nothing happened. It was so confusing."

COVERT PUT-DOWNS. 84% of adult children of narcissists had experienced covert put-downs.

Narcissistic parents often make cruel remarks in a backhanded or underhanded manner to diminish you. This is what I call the "insult with a smile." They use these covert put-downs to belittle you without taking accountability for their behavior. This form of verbal abuse instills harmful negative belief systems about the "self." For example, a narcissistic mother may have a habit of scrutinizing her daughter's clothing choices by saying, "You're wearing *that*? Well, you sure have creative taste," in a mocking voice. A narcissistic father may humiliate his son at a family event by sarcastically saying, "John's never been the athletic type. He likes to play with his *books*." It's not uncommon for narcissistic parents to mock and provoke their children with these comments in public, claiming they are just "teasing." This allows them to recruit other toxic members of the family or their community to join in collectively to rejoice in the child's humiliation.

Due to the cruel feedback of their caregivers, adult children of narcissists internalize false messages about themselves, and are unable to place the blame where it belongs due to how covert and insidious this method is. Instead, they often blame themselves, believing there must be something flawed within them to "provoke" these veiled insults. Covert put-downs cause adult children of narcissists to carry within them an overarching lack of faith in their abilities, talents, potential, and worthiness.

VERBAL ABUSE. 78% of adult children of narcissists experienced verbal abuse.

Verbal abuse includes overt put-downs, name-calling, and cruel insults regarding your appearance, personality, lifestyle choices, passions – anything and everything is fair game. The narcissistic parent is prone to instilling a sense of worthlessness and helplessness early on so that the child suffers from lifelong struggles with their self-image and self-esteem. As Dr. Susan Forward notes in her book, *Toxic Parents: Overcoming Their Legacy and Reclaiming Your Life*, "Most parents will occasionally say something derogatory to their children. This is not necessarily verbal abuse. But it is abusive to launch frequent verbal attacks on a child's appearance, intelligence, competence, or value as a human being." Verbal abuse causes the child to suffer from a lifelong Inner Critic which criticizes them no matter what they achieve; this becomes an internalized inner voice which continues the abuse, long after childhood.

MALIGNANT PROJECTIONS. 70% had experienced malignant projections from their narcissistic parent.

Narcissistic parents are prone to projecting their negative qualities, traits and behaviors onto you, all while avoiding accountability or responsibility for their own toxic behaviors. They may even call *you* selfish, abusive or full of yourself, even when these qualities better describe them. Malignant projections like these have the effect of creating chronic uncertainty in the victims of narcissists. Childhood abuse survivors may always question themselves and struggle with their sense of identity. The accusations of being selfish, narcissistic, or self-centered cause adult children of narcissists to fear setting boundaries with others. Since narcissistic parents condition their children to associate any form of healthy boundary-setting with punishment and projection, their children grow up believing that standing up for themselves is an inherently selfish act.

SABOTAGE AND PATHOLOGICAL ENVY. 73% had experienced sabotage and pathological envy.

Narcissistic parents attempt to sabotage your relationships, friendships, and career aspirations whether as a child or an adult. This can stem from pathological envy. Narcissistic mothers, for example, can put down the appearance of their youthful daughters out of jealousy and a warped sense of competition. Isolating the child from their true self, their social networks, and their dreams, has the effect of exerting the maximum amount of control over the child. It also instills in the adult child of a narcissist an intense fear of success and achievement, lest that achievement is taken away like it was in childhood.

HOT-AND-COLD BEHAVIOR (LOVE-BOMBING AND PUNISHMENT). 70% of adult children of narcissists had been on the receiving end of hot and cold behavior, such as love-bombing one moment, with punishment the next.

Narcissistic parents may pay excessive attention to you when they need something, only to rage or neglect you when they don't or when *you* refuse to be "obedient" to their demands. It is common for toxic parents to love-bomb and hoover their children when their children attempt to practice boundaries (especially as adults), and to devalue their children whenever they do not need anything from them. Since this type of love is rarely consistent, children of narcissists learn to associate unpredictable danger with intimacy and "chemistry" when they become adults. They crave the highs of excessive attention because it represents the only form of positive regard they received in childhood, but they learn to tolerate the harsh blows of hypercriticism, demeaning assaults, and rage attacks which inevitably come with any abuse cycle. This twisted form of love is what they internalize as the "norm."

RAGE ATTACKS AND OTHER FORMS OF EMOTIONAL ABUSE. 85% had experienced rage attacks and other forms of emotional abuse such as ignoring, contempt and insults disguised as jokes.

If you fail to obey a narcissistic parent's unjust demands, question their entitlement or sense of superiority in any way, you are subjected to rage attacks meant to control you and keep you in line. It's no wonder that many adult children of narcissists develop fawning and people-pleasing tendencies. They've been trained by the very real threat of physical or psychological violence to obey. Other forms of emotional abuse such as showing contempt for the child and ignoring the child creates an overwhelming sense of toxic shame. Children of narcissists who are habitually ignored learn to ignore their own needs as adults as they cater to others and walk on eggshells. The adult daughter of a narcissist may learn to placate angry men as a result of her father's abusive outbursts. The adult son of a narcissistic mother may find himself in relationships with emotionally volatile women.

MICROMANAGING. 62% of adult children of narcissists experienced micromanaging.

Narcissistic parents attempt to exert the maximum amount of control over every facet of your life. They invade your privacy and disallow you from doing things on your own even as a teenager. They may also attempt to control your friendships and relationships in a way that goes beyond healthy parenting, boundaries, and discipline. They're not above engaging in activities such as listening to your phone conversations, reading your diary, or attempting to infiltrate your social circles or personal spaces in order to do so. As one survivor, Angela, described, "There was a constant violation of boundaries in my family. For example, I was not allowed to close my bedroom door even when changing my clothes. For a tiny sliver of privacy, I had to huddle down in the corner out of direct view as best as possible to change my clothes. If I dared to close my door even partially, there was hell on earth to pay with raging from my parents. At times, they would even enlist my brothers to abuse me further for what they perceived as my defiance of their orders."

PHYSICAL DEPRIVATION. 61% of adult children of narcissists suffered from physical deprivation.

When children are not given basic nourishing touch or affection, it has serious implications and adverse effects for their neurobiological, social, cognitive and behavioral development. Narcissistic parents who physically deprive their children often refuse to touch their children and do not give them the necessary physical affection they need for healthy development.

In extreme cases, physical deprivation as well as neglect can lead to delays in cognitive function, motor development, and language, as well as deficiencies in socioemotional behaviors. Children who are physically deprived may also experience more psychiatric disorders. Dr. Nathan Fox, author of *Romania's Abandoned Children: Deprivation, Brain Development, and the Struggle for Recovery*, describes witnessing the horrors of physical deprivation when he first stepped into a Romanian orphanage:

"The most remarkable thing about the infant room was how quiet it was, probably because the infants had learned that their cries were not responded to. The babies laid in cribs all day, except when being fed, diapered or bathed on a set schedule. They weren't rocked or sung to. Many stared at their own hands, trying to derive whatever stimulation they could from the world around them."

The issues stemming from this kind of neglect led to poor impulse control, social withdrawal, dysfunction in emotional regulation and coping, low self-esteem, low academic achievement and self-punishment.

PHYSICAL ABUSE. 53% of adult children of narcissists reported being physically abused.

While not all narcissists are physically abusive, narcissistic parents who cross over to physical violence do so by engaging in slapping, hitting, shoving, kicking, punching, pushing aggressively, choking, or anything that causes physical harm. Children who are physically abused not only suffer immediate pain and medical problems, they also exhibit many emotional and behavioral problems such as aggression towards others, self-destructive behavior, getting into violent relationships, depression, low self-esteem, and drug or alcohol abuse.

TRIANGULATION. 71% of adult children of narcissists had been triangulated and unfairly compared to others in demeaning ways.

Triangulation is the act of bringing a third party into the dynamic of a relationship to further belittle you. This is when the narcissistic parent pits you against other siblings or peers, comparing you in cruel, demeaning, and unfair ways to others. They may also give you the silent treatment and choose to communicate to you through another person (like another sibling or parent). Triangulation causes adult children of narcissists to compare themselves excessively to others and to carry a persistent sense of not feeling "good enough." Adult children of narcissists are also taught to be highly competitive and to be the best at all costs.

As former FBI profiler Joe Navarro, writes in his book *Dangerous Personalities*, "As a parent, the narcissistic personality doesn't have the emotional bandwidth to be truly giving to children. Just as narcissists idealize themselves, so they may expect perfection from their children, pushing children to be the best, even at things the children don't like or aren't good at (but may try hard, attempting to win the parent's approval), and constantly raising the bar ("Why didn't you get an A?" "Too bad you didn't make varsity." "I know you can do better than that.").

As a result of this hypercriticism, overachieving adult children of narcissists fear imperfection and failure like the plague; they gain their sense of self-worth from their accomplishments and their ability to be on top. Unfortunately, this disables these adult children from cultivating their sense of self-worth from within, causing them to excessively compare themselves to others in unhealthy ways. If you have been the victim of triangulation, you might benefit from the recovery exercises in my section on Tapping Into Your Inner Child and Healing and Re-parenting the Inner Child.

SCAPEGOATING AND SMEAR CAMPAIGNS. 70% of adult children of narcissists had been scapegoated. 59% had endured smear campaigns.

The narcissistic parent makes you the primary target to dump all projections, blame, and abuse on. They chronically blame you for things you weren't at fault for, causing you to become the black sheep of the family. Other family members may be recruited as "flying monkeys" to further bully, silence, taunt and terrorize you.

Narcissistic parents may slander their children to other family members, peers, or other social networks, whether as an adult or a child. They might try to ruin your reputation among your own social circles to further isolate and scapegoat you if you choose to go No Contact with them as adults. Without social support, it's easy for adult children of narcissists to feel like they are the defective ones for not tolerating the abuse of their parents. However, it's important to remember that scapegoating and smear campaigns are manipulative tools used to belittle you in order to keep you under the narcissistic parent's control and power.

COVERT EMOTIONAL INCEST. 36% of adult children of narcissists had experienced covert emotional incest and parentification.

Covert emotional incest blurs psychological boundaries between parent and child. It reverses roles or assigns new roles which are inappropriate for the child to undertake. You may also become a surrogate wife or husband figure to your narcissistic parent. If your parent treats you as more of a partner or best friend rather than a child, this is covert emotional incest. Your narcissistic parent may talk about sexual subjects or their sex life in inappropriate ways, exposing you to sexual topics early on; they may ask you for advice on subjects that are not age-appropriate; they may share problems about their adult relationships or spousal difficulties. When a parent relies heavily on a child to get their emotional needs met, this is known as parentification. Parentification causes you to become the parent to your parent. Narcissistic parents may make you responsible as a "caretaker" for their addictions even as a child. This is common in dysfunctional households where one of the parents is an addict.

Melissa, a survivor from Florida, tells me about how she became a parent to her enabling mother even though she was an innocent child undergoing horrific abuse. She writes, "As a child, I developed the disease to please at an extremely young age. My mom was an enabler and a victim herself and because she was not getting her emotional needs met by my father, she parentified me from around the age of 6. So, I parented her and tried to meet her emotional needs while experiencing sexual abuse from my father and endured all of his other nasty covert manipulations. I hated conflict and did everything in my power to help keep the peace in my house."

SEXUAL ABUSE AND COERCION. 14% of adult children of narcissists had been sexually abused.

Narcissistic parents who are also sexual predators may violate the sexual boundaries of their children by assaulting and raping them, or "selling" their children in some way to other adults. Research has shown that those who endured familial sexual abuse reported higher levels of depression and anxiety than those who endure non-familial sexual abuse. Being violated by the very people meant to protect you adds another level of betrayal to the trauma – it increases cognitive dissonance in that the child cannot process the perpetrator also being their parent. To process this incongruity, they may internalize the sexual abuse as their fault. In whatever context sexual abuse takes place, childhood sexual abuse has numerous effects – increasing a sense of misplaced guilt, shame, self-blame in the child, and heightening the risk of issues with sexuality, dissociation, toxic relationships, repression and denial in adulthood.

Effects of Trauma for Adult Children of Narcissists

As we'll learn more about in the following essays, as a result of this abuse, adult children of narcissists tend to struggle with the following lifelong habits and behaviors:

SYMPTOMS OF TRAUMA: Adult children of narcissists struggled with the following symptoms of trauma.

83% had a heightened inner critic, meaning they either constantly heard the voice of their abusive parent or found themselves judging and criticizing themselves.

80% had a heightened sensitivity to criticism.

80% had a heightened sensitivity to rejection.

74% struggled with ruminating thoughts over the abuse.

77% struggled with toxic shame and self-blame.

68% had hypervigilance, an inability to trust others and their environment, as well as seeing danger or threats everywhere.

42% had nightmares.

40% reported having a trauma bond with the abusive parent, being unable to let go of their connection with them despite continued abuse.

SELF-IMAGE AND SELF-PERCEPTION.

93% of adult children of narcissists reported having struggled with their self-esteem.

62% suffered from self-sabotage.

77% of adult children of narcissists struggled with anxiety.

MENTAL HEALTH: Adult children of narcissists struggled with mood disorders, post-traumatic stress, and suicidal ideation.

65% of adult children of narcissists struggled with depression.

47% had Complex PTSD, while 38% had PTSD.

44% developed or had issues with eating disorders.

53% dealt with suicidal ideation.

37% had engaged in substance abuse or other addictions.

29% had engaged in physical self-harm due to childhood abuse.

RELATIONSHIPS, FRIENDSHIPS, AND BOUNDARIES: Adult children of narcissists struggled with boundaries, toxic relationships and self-isolation.

86% struggled with people-pleasing habits.

83% had problems setting boundaries with others.

77% of adult children of narcissists had trouble standing up for themselves when violated.

77% of adult children of narcissists tended to self-isolate due to fear or mistrust.

83% had toxic relationships with people who were similar to their parents.

73% had toxic friendships with people who were similar to their parents.

65% reported not trusting most people.

53% had issues with their sexuality and sex life.

51% had been in a constant search for a "rescuer," placing them in situations with dangerous people.

49% reported being emotionally unavailable in their relationships.

42% reported trusting people too easily.

56% had found themselves being taken advantage of multiple times in adulthood.

CAREER AND GOALS: ADULT CHILDREN OF NARCISSISTS EXHIBITED PERFECTIONISM, SELF-SABOTAGE AND OVERACHIEVING.

65% suffered from perfectionism and overachieving overall.

53% had engaged in some form of sabotage regarding their career.

39% became overachievers in their careers.

SOMATIC: ADULT CHILDREN OF NARCISSISTS HAD HEALTH PROBLEMS DUE TO THE ABUSE AS WELL AS ISSUES WITH WEIGHT.

44% had health issues due to the abuse.

33% had issues with losing weight.

22% had issues with gaining weight.

Vocabulary for Adult Children of Narcissists

As you read through this book, there are some terms you should become familiar with if you aren't already which can help you to contextualize your experiences as an adult child of a narcissist. I list them below with brief explanations and you will see many of them discussed throughout the book as well.

Abandonment Trauma / Abandonment Depression.

Trauma therapist Pete Walker writes, "Chronic emotional abandonment is one of the worst things that can happen to a child. It naturally makes her feel and appear deadened and depressed. Functional parents respond to a child's depression with concern and comfort; abandoning parents respond to it with anger, disgust and further abandonment, which in turn create the fear, shame and despair that become characteristic of the abandonment depression."

The traumas of abandonment in childhood often lead to self-abandonment in adulthood, usually in the form of self-destructive and maladaptive defensive behaviors. When an adult child of a narcissist is already feeling worthless and unloveable, he or she can be easily triggered by the fear of abandonment and overwhelmed by the voice of the Inner Critic. This survivor might then launch into one of the 4 F responses (fight, freeze, fawn and flight), only to be met with further "reasons" for self-hatred when they lash out and experience further abandonment and trauma. The compounded traumas of abandonment continue the vicious cycle of depression originating in childhood.

Adult children of narcissists can suffer from a wide range of emotional ailments due to this type of trauma, including intense anxiety, insecurity, fear of being abandoned by others, avoidance of significant relationships, a need for control, self-judgment and self-harm.

Adverse Childhood Experiences (ACEs).

Adverse childhood experiences refer to stressful or traumatic events in childhood such as abuse or neglect. They can include physical abuse, sexual abuse, emotional abuse, physical or emotional neglect, witnessing domestic violence, having a family member with a mental illness or addiction, parental separation or divorce, having a mother being treated violently, and the incarceration of a family member. The CDC-Kaiser Permanente Adverse Childhood Experiences (ACEs) study[3] was one of the largest studies done on those who had suffered child abuse and neglect. It evaluated the effects of the abuse on health and well-being in adulthood. It discovered that those who had suffered a number of ACEs were more at risk for chronic health problems, substance abuse, self-harm, and suicidal ideation. You can take an ACEs quiz on NPR here to assess your own ACEs score.

Attachment Styles.

Attachment styles are models of behaving and interacting in relationships. Attachment theorist John Bowlby described attachment as the "lasting psychological connectedness between human beings." He believed that early childhood experiences (especially the infant/caregiver relationship) deeply affected development and social behavior in adulthood.

Bowlby believed there were four characteristics of attachment: 1) *Proximity Maintenance* – the tendency to want to be near the people we are bonded to. 2) *Safe Haven* – Returning to the person we are attached to for comfort in times of fear, distress, or threat. 3) *Secure Base* – The person we are attached to serves as a secure base which allows the child to safely explore their environment and learn from it. 4) *Separation Distress* – Any anxiety we experience in the absence of our attachment figure.

When children are raised in a secure attachment in which a caregiver is responsive and available to them, this gives them the confidence to explore new environments and healthily depend on others. Secure children have similar expectations for the same kind of responsiveness they received as children as they grow to be adults navigating relationships.

In the 1970s, psychologist Mary Ainsworth conducted the "Strange Situation" study. This study explored and expanded on Bowlby's theories. She tested what would happen when a mother and child entered a new room with toys. The child had time to explore the room and get settled. A stranger then entered the room while the mother snuck off, before returning minutes later. Researchers in this study were interested in how the child behaved when the parent left the room (especially whether or not the child still explored the new environment) and how the child would react when the parent returned to comfort the child (whether the child showed signs of distress and was easily comforted).

Based on this study, she concluded there are three major styles of attachment in children:

1) Secure Attachment – Securely attached children feel confident that the parent will remain a safe base for them to come back to as they explore new environments. They seek the parent in times of distress and are easily soothed by the parent when they return. Secure attachment occurs when the caregiver has been responsive and sensitive to the child's needs.

2) Avoidant-Insecure Attachment – Those who fall into the avoidant-insecure category of attachment are more physically and emotionally independent of the parent. They don't try to seek the parent in times of distress, because they've learned they will be punished or rejected when they do. These children often have parents who are insensitive to the child's needs and have shown them that they will not respond to their needs appropriately.

3) Insecure-Ambivalent – Insecure-ambivalent children will seek out and become clingy or dependent on their caregivers, but will then reject them when their caregiver attempts to engage with them. They find it difficult to explore the new environment and are unable to be soothed by the caregiver. This form of attachment frequently results from inconsistent responsiveness from their caregiver.

4) Disorganized-Insecure Attachment – This was an additional style of attachment added by researchers Main and Soloman in 1986. Children who exhibit disorganized-insecure attachment do so when their caregivers are abusive, confusing or unpredictable in their responses to the child in some way. Disorganized-insecure attachment is known as the attachment style which arises from "fright without a solution." The parent, who is supposed to be the source of comfort in times of distress, instead becomes the *source* of distress. As a result, children may still approach the parent, but then become avoidant of the parent and fearful.

Adult Attachment Styles

Your attachment style is usually established through these early childhood relationships and they can continue to be a working model for your relationships in adulthood as well. Psychologists have concluded that there are four main styles of attachment which adults can fall into that correspond with the attachment styles we observe in childhood. These are:

Secure - Much like children who are securely attached, adults who are securely attached are able to "explore" on their own. They remain autonomous in a healthy way and know that their partner will be there for them when they return. They do not fear intimacy with their partners nor do they fear being abandoned. They can create a healthy, mutual dependency on their partners without becoming excessively preoccupied with the relationship.

Anxious-Preoccupied – Adults who are anxious-preoccupied in their attachment styles long for intimacy and closeness, but they are very insecure and overly preoccupied with their intimate relationships. They search for someone to rescue and complete them – a savior. They have an intense fear of abandonment and may become too dependent on their partners and the relationship. This can actually drive their partners away and leads to a vicious cycle of self-fulfilling prophecies. When the fear of abandonment is confirmed, the anxious-preoccupied individual unfortunately becomes more adamant in their anxiety.

Dismissive-Avoidant – Dismissive-avoidant adults are emotionally distant in relationships. They prioritize independence and associate intimacy with the loss of independence. As a result, they exhibit emotionally unavailable behaviors. They avoid conflict, and they avoid talking about emotions.

Fearful-Avoidant – Fearful-avoidant individuals exhibit behavior very much like the disorganized-ambivalent children we discussed earlier, but as adults. They are ambivalent towards intimacy in that they know they must be with others to get some of their needs met, but they also associate relationships with pain. They can become dependent on their partners when they feel rejected but also feel trapped when they get too close to their partners.

It's very likely that if you were the child of a narcissist, you fit into one or two of the styles that were insecure due to the abuse you endured from your parents. As you grew up, you may have also had relationships with narcissists in adulthood, which could've influenced you to become anxious-preoccupied, dismissive-avoidant or fearful-avoidant rather than securely attached as an adult.

Black Sheep / Scapegoat.

The scapegoated child or the black sheep is the child in the family who often suffers the most abuse, blame, and neglect. The scapegoat may also be punished by other family members seeking to project their own issues onto a convenient victim. This role can be either permanent or shifting, much like the golden child role.

Childhood Emotional Neglect (CEN).

Emotional neglect refers to the parent's inability to notice, attend to, validate, or respond appropriately to a child's feelings. Children who suffer childhood emotional neglect have difficulty trusting or understanding their feelings in adulthood. While not all parents who emotionally neglect their children do so deliberately, narcissistic parents tend to use emotional neglect to belittle their children. Emotional neglect is a natural product of their lack of empathy and inability to attune to the feelings of their children with respect and compassion. Emotional neglect is just one of the many weapons in the arsenal of a narcissistic parent.

Codependency.

Adult children of narcissists may have developed codependent tendencies due to the ways they were raised; however, it is important to note that not all adult children of narcissists or survivors of narcissists are codependent. Some would better be described as traumatized and trauma-bonded. Codependency was historically a term used to describe the traits and behaviors of enablers who lived with an addict (such as a family member or spouse). It has since been expanded to include those in toxic and abusive relationships and used to describe individuals who have an unhealthy dependence on relationships as a source of self-esteem.

Codependents will often do anything to maintain a relationship to avoid feelings of abandonment. They have an excessive need for approval and attention, and a pattern of getting involved in one-sided, dysfunctional relationships where they are the "savior" to someone who cannot meet their needs.

Codependents who are involved with or have a family member who is an addict typically engage in caretaking behaviors as they sacrifice their own needs to "rescue" the addict. This form of caretaking is often compulsive, self-destructive, and rather than saving the addict, it only prevents the addict from facing the consequences of their behaviors. These codependent behaviors may have been encouraged for some adult children of narcissists who grew up taking care of an alcoholic parent who was also a narcissist.

Complex Trauma / Complex PTSD.

Trauma that is prolonged, ongoing, and repeated, creating a perceived inability to escape is known as complex trauma. Chronic childhood bullying, abuse by a parent, sexual abuse or exploitation, as well as retraumatization in adulthood, are all examples of experiences which can cause complex trauma. Complex Trauma can result in Complex PTSD. Complex PTSD causes disruptions in our emotional regulation, consciousness, and self-perception. It also causes distorted perceptions of our perpetrators, dysfunction in our relations with others and in the ways we view the world. I discuss Complex PTSD in this section of the book. To learn more about the differences between Complex PTSD and PTSD, read my article on it here[4]. Also be sure to read my article on The Meadows[5] about complex trauma and bullying if you are a survivor of bullying by peers as well as narcissistic parents.

Emotional Flashbacks.

Emotional flashbacks are a symptom of Complex PTSD. These are flashbacks that occur without a visual component and they cause the survivor to regress back into the painful and overwhelming feelings of childhood. Trauma therapist Pete Walker calls emotional flashbacks "amygdala hijackings." These happen automatically and can cause survivors to feel the same intense fear, helplessness, rage, and humiliation they may have experienced in the abandonment they suffered in childhood. Emotional flashbacks can cause us to feel so powerless that we may fail to stand up for ourselves when we are being taken advantage of *or* we may even aggressively attack or flee when we perceive any kind of threat or danger. These regressions can be so intense that we feel frozen in the same states of horror and shame we felt in our earliest experiences of abuse.

Golden Child.

The golden child is the favored child in a household with a narcissistic parent or two toxic parents. They are often doted upon, spoiled, overvalued, idealized and used as a point of comparison for the scapegoated child or the black sheep. This role may change, however, if the golden child decides to stand up to the narcissistic parent, become independent of them, or if something else changes in terms of what the narcissistic parent needs from their children.

Flying Monkeys.

Flying monkeys are recruited by narcissistic individuals to do their dirty work on their behalf. Narcissistic parents may enlist other relatives, siblings, or friends to act as flying monkeys to further exploit, gaslight, and abuse their children.

Fear/Obligation/Guilt (FOG).

Popularized by psychotherapist Susan Forward, FOG is the triad of the emotions we often feel when we've become trauma bonded to an abuser who tries to emotionally blackmail us. Narcissistic parents induce these emotions in us to better control us. Learn more about emotional blackmail in the chapter, *6 Manipulation Tactics of Narcissistic Parents And How To Respond Effectively.*

The 4 F responses (Fight, Flight, Freeze, Fawn).

Trauma therapists believe that there are certain defensive modes we can maladaptively resort to, especially when we've been traumatized in childhood. These are fight, flight, freeze, and fawn. Children who are raised in healthy households can access their defensive responses when it is appropriate to do so (for example, fleeing in the face of true danger, or fighting back when it is needed in a life or death situation). Children raised by narcissists, however, learn to survive by depending on one or two defensive modes to the exclusion of others in unhealthy ways. For them, these defensive modes can be launched even in situations which do not warrant it.

- *Fight* **types** are fixated on power and control, often becoming aggressive and narcissistic to achieve a sense of safety.

- *Flight* **types** are excessively avoidant of their trauma and they channel their fears of abandonment into perfectionism, overachieving, workaholism, or running away completely to keep themselves away from the threat of abandonment.

- *Freeze* **types** are the isolators who attempt to "hide" themselves to circumvent further pain; they dissociate and they self-isolate from others as a way to avoid abandonment and reminders of the traumas they've experienced.

- *Fawn* **types** are the people-pleasers prone to codependency; they learned in early childhood that they had to cater to the needs of others in order to stay safe. In adulthood, they walk on eggshells trying to meet everyone else's needs while abandoning their own. Some survivors will demonstrate "hybrids" of these defensive types.

The Inner Critic.

In the context of childhood narcissistic abuse, the inner critic is the internalized voice of our abusers and a maladaptive protective mechanism meant to keep us away from abandonment or failure. The inner critic is usually harshly judgmental of us, attempting to keep us down in order to "protect" us from achieving our goals or feeling good about ourselves, lest such things are taken away from us as they frequently were in childhood.

The inner critic which causes emotional flashbacks originates from an abusive childhood and can take on the characteristics of our earliest abusers. For example, you may have an Inner Critic that judges everything you do harshly and speaks in the same kind of tone or voice that your abusive mother or father did. Perhaps it even regurgitates the same negative messages. The Inner Critic may be attempting to protect you from failure or abandonment, but it has many maladaptive means to do so and it actually prevents you from reaching your full potential.

Inner Parts.

Trauma can create disparate inner parts within us. These parts usually serve different defensive mechanisms and protective roles to keep us from confronting the intense grief and vulnerability that underlies trauma. Dr. Richard Schwartz, the founder of the Internal Family Systems model, notes that we have three types of "inner parts" which protect us: exiles, managers, and firefighters. *Exiles* are the wounded inner parts which carry the emotions and memories of our childhood wounds. *Managers* are the hypercritical, controlling inner parts which attempt to protect our exiles from being triggered. *Firefighter* inner parts also help to hide the vulnerable exile parts from coming into our consciousness but they do so by dousing out the "fires" (triggers) immediately by causing us to engage in addictive, compulsive, and self-harming behaviors to escape the pain. To learn more about these parts and their functions, read my chapter, *Healing Modalities for Adult Children of Narcissists.*

To begin learning more about your Inner Parts, see my exercise here.

Inner Child.

Even as many of us reach adulthood, we carry a wounded Inner Child within us that bears the burdens of abandonment and shame. For the healing journey of adult children of narcissists, healing and re-parenting that inner child with the kindness, compassion, validation, and space for grief is essential to healthily re-integrating this part of ourselves into our psyches.

Once we've worked to re-parent and heal the inner child, we can regain the childlike qualities that our healthy Inner Child was forced to bury beneath the trauma: qualities like curiosity, playfulness, compassion, spontaneity, and the joy of being alive.

Narcissistic Fleas.

When we've been raised by narcissists, it's quite common to have a few narcissistic fleas – traits or behaviors we adopt which are similar to our abusers. Adult children of narcissists, for example, might imitate the behavior of their parents by becoming hypersensitive to any perceived criticism. They might become overly rageful or aggressive with their parents, or attempt to manipulate their caretakers in maladaptive ways rather than detaching from them.

I must stress that these behaviors do not necessarily mean you have a full-fledged personality disorder. Many adult children of narcissists (or survivors of narcissistic abuse in romantic relationships) often turn inward in self-blame, questioning whether or not *they* are the ones who are the narcissists. This kind of self-doubt occurs after much gaslighting and projection from our abusers and it is usually not grounded in reality. However, there can be narcissistic tendencies or habits that we pick up from long-term experiences with disordered individuals. These are called "narcissistic fleas."

Narcissistic fleas are temporary defense mechanisms and characteristics which developed out of the need to survive the abuse. These fleas can dissolve with inner work, healing, and the fresher air of a healthier environment. They dissipate once we've left the toxic environment of our abusers and once we are free to work on ourselves without the interference of our abusive parents or partners.

Parentification

Parentification is the process where a child takes on the parent role, taking on adult responsibilities that surpass their emotional capacities and abilities. As Dr. Karyl McBride[6] describes, "In the narcissistic family usually the parental hierarchy is reversed so the child is taking care of the parent instead of the other way around. When a child is put in the position of parental caretaking, they are being asked to do a job they cannot do based on their maturity and development." Parentification is also common in families with an alcoholic parent, where the children are forced to look after the addicted parent and take on the burden of caretaking rather than being cared for or looked after. Parentification leads children of narcissists to lose many essential aspects of their childhood, because they are forced to become adults at such a young age.

Toxic shame and self-blame.

In his book *Homecoming*, psychologist John Bradshaw distinguishes between healthy shame and toxic shame. He writes, "Healthy shame is simply an emotion of limits. It gives us permission to be human, to be imperfect. We don't need much shame – just enough to know that we are not God...toxic shame forces us to be more than human (perfect) or less than human...healthy guilt is moral shame. Healthy guilt is the basis of a healthy conscience, which our inner child needs."

Toxic shame is the shame that is spawned from an abusive childhood, instilling in us a core wound and belief that we are somehow unloveable, defective, or unworthy, that we are to blame. This belief is internalized due to the abuse and mistreatment we suffered as innocent children. As children, we had no way of making sense of the horrific behavior we were subjected to. Innocent children do not have the emotional equipment to conceptualize that a parent's abuse could be related to the parent's disordered ways of thinking and behaving in the world, so they develop a belief system which places them at fault. Toxic shame carries with it the misguided belief that we are somehow at fault for the abuse, that we must have caused or provoked the abuse in some way.

Unfortunately, self-blame is a maladaptive way that adult children of narcissists regain a sense of control over experiences where they otherwise lacked power and control. After all, if we are to blame, we can also somehow "change" the abuser's behavior towards us – or so we think. Toxic shame and self-blame prevent us from placing the blame where it really belongs: on our abusive parents.

Trauma bonding.

Also called a "betrayal bond" by Dr. Patrick Carnes, a trauma bond is a strong bond we form with our abusers during intense emotional experiences. For adult children of narcissists, this bond is formed due to the need for survival in childhood. A helpless and innocent child cannot survive without the food, shelter, nourishment and physical touch of a parent. They thus bond with their narcissistic parent, become obedient to them and compliant, just in order to survive. Trauma bonding is very much like Stockholm Syndrome where those taken hostage show a strange but unflinching loyalty, love, and devotion to their captors.

Trauma repetition / Trauma Reenactment

Trauma repetition or trauma reenactment is the phenomenon where an earlier trauma is repeated or reenacted in adulthood, usually with the subconscious hope for resolution. Adult children of narcissists are prone to having traumas reenacted through toxic relationships with narcissistic partners, friends, even co-workers or bosses. They may also reenact the trauma in other ways, such as through self-harm or addiction. You can read more about this vicious cycle in the chapter, *Trauma Reenactment: Adult Children of Narcissists and the Trauma Repetition Cycle.*

Subconscious Wounding.

Core wounding from childhood which we are not cognizant of drives our belief systems and behavior. This is known as subconscious wounding. Unlike wounding which we *know* exists, we are not usually aware of subconscious wounding. These wounds are more difficult and take a longer time to heal because in order to address them, they must first come to the surface. Certain triggers, traumas, or episodes of abandonment may bring up subconscious wounding so we can finally process them and heal.

How to Use This Book

This collection features some of my most widely read essays on adult children of narcissists, along with new thought pieces and exercises for recovery and healing. It covers everything from what it's like to be raised by a narcissist to the strategies we can use to survive, heal and thrive after the experience.

While the first sections of the book focus on highlighting the effects of childhood abuse, the last few chapters of the book are dedicated solely to re-parenting the inner child, exploring healing modalities, going No Contact, as well as in-depth and practical exercises for recovery. I encourage you to spend some substantial time on these last chapters and preferably, work with a trauma-informed therapist while doing these exercises.

You will also find insights from the hundreds of adult children of narcissists that I surveyed throughout the book, as well as some tips from therapists who work with adult children of narcissists. Near the end of certain essays, you will find a set of exploratory exercises which will guide you to reflect on what you have just read and apply these understandings to your daily life. These "miniature" reflection exercises are meant to be the appetizers to the longer and more extensive exercises you'll find at the end of this book.

While narcissistic mothers and narcissistic fathers have their own set of essays, please note that many of the healing tools discussed will be explored in my essays, "Healing Modalities for Adult Children of Narcissists," "Re-Parenting the Inner Child," and my "Daddy Issues" series.

You can learn more about the organization of this book in the Author's Note.

A Note About Links in the Paperback Version

If you are reading the paperback version of this book, any mention of relevant embedded links throughout the book will be supplied as footnotes, which you can view as a list at the end of the book.

If you purchased the paperback copy directly from Amazon, you are eligible for the Kindle Matchbook program, where you can easily access these links by reading the Kindle version of the book on Amazon for free. Simply access the Kindle version of the book through your Amazon account by using the link provided on www.adultchildrenofnarcissists.org.

Professional Support

As a disclaimer, this book is not meant to be a substitution for therapy. It is meant to be an educational resource for those who have experienced childhood narcissistic abuse. If you are experiencing any symptoms of PTSD or Complex PTSD, it's highly advised that you work with a trauma-informed therapist while working through this book so you can safely navigate your triggers with a licensed professional.

If you are not currently in therapy but would like to explore different options for healing, you can read more about different types of therapies and healing modalities in my essays, "Healing Modalities for Adult Children of Narcissists" and "Healing and Re-parenting the Inner Child."

References

American Psychiatric Association. (2013). *Diagnostic and statistical manual of mental disorders* (5th ed.). Arlington, VA: American Psychiatric Publishing.

Bradshaw, J. (1990). *Homecoming: Reclaiming and championing your inner child.* London: Piatkus.

Bruce, J., Gunnar, M. R., Pears, K. C., and Fisher, P. A. (2013). Early adverse care, stress neurobiology, and prevention science: Lessons learned. *Prevention Science, 14*(3), 247–256.

Felitti, V. J., Anda, R. F., Nordenberg, D., Williamson, D. F., Spitz, A. M., Edwards, V., . . . Marks, J. S. (1998). Relationship of Childhood Abuse and Household Dysfunction to Many of the Leading Causes of Death in Adults. *American Journal of Preventive Medicine,14*(4), 245-258. doi:10.1016/s0749-3797(98)00017-8

Hare, R. (1999). *Without Conscience.* The Guilford Press.

Kernberg, O.F. (1975). Treatment of narcissistic personalities. *Int. J. Psychoanal.,* 56:245-248.

Main, M., & Solomon, J. (1986). Discovery of an insecure-disorganized/disoriented attachment pattern. In T. B. Brazelton & M. W. Yogman (Eds.), *Affective development in infancy* (pp. 95-124). Westport, CT, US: Ablex Publishing.

Međedović, J. & Petrovic, B. (2015). The Dark Tetrad. *Journal of Individual Differences.* 36:228-236. 10.1027/1614-0001/a000179.

Nelson, C. A., Fox, N. A., and Zeanah, C. H. (2014). *Romania's abandoned children: Deprivation, brain development, and the struggle for recovery.* Cambridge, MA, and London, England: Harvard University Press.

Nelson III, C. A., Zeanah, C. H., Fox, N. A., Marshall, P. J., Smyke, A. T., and Guthrie, D. (2007). Cognitive recovery in socially deprived young children: the Bucharest Early Intervention Project. *Science, 318*(5858), 1937–2940.

Sethi, A., Gregory, S., Dell'acqua, F., Thomas, E. P., Simmons, A., Murphy, D. G., . . . Craig, M. C. (2015). Emotional detachment in psychopathy: Involvement of dorsal default-mode connections. *Cortex, 62*, 11-19. doi:10.1016/j.cortex.2014.07.018

Shin LM, Rauch SL, & Pitman RK (2006). Amygdala, medial prefrontal cortex, and hippocampal function in PTSD. *Annals of the New York Academy of Sciences, 1071*, 67-79

Teicher, Martin H., et al. "The Neurobiological Consequences of Early Stress and Childhood Maltreatment." *Neuroscience & Biobehavioral Reviews*, vol. 27, no. 1-2, 2003, pp. 33–44., doi:10.1016/s0149-7634(03)00007-1.

Teicher, M. (2006). Sticks, Stones, and Hurtful Words: Relative Effects of Various Forms of Childhood Maltreatment. *American Journal of Psychiatry Am J Psychiatry, 163*(6), 993. doi:10.1176/appi.ajp.163.6.993

Wai, M., & Tiliopoulos, N. (2012). The affective and cognitive empathic nature of the dark triad of personality. *Personality and Individual Differences, 52*(7), 794-799. doi:10.1016/j.paid.2012.01.008

Exploratory Questions: Introduction

Which of the manipulation tactics listed in this chapter (ex. Gaslighting, stonewalling, covert put-downs, sabotage, triangulation, etc.) did you experience most frequently from your narcissistic parent(s)?

What defense mechanisms did you develop as a result? (Examples might look like: "I became overly perfectionistic in response to the put-downs," "I have a heightened sensitivity to criticism," "I am guarded with people" or "I feel unable to trust myself or my reality, so I am always second-guessing my decisions or what I experienced.")

What mental health or chronic health problems did you develop as a result of the abuse you endured? (ex. I struggled with self-harm and suicidal ideation all my life, I suffered from severe migraines, I turned to drugs to fill the persistent sense of emptiness, etc.)

What did you wish you *had* received from your narcissistic parent? (ex. affection, healthy attention, unconditional positive regard, support, emotional validation).

What healthy substitutes can you think of to receive what you did not get in childhood? (ex. Pursuing a personal passion or mission that gives back to the world, finding a healthy support network to get relational healing and validation, practicing self-love and self-compassion meditations and affirmations, etc.)

The Trauma of Adult Children
of Narcissists

Essays on the traumatic effects of
childhood trauma and narcissistic parenting.

Five Damaging Lies

We Learn From Narcissistic Parents

The adult children of narcissists are very much like emotional orphans. Their biological parents may still be alive, but they fail to provide their children with the unconditional positive regard, love, empathy and compassion all children need in order to possess a healthy sense of self. Parents are meant to mirror unconditional positive regard for their children as they grow; they are meant to provide the psychological equipment necessary for healthy development.

The effects of childhood trauma, including emotional neglect or abuse in childhood, can have alarmingly potent effects on our psyche as we enter adulthood, even to the extent of rewiring our brains. When emotional abuse takes place in childhood, it wreaks havoc on the mental architecture of the brain, affecting areas such as the amygdala, the hippocampus, and the prefrontal cortex. These areas of the brain help with emotional regulation, learning, memory, focus, cognition, and planning.

The children of narcissistic parents, those who meet the diagnostic criteria for Narcissistic Personality Disorder, know this all too well, having been raised by someone with a limited capacity for empathy and an excessive sense of grandiosity, false superiority and entitlement (Ni, 2016).

Children of narcissistic parents are programmed at an early age to seek validation where there is none, to believe their worthiness is tied to the reputation of their families, and to internalize the message that they can only sustain their value by how well they can 'serve' the needs of their parents. They have lived an existence where love was rarely ever unconditional, if given at all.

This is not to say that childhood survivors of narcissistic abuse cannot rise above their childhood conditioning. In fact, they can be stronger survivors and thrivers as a result of the resilience they are capable of developing and the ways in which they channel their traumas into transformation (Bussey and Wise, 2007). It takes real inner work and bravery to unravel the traumas that we've had to endure as children as well as address any retraumatization as adults. Being able to understand our relationship and behavioral patterns, as well as any negative self-talk which has arisen as a result of the abuse, can be revolutionary in challenging the myths and falsehoods we've been fed about our worth and capabilities.

As children of narcissistic parents, we often learn the following from a very young age:

1. Your worth is always dependent on conditional circumstances.

As the child of a narcissistic parent or parents, you were taught that you were not inherently worthy, but rather that your worth depended on what you could do for the narcissistic parent and how compliant you were. The emphasis on appearance, status, reputation is at an all-time high in households with a narcissistic parent. Due to the narcissistic parent's grandiosity, false mask and need to be the best, you were probably part of a family that was 'presented' in the best possible light, with abuse taking place behind closed doors.

Within the home was a different story than the one presented to the public: you may have witnessed the horrific dynamics of seeing one parent verbally or even physically abuse the other, been subjected to the abuse yourself, and/or experienced both parents working together to undercut you and your siblings. If you ever dared to threaten the perfect false image of the family or did anything to speak out about the abuse, you were most likely punished.

The emotional and psychological battery children of narcissistic parents endure when going against the expectations and beliefs of the family can be incredibly damaging. It can have life-long effects on their self-image, their agency and their faith in themselves. They are taught that they are not independent agents, but instead objects here to serve the narcissistic parent's ego and selfish agendas.

(2) You need to be perfect and successful, but you should never be rewarded for it or feel 'enough.'

Narcissists are masters of moving the goalposts so that nothing their victims do is ever enough. As childhood abuse survivors, we are no exception to that rule. Our accomplishments were rarely acknowledged unless they met some arbitrary criteria for what looked best to society or confirmed the narcissistic parent's own grandiose fantasies. Our abusive parent was never genuinely proud of us unless he or she could claim credit for that particular success. Some narcissistic parents can even envy or look down upon the success of their children, especially if that success enables that child to become independent of their parents, outside of their realm of power and control.

It is not uncommon for these types of parents to attempt to sabotage the success and happiness of their children if that success interfered at all with their grandiose self-image. This is especially true if their success challenges the narcissist's own ideas of what 'happiness' should entail (usually whatever makes *them* look good rather than what makes their children feel good) or makes their children too independent. To a narcissistic parent, the independence of their children serves as a viable threat to their compulsion to micromanage and control every facet of their children's lives.

In the sick mind of the narcissistic parent, it would have been better if their children did not exist at all, rather than be unable to do their bidding and 'perform' the identity that the parent wished their children to embody - or achieved the exact goals they wanted their children to achieve. Even if they were the perfect daughters or sons, the goal posts would again shift - and the child's level of perfection would still never be good enough in the eyes of the narcissistic parent.

(3) There is always someone better, and you must beat them – starting with your own siblings.

Children of narcissistic parents are often turned against their siblings in a competition to vie for the affection and love they always craved but never received. Narcissistic parents are well-known for 'triangulating' children against one another as an attempt to unnecessarily compare them, demean them and feed their own sense of power and control over their children. Triangulation is a technique that narcissists use to bring the presence of a third party into the dynamic of a relationship to destabilize all individuals involved.

Usually there is a golden child and a scapegoat, and sometimes the roles are reversed depending on what the narcissistic parent needs to meet their agenda (McBride, 2011). Scapegoated rebel children are often truth-seekers who desire an authentic connection with their family members, but fail to remain silent about the abuse that occurs when they do not meet the absurd expectations of their parents. The golden child, on the other hand, is usually lauded as the 'standard,' but this too can quickly take a turn should the golden child ever exercise his or her agency and do something outside of the parent's control. We are taught at a very young age that we will never be good enough, that we must always compare ourselves to others, and fail to acknowledge our inherent worthiness and value.

As adults, we learn that we do not have to compete with anyone in order to be worthy or valuable, nor do we necessarily have to be the best at everything. Cultivating a sense of unconditional self-love, as well as an appreciation of our unique skills and abilities, can go a long way in combating these harmful internalizations from abuse and replacing them with a healthy level of pride and self-sufficiency.

(4) Contempt is a part of love and 'normal' in a relationship.

Narcissistic parents can subject their children to periods of idealization when they need them, quickly followed by contempt and terrifying narcissistic rage when they 'disobey' and threaten their excessive sense of entitlement (Goulston, 2012). The condescension, contempt, and hatred with which a narcissistic parent uses to berate their children are not only immensely hurtful, they retrain the mind into accepting abuse as a new normal.

This pattern of idealization and devaluation teaches us that love is unstable, frightening, and ultimately unpredictable. It causes us to walk on eggshells, fearful that we may displease others. It also desensitizes us and makes us tone-deaf to verbal abuse later on in adulthood (Streep, 2016). Although we may learn to identify emotional and verbal abuse, we will be less likely than someone who had a healthy upbringing to recognize how damaging it can be or how unacceptable it truly is, because it unfortunately is 'familiar' to us as the only version of love we've been shown.

We may become 'trauma bonded' to our abusive parents and more prone to bonding with abusive partners in adulthood as a result (Carnes, 1997). We may even go to the other end of the spectrum and shut out anyone who resembles our parents in tone or attitude – some of this may be hypervigilance, but much of it is self-protection and intuition about the behaviors that have traumatized us in the past.

Children of narcissistic parents can re-sensitize themselves to the fact that abuse is not a normal or healthy part of any relationship by addressing their people-pleasing habits, doing important boundary work, and replacing old narratives of unworthiness with empowering ones about the type of love and respect they truly deserve. They can essentially 'reparent' themselves in a safe, protective space (Walker, 2013).

(5) Your emotions are not valid.

Narcissistic parents, much like narcissistic abusers in relationships, pathologize and invalidate our emotions to the point where we are left voiceless. We are not allowed to feel, so we end up going to extremes: we either become repressed and numb or we become rebel children who 'feel' too much, too soon. Our emotions become overwhelming either way because our grief is not processed in a healthy way, starting from childhood. In adulthood, we gain the opportunity to validate our own emotions and recognize that what we feel, and have felt all along, is entirely valid. We learn how to process our emotions, our trauma, and the grief of being unloved as children and adolescents. We learn that we have opportunities to detach from our abusive parents, whether it be through Low Contact (minimum contact only when necessary) or No Contact at all.

We experiment with using our agency to separate ourselves from the identity erosion that has occurred in our childhoods. We learn to separate the narcissistic parent's harmful beliefs about us and our own burgeoning faith. Most of all, we learn that it is okay to believe in ourselves and to welcome good things into our lives. We learn that we are deserving of all that is good.

It is important to remember that as children of narcissistic parents, we carry the legacy of our wounds, but that these wounds can become portals to deeper and richer healing. We do not have to burden the next generation with our wounding, but rather use it as a way to nurture and validate future generations. We have options as to how we can channel this trauma for our own growth, rather than our destruction. These wounds cannot heal if they are not addressed or if we refuse to be awake; at the same time, our timeline for healing will be unique, and our journey cannot be compared to that of others. Self-awareness and self-compassion is needed on the healing journey more than ever.

As children of narcissistic parents, we have to learn to protect ourselves from further abuse and set up a plan to better engage in self-care. Falsehoods about parents always being loving and having our best interests at heart simply do not cut it when it comes to manipulative, toxic and abusive parents. These parents are incapable of empathy and are likely to 'hoover' you back only when they need to use you as a source of narcissistic supply (Schneider, 2015).

We must allow ourselves to grieve for the loss of our childhoods. We must embrace the truth that our parents may have never loved us in the ways we deserved to be loved or wanted the best for us, but that we *can* 'reparent' ourselves the best ways we know how – through empathy, compassion, self-acceptance, and self-love.

Make no mistake: when you are the child of a narcissistic parent, the idea that you never deserved this love, is perhaps the biggest lie of all.

References

Bussey, M. C., & Wise, J. B. (2007). Trauma transformed: An empowerment response. New York: Columbia University Press.

Carnes, P. (1997). The betrayal bond: Breaking free of exploitive relationships. Deerfield Beach, FL: Health Communications.

Goulston, M., MD. (2012, February 8). Rage – Coming Soon From a Narcissist Near You. Retrieved March 04, 2019, from https://www.psycholog ytoday.com/blog/just-listen/201202/rage-coming-soon-narcissist-near-you

McBride, K. (2011, May 1). The Narcissistic Family Tree. Retrieved March 04, 2019, from https://www.psycholog ytoday.com/blog/the-legacy-distorted-love/201105/the-narcissistic-family-tree

Ni, P. (2016, February 28). 10 Signs of a Narcissistic Parent. Retrieved March 04, 2019, from https://www.psycholog ytoday.com/blog/communication-success/201602/10-signs-narcissistic-parent

Schneider, A., LCSW. (2015, February 13). 'Hoover Maneuver': The Dirty Secret of Emotional Abuse. Retrieved March 04, 2019, from http://www.goodtherapy.org/blog/hoover-maneuver-the-dirty-secret-of-emotional- abuse-0219154

Streep, P. (2016). Why Unloved Daughters Fall for Narcissists. Retrieved March 04, 2019, from http://blogs.psychcentral.com/knotted/2016/09/why-unloved-daughters-fall-for-narcissists/

Van der Kolk, B. (2014). The body keeps the score: Brain, mind, and body in the healing of trauma. New York: Viking.

Walker, P. (2013). Complex PTSD: From surviving to thriving. Lafayette, CA: Azure Coyote.

Exploratory Questions: Five Damaging Lies We Learn From Narcissistic Parents

Which emotions did your narcissistic parent(s) invalidate the most? Are there situations where you find yourself invalidating your own emotions as an adult? How can you start to better self-validate?

Example: I was always invalidated whenever I brought up that I was hurt by a cruel comment my toxic mother made. Now, in adulthood, I try to hide it from others when I am upset at insensitive remarks or brush it off with a laugh. To better self-validate, I might journal about my emotions or gently call out someone when they have made me feel uncomfortable rather than hiding it.

Were there goals, hobbies or pursuits your parents discouraged? Are there small ways to reconnect with these now?

Example: My narcissistic father always discouraged me from drawing even though I had a natural talent for it. He would only show off my artwork when I won a contest. I became a doctor to fulfill his expectations of me. To reconnect with my past passion, I am going to start taking art classes during my free time.

How often have you encountered people in your life who treat you with contempt or make you feel the same way your narcissistic parent did? What are your usual reactions to them?

Example: I've encountered a lot of people in dating and friendships who show contempt. In the past, I've responded by trying to please them. Now I know their contempt is indicative of their character, and it means they are not the type of person I want in my life.

In the past, what red flags or "first signs" of toxicity did you notice in friends and partners that you tended to minimize, deny, rationalize or ignore? Write down a list and next to each red flag, write down how you reacted as well as the boundary you will set for the future when you see this red flag pop up.

Example: A red flag I often experience early on is the telling of a cruel insult told as a joke. In the past, I would laugh it off nervously and tell myself I was being too sensitive, even though this person would later escalate with even more cruel comments. Now that I know it's a sign of toxicity, I will either call it out if I feel comfortable doing so and see whether they stop, or I will cut off contact immediately if I haven't yet begun to invest in this person. The sooner, the better.

The Children of Narcissists

Face An Invisible War Zone In Childhood

"Adverse childhood experiences are the single greatest unaddressed public health threat facing our nation today." – *Dr. Robert Block, MD, former President of the American Academy of Pediatrics*

Much of society associates the terms "trauma" and "PTSD" with war veterans. Yet we forget about the children who grow up in war zones at home, who suffer psychological scarring at vulnerable developmental stages of their lives. Neglect, mistreatment, abandonment and/or any form of sexual, emotional and physical abuse (such as the type imposed by toxic, narcissistic parents) have been proven by research such as the Adverse Childhood Experiences study[7] to leave an impact that is destructive and long-lasting.

According to researchers, early childhood trauma can affect our brains in the following ways:

- Our amygdala, which controls our fight/flight response, emotional regulation, and our moods, becomes **hyperactive**

and enlarged as a result of trauma. We can become extremely emotionally responsive and hypervigilant to potential threats in our environment due to trauma.

- Our hippocampus, the part of our brain that deals with learning and memory, **shrinks** after a period of time. This makes integrating traumatic memories problematic and also disrupts our learning. The traumatic impact of those memories can remain a great deal more impactful.

- Trauma can **inhibit the prefrontal cortex**, the center of our executive functioning, decision making and judgment. This can affect our ability to regulate our emotional responses as well as plan, focus and organize.

The good news is, healing can help to mitigate some of these effects. Brains can also be rewired in the other direction – meditation, for example, has been shown by studies to produce the opposite effects in the same areas of the brain that trauma affects. Yet the brains and psyches of children are so malleable that the effects of chronic emotional/verbal abuse, let alone physical abuse, leaves a frightening mark beyond childhood. It creates the potential for complex trauma to develop, especially when one is later re-violated in adulthood.

Without proper intervention, support, validation and protective factors, this form of violence has the potential to shift the course of one's life-course trajectory. There are five common "battle wounds" adult children of narcissists face as a result of this type of abuse:

(1) Your life resembles a reenactment of old traumas.

Freud dubbed it "repetition compulsion[8]," psychologists refer to it as the effects of childhood "conditioning" or "trauma reenactment" and survivors call it, "Oh God, not this again." The trauma repetition cycle is real. It's destructive. And it's birthed in the ashes of a violent childhood.

Ever wonder why some people always seem to be drawn to toxic people, yet perceive more stable individuals as "boring"? They may have a history of childhood trauma.

For childhood abuse survivors, chaos becomes a new "normal" as they become accustomed to highly stimulating environments which shape their nervous system and their psyches. Their fight for survival in childhood leaves a void in adulthood that is often filled with similar struggles.

Chaos becomes our new normal.

What we have to remember is that narcissistic parents aren't all that different from narcissistic abusers in relationships. They love-bomb (excessively flatter and praise) their children when they need something from them, they triangulate them with other siblings by pitting them against each other and they devalue them with hypercriticism, rage attacks, verbal and emotional abuse.

They engage in intermittent reinforcement as well[9] – withdrawing affection at critical periods while also giving their children crumbs to make them hope that they'll receive the love they always desired.

> "The family environment allows children to become comfortable with deprivation. The neglect of children becomes self-neglect in adults. Couple it with high arousal events such as domestic violence or sexual abuse and you have a neurochemical cocktail that is hard to beat. The antidote to being out of control is to be in supercontrol. Maybe the only way to control survival is to freeze like a hunted animal. Ask nothing. Do nothing. Attract no attention. Yet fear mobilizes the body. Adrenaline, cortisol, endorphins and norepinephrine pour into the body. In a constant state, it can become addictive." – Dr. Patrick Carnes, *The Betrayal Bond*

As children, our bodies become so addicted to the crazy-making effects of emotional abuse that we find ourselves more intensely attached to partners who tend to replicate a similar chaotic effect on our bodies as our narcissistic parents.

We feel biochemically attracted[10] to those who resemble our early childhood predators because they mirror the severe highs and lows our bodies went through in childhood. When love-bombing turns into devaluation, our body becomes biochemically bonded to our present-day abusers.

This biochemical addiction leaves us reeling.

In the realm of adult relationships, there are all sorts of chemicals being released when we're in a bond with a predator. They create a very powerful attachment that's actually strengthened by intermittent cruelty and affection, pleasure and punishment.

Dopamine, oxytocin, adrenaline, cortisol and our serotonin levels are being affected in any type of intimate partnership; these are involved in attachment, trust, fear, and stress. In fact, children who have endured maltreatment tend to have lower oxytocin levels due to the abuse, which leads to a greater number of indiscriminate relationships in adulthood (Bellis and Zisk, 2014).

There's also a psychological component to this addiction.

When we are the children of narcissistic parents, emotionally abusive people fit the profile of what our subconscious has been primed to seek. Yet they often come disguised as our saviors.

Complex trauma survivors, as trauma expert Dr. Judith Herman notes, are in a 'repeated search for a rescuer.'

"Many abused children cling to the hope that growing up will bring escape and freedom. But the personality formed in the environment of coercive control is not well adapted to adult life. The survivor is left with fundamental problems in basic trust, autonomy, and initiative. She {or he} approaches the task of early adulthood—establishing independence and intimacy—burdened by major impairments in self-care, in cognition and in memory, in identity, and in the capacity to form stable relationships. She {or he} is still a prisoner of childhood; attempting to create a new life, she re-encounters the trauma." –Judith Lewis Herman, *Trauma and Recovery: The Aftermath of Violence – From Domestic Abuse to Political Terror*

Love-Bombing Pulls Us In And Keeps Us Trapped In Loveless Relationships

The children of narcissists are drawn to narcissists in adulthood to fill a void. They are looking for the validation they never received in childhood and narcissists, on the onset, present us with a lot of it in the love-bombing stage when they are "grooming" us into believing that we're the perfect partners for them. We crave their excessive praise because we lacked the unconditional positive regard we deserved in childhood but never received.

As children, we learned to associate betrayal with love and we were conditioned to see mistreatment as a form of connection. In fact, it was the only form of connection offered to us. Survivors of narcissistic parents have an extra layer of healing to undergo. Not only do we have to unlearn all of the unhealthy belief systems, we also have to clear our bodies and our minds of its familiarity with toxicity.

When the fears from our childhood are finally removed, we meet peace and stability with resistance; our bodies and our minds have to readjust to baseline levels of safety and security before we even begin to find healthy relationships appealing.

> "The drive to complete and heal trauma is as powerful and tenacious as the symptoms it creates. The urge to resolve trauma through re-enactment can be severe and compulsive. We are inextricably drawn into situations that replicate the original trauma in both obvious and nonobvious ways…Re-enactments may be acted out in intimate relationships, work situations…adults, on a larger developmental scale, will re-enact traumas in our daily lives." –Peter A. Levine, *Waking the Tiger: Healing Trauma*

For example, a daughter who is unloved by her abusive father may end up with emotionally unavailable – or even sociopathic – partners in adulthood due to an instilled sense of unworthiness. To her, cruelty is all too familiar and abusers feed on her resilience and ability to 'bounce back' from abusive incidents. She is used to taking a caretaking role – catering to someone else's needs while neglecting her own. She has been subconsciously "programmed" to seek dangerous people because they are the "normal" which causes her to associate relationships with torment.

Survivors who are abused as children can later get married to and have children with abusive partners as adults, investing time, energy and resources into people who ultimately seek to destroy them.

I have read countless letters from survivors who have been raised by toxic parents and ended up in long-term abusive marriages.

If these wounds are not addressed and the cycle is never disrupted, the first eighteen years of life can literally affect the *rest* of your life.

(2) Verbal and emotional abuse has conditioned you toward self-destruction and self-sabotage.

Narcissistic parents subject their children to hypercriticism, cruel punishment and a callous disregard for their basic needs as human beings. In order to survive, children of narcissists have to depend on their caretakers for food and shelter – which means they have to play by the rules of their toxic parents if they want to live. This creates what Dr. Seltzer calls maladaptive "survival programs" that we carry onto adulthood – habits like people-pleasing, sacrificing one's needs to take care of others, feeling "selfish" when pursuing our goals and dimming our light so we don't become noticeable enough to be targeted.

"You may have internalized early in your life that your needs were not as important as others' needs were. Lack of empathy from a parent or caretaker, neglect, blame, criticism, failure to accept you as you are and appreciate your qualities and other such experiences have shaped your belief that others' needs should come before your own." –Nina W. Brown,

A lack of safety and security in the crucial developmental stages of life can create destructive, insecure attachment styles when we are adults, causing us to gravitate towards people who will fail to meet our needs and disappoint us, time and time again.

It can also drive children of narcissists to sabotage themselves, due to the put-downs experienced during a time when the brain is highly susceptible to the harmful effects of trauma. In response to psychological violence, children of narcissistic parents develop a sense of toxic shame, self-blame and an unyielding inner critic[11] that makes them feel as if they're not worthy of the amazing things life has to offer.

Children of narcissists may be convinced they're not good enough, or they may go in the other direction: they may become overachieving perfectionists in an effort to prove themselves. Either way, they are lacking the self-validation and internal sense of stability which can only come from healthy self-love.

(3) Addictions and dissociation become default coping mechanisms.

Trauma can affect the reward centers of our brain, making us more susceptible to substance abuse or other addictions (Bellis and Zisk, 2014). When we've been traumatized at such a young age, dissociation, a survival mechanism which detaches us from our experiences, our bodies and the world – can become a way of life. It's not uncommon for abused children to create fantasy worlds they can escape into, especially during periods of horrific violence. Depending on the severity of the trauma, survivors of childhood abuse may also struggle with addictive behavior as adults.

> "The human brain is a social organ that is shaped by experience, and that is shaped in order to respond to the experience that you're having. So particularly earlier in life, if you're in a constant state of terror; your brain is shaped to be on alert for danger, and to try to make those terrible feelings go away. The brain gets very confused. And that leads to problems with excessive anger, excessive shutting

down, and doing things like taking drugs to make yourself feel better. These things are almost always the result of having a brain that is set to feel in danger and fear. As you grow up an get a more stable brain, these early traumatic events can still cause changes that make you hyper-alert to danger, and hypo-alert to the pleasures of everyday life...

"If you're an adult and life's been good to you, and then something bad happens, that sort of injures a little piece of the whole structure. But toxic stress in childhood from abandonment or chronic violence has pervasive effects on the capacity to pay attention, to learn, to see where other people are coming from, and it really creates havoc with the whole social environment. And it leads to criminality, and drug addiction, and chronic illness, and people going to prison, and repetition of the trauma on the next generation."
–Dr. Van der Kolk, *Childhood Trauma Leads to Brains Wired for Fear*[12]

This addictive behavior is not just limited to alcohol or hard drugs; it can range from gambling to sex addiction to unhealthy relationships or even self-harm. Survivors of toxic parents can overeat or undereat as a way to regain control and agency over their bodies; they may develop eating disorders, a penchant for risky sexual behavior or other compulsive behaviors to soothe their unresolved grief.

It's not necessarily about the specific addiction, but the fact that the addiction provides a convenient escape from the day-to-day realities of immense pain, depression, anxiety and rage that often lie in the aftermath of unresolved childhood wounding.

(4) Suicidal ideation is devastatingly common and pervasive among childhood abuse survivors.

Suicidality increases as ACEs score (Adverse Childhood Experiences score) increases and so does the risk of developing chronic health problems in adulthood.

When one has been traumatized as a child and then later re-victimized multiple times in adulthood, a pervasive sense of hopelessness and perceived burdensomeness can result (Joiner et al.,

2002). Survivors of chronic, complex trauma are especially at risk for suicidal ideation and self-harm as adults, because they have witnessed time and time again the cycle repeating itself.

In fact, survivors who have four or more adverse childhood experiences are twelve times more likely to be suicidal.

This learned helplessness lends itself to belief systems which cause survivors to feel as if nothing will ever change. They may feel "defective" or different from others because of the immense adversity they experienced. The future may look bleak if a survivor has not been properly validated or gotten the professional support needed in order to heal.

(5) There are disparate inner parts that develop which seem out of alignment with your adult self.

While many people have heard of the "inner child," fewer people address the fact that there can be *multiple* inner parts that can develop as a result of chronic abuse. Some of these parts are those we've hidden, sublimated or minimized in an attempt to mitigate the risk of being abused – for example, when victims of abuse shy away from the limelight to avoid being punished or criticized for their success.

Then there are "parts" which are defensive responses to the trauma itself. These parts manifest in self-sabotaging ways, but they are actually misguided attempts to protect us. Complex trauma survivors may be so protective of sharing who they really are with the world that they close themselves off from the people who might really "see" and appreciate them. This ruins the possibility of authentic connection or vulnerability with others. This defensive strategy may have been a survival mechanism they developed when younger to avoid the threat of being harmed by a violent parent. It served them as helpless children, but it can cause them to shut out the possibility of intimacy with others as adults.

That being said, there are many ways in which self-sabotage can present itself depending on context and even the type of abuse endured. For example, a male complex trauma survivor may find himself developing a hypermasculine side to himself to ward off memories of sexual abuse. The daughter of a hypercritical narcissistic mother may develop an inner part which is overly angry and defensive to criticism, whether constructive or destructive.

Whether they stemmed from childhood or adult traumas, these 'parts' have much to tell us. Silencing or repressing them only makes them stronger in their resolve to protect us – so instead, we have to listen to what they want us to know. Integrating these parts in a healthy manner requires that we learn what they are trying to protect us from and find alternative ways to create a sense of safety in the world moving forward.

Cutting the Emotional Umbilical Cord and Recovery

The children of narcissistic parents can begin their healing journey by working with a trauma-informed professional to navigate their triggers, process their traumas and learn more about healthier boundaries. Using mind-body healing techniques can also be helpful to supplement therapy; trauma-focused yoga and meditation have been scientifically proven to help heal parts of the brain affected by early childhood trauma.

A daily exercise regimen is also a great way to replace the unhealthy biochemical addiction we developed to toxicity. It's a natural way to release endorphins and gives us that "rush" of feel-good chemicals *without* inviting toxic people into our lives.

We talk more specifically about these healing modalities in greater detail later on in the section, *"Healing Modalities for Adult Children of Narcissists."*

There are also tremendous benefits from going No Contact or Low Contact with toxic parents as we heal – this is another aspect we will explore later on in the essay regarding low contact. Minimum contact with a narcissistic parent along with strong boundaries can help us to detox from the effects of their cruelty and in essence learn how to breathe fresher air. Grieving our complex emotions is also necessary to recovery, as we are likely to feel a very powerful bond to our parents despite the abuse (and in fact *due* to the abuse) we endured. Seek positive role models, especially of the gender of your toxic parent, who can help remodel what you are looking for in an intimate relationship.

Address subconscious behavior patterns by bringing the true beliefs underlying them to the surface. Many children of narcissistic parents are trained to believe in their unworthiness; it's time to start rewriting these narratives. Use positive affirmations, journaling, and speak directly to any repressed inner parts which may be sabotaging your success. It is only when you feel truly worthy of respectful, compassionate love on a subconscious level, that you will be able to run in the other direction when you encounter toxicity.

Despite the challenges on their journey, childhood abuse survivors of narcissistic parents have incredible potential to lead victorious lives. They can channel their adversity into freedom, peace, and joy. They have tremendous resilience, an extraordinary ability to adapt and a knowledge of coping mechanisms that will serve them well as they begin to heal.

References

Bremner, J. D. (2006). Traumatic stress: effects on the brain. *Dialogues in Clinical Neuroscience, 8*(4), 445–461.

Bellis, M. D., & Zisk, A. (2014). The Biological Effects of Childhood Trauma. *Child and Adolescent Psychiatric Clinics of North America, 23*(2), 185-222. doi:10.1016/j.chc.2014.01.002

Brown, N. W. (2008). Children of the self-absorbed: A grown-up's guide to getting over narcissistic parents. Oakland, CA: New Harbinger Publications.

Choi, J., Jeong, B., Rohan, M. L., Polcari, A. M., & Teicher, M. H. (2009). Preliminary Evidence for White Matter Tract Abnormalities in Young Adults Exposed to Parental Verbal Abuse. Biological Psychiatry, 65(3), 227-234. doi:10.1016/j.biopsych.2008.06.022

Harris, N. B. (2014, September). How childhood trauma affects health across a lifetime. Retrieved November 15, 2017.

Herman, Judith Lewis. *Trauma and Recovery: the aftermath of abuse – from domestic violence to political terror.* Basic Books, 1997.

Joiner, T. E., Pettit, J. W., Walker, R. L., Voelz, Z. R., Cruz, J., Rudd, M. D., & Lester, D. (2002). Perceived Burdensomeness And Suicidality: Two Studies On The Suicide Notes Of Those Attempting And Those Completing Suicide. *Journal of Social and Clinical Psychology, 21*(5), 531-545. doi:10.1521/jscp.21.5.531.22624

Levine, P. A. (1997). *Waking the tiger: Healing trauma.* Berkeley, CA: North Atlantic Books.

Lazar, S. W., Kerr, C. E., Wasserman, R. H., Gray, J. R., Greve, D. N., Treadway, M. T., . . . Fischl, B. (2005). Meditation experience is associated with increased cortical thickness. *NeuroReport, 16*(17), 1893-1897. doi:10.1097/01.wnr.0000186598.66243.19

Schulte, B. (2015, May 26). Harvard neuroscientist: Meditation not only reduces stress, here's how it changes your brain. The Washington Post. Retrieved September 5, 2017.

Shin, L. M., Rauch, S. L., & Pittman, R. K. (2006). Amygdala, Medial Prefrontal Cortex, and Hippocampal Function in PTSD. *Annals of the New York Academy of Sciences, 1071*(1), 67-79. doi:10.1196/annals.1364.007

Seltzer, L. F. (2011, January 07). The "Programming" of Self-Sabotage (Pt 3 of 5). Retrieved November 15, 2017.

Substance Abuse and Mental Health Services Administration. (2017, September 5). Adverse Childhood Experiences. Retrieved October 10, 2017.

Teicher, M. (2006). Sticks, Stones, and Hurtful Words: Relative Effects of Various Forms of Childhood Maltreatment. American Journal of Psychiatry, 163(6), 993. doi:10.1176/appi.ajp.163.6.993

Van der Kolk, B. (2015). *The body keeps the score: Brain, mind, and body in the healing of trauma.* NY, NY: Penguin Books.

Van der Kolk, Bessel. Childhood Trauma Leads to Brains Wired for Fear. 3 Feb. 2015. Accessed 15 Nov. 2017

Trauma Reenactment:

Adult Children of Narcissists and The Trauma Repetition Cycle

At the root of the life-course trajectories of adult children of narcissists, we often find some form of what psychologists call **trauma reenactment** or *repetition compulsion*. This is a repetition of the traumatic event in one's adulthood. Dr. Patrick Carnes, author of *The Betrayal Bond*, writes:

> "Therapists use the term repetition compulsion which means repeating behaviors and/or seeking situations or persons that re-create the trauma experience...Some people will find themselves in the same situation, with the same type of person, over and over again in their lives. Yet...they may never link their behavior to the original betrayal and trauma. Reenactment is living in the unremembered past."

While trauma reenactment on the surface could be mistaken as a set of conscious choices, it is often anything but. It is usually driven by our subconscious and can be quite inadvertent and involuntary. We may not even be aware that we're in a trauma repetition cycle until we observe the larger patterns in our lives.

Repetition compulsion often has an addictive, reflexive and seemingly unstoppable quality to it. As Dr. Whitfield notes:

"Such compulsive actions range across a wide spectrum of possible behaviors, from heavy use of alcohol or other drugs, to short-term, intense relationships, to trying to control another person. It may involve overeating, oversexing, overworking, overspending...this compulsive behavior tends to be negative in some way, such as self-destruction or other-destruction. It may produce a crisis as a side effect or may precipitate a crisis for self and for others. While we can control the behavior to some extent—we have some degree of willpower over it, in that we may even plan it—it often occurs impulsively and automatically, as if by reflex."

Perhaps one of the most common forms of repetition compulsion lies within the realm of our relationships in adulthood. It should come to no surprise that 83% of the adult children of narcissists I surveyed had toxic relationships in adulthood with those who resembled their parents. Certainly, we should not engage in any form of self-blame just because we were re-traumatized. Nor should we use trauma reenactment as a sign that there is something so defective about us that it detracts from the responsibility of the predators who have victimized us.

Regardless of our childhood wounding, abuse is and will always be the fault of the perpetrator who inflicts it. We can take responsibility for healing ourselves without blaming ourselves for the abusive actions of others. We also know that anyone, regardless of their childhood upbringing, can be targeted by a narcissistic individual. Predators who seek to terrorize individuals who've already been wounded are all the more dangerous and sick for doing so, and should be held fully accountable for their actions.

Nevertheless, an understanding of trauma repetition is crucial if we want to learn how to break the cycle and become more aware of when we're in the cycle in the first place. An understanding of how our childhood upbringing strengthens present trauma bonds, how we've come to normalize abusive behaviors, and what childhood wounds we can heal to better detach from abusers is essential to our healing journey as adults.

According to Dr. Levy, there are usually several reasons for trauma reenactment, including attempting to subconsciously master the trauma as well as inadvertent repetition due to subconscious defenses and wounds. As he writes in his article, "A Helpful Way to Understand and Conceptualize Reenactments":

"Other writers understand reenactments as a means of achieving mastery: a traumatized individual reenacts a trauma in order to remember, assimilate, integrate, and heal from the traumatic experience... there is something uncanny about reenactments. While they often appear to be consciously chosen, they have a quality of involuntariness. In addition, although it has been theorized that reenacting a past trauma is a way an individual attempts to master it, lifelong reenactments and re-exposure to trauma rarely result in resolution and mastery."

Mastery of the Trauma

This is perhaps the realm of trauma reenactment in which individuals appear to exercise agency the most consciously. Individuals may be driven to "master" their trauma by gravitating towards similar types of scenarios they experienced in childhood in an attempt to find some form of resolution or to channel that experience differently.

For example, in graduate school, I interviewed teachers who had been bullied in childhood. They attempted to "master" their trauma by going to the original "scene of the crime" – schools. Many of them implemented anti-bullying curricula and programs in the schools where they taught, thus successfully adapting and channeling their traumas into the greater good. They helped to prevent other children from being bullied as they were. This would be considered by Dr. Levy as a successful "adaptation" or an example of mastery over their traumas. Not only did they become active agents in creating more empowering narratives about their experiences, they also empowered victims just like them.

On the other hand, mastery of the trauma can also present itself in maladaptive ways. Some of these same bully victims, while successful in their careers, tended to end up with narcissistic individuals as dating partners in adulthood. Their experiences of being bullied still affected them interpersonally, which led to diminished self-esteem and a need for validation from toxic people. In an attempt to subconsciously master the trauma of being terrorized, they were inadvertently re-traumatized in their social and intimate relationships.

The maladaptive aspect of "mastery" can come into play quite frequently in the adult relationships of those who've been raised by narcissistic parents. Not only is our subconscious attempting to find a successful resolution to the trauma experienced, the familiarity of abuse and how normalized it is causes us to gravitate towards individuals who, while on the surface may appear charming, are actually quite predatory and similar to our early caretakers.

As Levy says:

"Trauma survivors may also be drawn to establish relationships that are similar to past significant relationships because there is comfort in familiarity. For example, a man who was emotionally abused by his aloof, distant mother ends up in a relationship with a woman with similar traits. Another woman who was sexually abused by her father and brothers acts in sexually provocative ways with others. It has been found that when animals are hyperaroused, they tend to avoid novelty and perseverate in familiar behavior regardless of the outcome. However, in states of low arousal they seek novelty and are curious. For many victims of childhood abuse, dealing with other people on an intimate basis is a high-arousal state because past relationships have been marked by terror, anxiety, and fear."

It makes sense that since many adult children of narcissists are in a high arousal state due to unhealed trauma that they would subconsciously seek the familiarity of abusive relationships rather than the novelty of healthier ones – even if they are unaware of this pattern. Although this connection is explored in a rather straightforward, linear way by psychologists, I believe it is far more complex and multifaceted. It's true that our subconscious can choose partners who are very much like our early caretakers, in an attempt to find resolution to the horrific traumas we experienced in childhood. However, many victims of narcissists in adulthood do not fall for predators who are outwardly violent or like their parents on the surface. Rather, they fall for the "knight in shining armor" – the person who appears to be there to rescue them. That is why love-bombing by narcissists works so well: it disarms us, because it symbolizes the unconditional positive regard we never received in childhood. Every child deserves this unconditional positive regard, but unfortunately, not all children receive it. There is nothing wrong with that desire. It does, however, leave us vulnerable when we don't acknowledge when our desire may be getting in the way of accurately seeing our partners for who they truly are, rather than who they pretend to be.

Covert abusers break down our defenses slowly and erode our boundaries bit by bit until we realize that the charming savior was actually a charlatan all along. By that time, it's too late – we've already been violated, retraumatized and trauma bonded to this individual.

Reenactments Caused By Rigid or Dissociative Defenses

As we know, those who've been abused by narcissistic parents in adulthood can develop insecure, anxious, disorganized or avoidant attachment styles. Many of us struggle with abandonment wounds as well. In relationships with abusive narcissists in adulthood, these abandonment wounds become exacerbated and cemented. Each new relationship with a toxic individual dumps salt on existing wounds. We feel even more paralyzed and helpless because even if we do know we are being abused, the terror of abandonment is one that might have meant life or death in our childhood.

Remember that our brains are wired to survive in dangerous situations; as a child, our brain becomes so overwhelmed by the toxic stress inflicted by our abusive parent that it uses most of our mental and psychological resources to survive the abuse. As a result, we have fewer resources spent on learning, planning, regulating our emotions and productive decision-making – all crucial ingredients for healthy development. As we grow into adults, our abilities to attach to others in healthy ways can be disrupted. So, we may automatically react to the threat of abandonment in ways that could be people-pleasing, ambivalent, avoidant, or a hybrid of all insecure attachment styles.

Perhaps we self-isolate or withdraw from others to avoid abandonment. Yet by doing so, we lack the supportive relationships which might make us feel loved. Maybe we get involved with emotionally unavailable partners or those who initially don't present as much of a "threat" to our nervous system because we already sense they're not compatible with us in some way. This could be a protective mechanism meant to avoid rejection and emotional overwhelm by someone we're *actually* interested in. After all, if we pick someone who can never commit to us or who we aren't truly interested in, we "avoid" being rejected. Yet, inadvertently, what happens is that we might still be abandoned by this person and it *still* brings up all of our childhood wounds. We are still rejected – by someone we weren't even interested in!

We may also have dissociative defenses we developed in childhood, where we dissociated from the reality of the abuse in order to survive the experience. As a child who grew up witnessing and being subjected to severe emotional abuse by a narcissistic parent, I remember having to put my hands over my ears to tune out the screaming matches which woke me up every morning. I would also have to mentally tune out and dissociate while witnessing the horrific verbal abuse my narcissistic parent used to control our family. Since I was also severely bullied by peers at the time at school, I would disappear into daydreaming for hours, creating imaginary worlds and escaping into fantasy scenarios instead of connecting with the reality of the abuse around me. These dissociative defenses can also come up when we end up in toxic relationships in adulthood. We might find ourselves denying, minimizing, or disappearing into a fantasy of the ideal relationship even while being abused, mistreated, and violated.

This was a survival mechanism which was birthed in our violent childhoods, but it does not serve us in adulthood. Instead, it keeps us further entrenched in toxic relationships. It continues the cycle.

To better understand how to break the cycle, I've created an acronym which will help to remind you of which areas to target when you're working to heal from trauma repetition. *This acronym is a short and sweet summary of some of the work we'll be doing throughout the book and is only the beginning.* You will find more specific healing modalities to address these aspects discussed in the sections "Healing and Re-parenting the Inner Child" and "Healing Modalities for Adult Children of Narcissists."

BREAK THE CYCLE – My Acronym for Adult Children of Narcissists

Breath and bodywork.

Relationship choices.

Evaluate patterns.

Addictions.

Kindness towards self.

Trauma bonds.

Hidden selves.

Exit toxic situations.

Cry and grieve.

Yield.

Child (Inner Work).

Liberation from unhealthy belief systems.

Emotions.

Breath and bodywork. As we'll discuss in many of the essays, mindfulness is important and essential to healing the brain which has been formed by childhood abuse. Interacting with people and making decisions can be inevitably triggering to us, hijacking the very parts of our brain which cause us to regress back to childhood. Remembering to take a few minutes to breathe, bring our mind and body back to baseline levels of safety whenever we're dealing with triggering interpersonal situations can help us to ensure that we are operating from what therapist Dr. Marsha Linehan calls "wise mind." That way, we are not constantly in fight, flight, freeze or fawn mode, but rather, approaching situations with an awareness of our boundaries and an ability to be assertive. Bodywork is also important to this, because, as Dr. Van der Kolk suggests, our body does indeed "keep the score" on the traumas we experience. Trauma-informed yoga, healing massage, Reiki therapy, acupuncture, mindful body scans and somatic reexperiencing can all be a part of healing the physical aspects of the trauma which may still be trapped within us.

Relationship choices. While we know that any type of abuse is not our fault, it is still productive to look at the relationship partners and friendships we've had. When we see the similarities among these partners and friends, we can pinpoint the qualities which may have subconsciously caused us to gravitate towards those people, triggering ancient destructive beliefs and abandonment wounds.

Evaluate patterns. Evaluating the patterns in our lives is essential to understanding how these cycles begin and how they end. Imagine that there are multiple cycles being repeated, one with each toxic person you've encountered. How did each cycle begin? What factors helped to keep the cycle going? How did the cycle with that person end (or, if it's still continuing, evaluate what factors are causing you to remain entrenched)? We also need to evaluate the other patterns in our lives and the cycles. Are there cycles of sabotage, and if so, which areas of your life are most affected by it?

Addictions. Address any addictive behaviors you might engage in as a way to fulfill the void that childhood emotional abuse has left. Do you overeat or undereat? Do you engage in compulsive shopping, gambling, or risky sexual activities? Do you find yourself feeling somehow "addicted" to dangerous situations or people? Are you addicted to overachieving or perfectionism?

Kindness towards self. Self-compassion during the healing journey is paramount, and it is crucial when you're doing the inner work to break cycles like these. Notice when you're engaging in negative self-talk. Track when that inner critic pops up and what it says. Gently steer yourself back into a self-compassionate stance whenever you find yourself going down the rabbit hole of toxic self-blame and shame. If you're harshly judging yourself, remind yourself that the abuse you suffered was not your fault. You were an innocent child who did not learn the healthy coping mechanisms which would've served you as an adult. You do not deserve any more cruelty, especially from yourself – you have already suffered enough. Know that you deserve a positive inner voice.

Trauma bonds. Assess the trauma bonds you have with your narcissistic parents as well as your subsequent abusive partners, friends or colleagues. Do you still find yourself protecting or defending them or other abusers in your life? Do you still suffer from fear, obligation and guilt whenever you interact with them? On a scale of 1-10, how attached do you still feel to these toxic people?

Hidden selves. As children, we were not allowed to grow into our authentic selves. Instead, we were encouraged to inhabit a false self in an attempt to please our parents or in an attempt to avoid abuse. As adults, we may struggle with a fragmented sense of identity. There may be "hidden selves" or disparate inner parts, each of which represents a facet of ourselves. Some parts carry the direct emotional charges and wounds of childhood, while others stem from defenses that arose due to trauma. Some parts represent aspects we were not allowed to express or take ownership as children, while others are false selves created from the brutal conditioning inflicted by our parents. Write down "names" for these different parts and their characteristics to help better identify them when they come up.

For example, as I discuss more in-depth in the Inner Parts exercise, one of my parts include "The CEO," an overly perfectionistic aspect of myself that developed as an overachiever in response to abusive and bullying tactics. They also include "The Party Girl" and "The Fawner."

Exit toxic situations. What are the situations which are currently exacerbating your wounds? Are your social circles toxic to your psyche? Is your current work environment bringing out all of your toxic people-pleasing habits? Brainstorm ways to exit, or at the very least, lessen the impact of these situations until you can (for example: meditating and saving money while planning to leave your draining job, gradually decreasing contact with friends who are unsupportive).

Cry and grieve. Grieving is an integral part of the healing journey. We need to heal our childhood wounds, the traumas which reinforced these wounds in adulthood, and grieve for the childhood and supportive parents we never had. This requires confronting intense emotions without attempting to repress them (preferably with the help of a trauma-informed counselor). The more we attempt to shut down our grief or numb our emotions, the more our grief festers, and the more healing that needs to be done. Think of it like a psychological debt which accumulates interest over time. When we don't "pay" the emotional debt or relieve and experience the pain of it, it then becomes strengthened with similar life experiences which add to the original wound. The grieving we do not do now, we will inevitably have to grieve for later, often even more compounded with extra layers of trauma.

In his book, *Healing the Child Within*, Dr. Whitfield describes this as "unresolved grief." He writes:

> "Unresolved grief festers like a deep wound covered by scar tissue, a pocket of vulnerability ever ready to break out anew. When we experience a loss or trauma, it stirs up energy within us that needs to be discharged. When we do not discharge this energy, the stress builds up to a state of chronic distress...with no release, this chronic distress is stored within us as discomfort or tension that may at first be difficult for us to recognize.
>
> We may feel it or experience it through a wide range of manifestations, such as chronic anxiety, tension, fear or nervousness, anger or resentment, sadness, emptiness, unfulfillment, confusion, guilt, shame or, as is common among many who grew up in a troubled family, as a feeling of numbness or "no feelings at all." These feelings may come

and go in the same person. There may also be difficulty sleeping, aches, pains and other somatic complaints, and full-blown mental-emotional or physical illness, including PTSD, may result. In short, we pay a price when we do not grieve in a complete and healthy way."

Yield. Yield to what has been, rather than what we wished it had been. As a defensive mechanism, adult children of narcissists might attempt to sweep the trauma they went through under the rug, spiritually bypass the pain, look at their childhood through rose-colored glasses, or ignore the effects of the abuse they endured altogether. We don't have to approve of what happened to us in the past in order to radically accept or confront it in the present. We can acknowledge how unjust, how unfair, how terribly brutal it was, even while surrendering to the reality of it. Denying, rationalizing, or minimizing the destructive impact our childhood had on us can halt the grieving process and delay true healing. It can cause us to feed into trauma bonds with our toxic parents and subsequent partners, disabling us from setting healthier boundaries and living the life of freedom we truly deserve.

Child (Inner) work. Working with our inner child and "re-parenting" it by giving it the love, acceptance and unconditional positive regard we did not get in childhood can significantly alter our life-course trajectory. A child raised in a healthy home learns that he or she is inherently worthy and deserving of all that is good. In re-parenting ourselves, we have to give ourselves the soothing words and actions we did not receive in childhood. When we perceive ourselves as worthy, loveable, and deserving, we're less likely to fall into the trap of shortchanging ourselves, our values, and our boundaries. You'll learn how to do this in Re-parenting the Inner Child.

Liberation from unhealthy belief systems. As children of narcissistic parents, we learn numerous unhealthy belief systems which are stored in us at a subconscious and bodily level. We may not even be aware which belief systems dominate our everyday decisions, but they do in fact filter the ways in which we view the world, ourselves, and others. For example, a common belief that many adult children of narcissists share is, "I am not good enough." This is a core belief which drives our behavior in adulthood, causing us to settle for less than what we deserve, sabotage ourselves, and always search for a rescuer to complete us. Liberating ourselves from unhealthy belief systems takes work and effort; we have to first identify that these toxic beliefs exist in the first place. A good way to start is to imagine that a friend of yours is the one who holds these beliefs, such as, "I am not worthy" or "I am not capable." What would you tell *them*? How would you convince them otherwise? Then, turn the advice to yourself: what evidence contradicts this belief?

Emotions. Learning to express, release, channel, validate and take care of your emotions in healthy ways is vital. Emotion management, regulation and self-care are part of the life skills which any adult child of a toxic parent will need to focus on developing throughout their lives. Validate any and all of your emotions as they come up. They don't have to be "rational" in order to be validated. Whatever you're feeling is okay and deserves attention. Mindfully keep track of your emotions and note where you might require some physical release. Do you have an excess of rage that you need to express in a safe holding environment with a therapist or a kickboxing session? Do you have a deep sadness that might be constructively expressed through journaling, a creative project or art therapy? If you could label your emotions, what would they be? If you could visualize your emotions, how would they look? If you could truly honor and love your emotions, rather than repressing or shaming them, how would you feel?

Healing and the True Self

When complex trauma survivors begin to grieve and heal their core wounds, something magical occurs. The toxic people and situations that once triggered them and made them regress into intense states of powerlessness and toxic shame begin to hold less power. Their emotional responses to predatory people become neutralized, replaced with the knowing that the malignant projections of others have nothing to do with them. In the midst of healing, you begin to feel a beautiful and glorious detachment. You no longer seek an external savior – you save yourself. Self-love and the "true self" – wise, self-compassionate, calm, and in control – emerge.

Once buried beneath the ashes of trauma, who we really are and who we were truly meant to be is finally uncovered. You are reborn.

References

Carnes, P. P. (2015). *Betrayal Bond: Breaking Free of Exploitive Relationships*. Deerfield Beach, FL: Health Communications, Incorporated.

Levy M. S. (1998). A helpful way to conceptualize and understand reenactments. *The Journal of psychotherapy practice and research*, *7*(3), 227-35.

Whitfield, C. L., & Nuckols, C. C. (2015). *Healing the child within: Discovery and recovery for adult children of dysfunctional families*. Deerfield Beach, FL: Health Communications.

Exploratory Questions: The Trauma Repetition Cycle

As you read through the BREAK THE CYCLE acronym, get out a notebook or pull up a document on your computer and work through the following questions.

What type of compulsive behaviors did you engage in as both a child and later as an adult? (ex. Overeating, undereating, using drugs, getting into relationships with toxic people).

Whatever your compulsive behaviors were, write them down and next to each behavior, write down which emotions, thoughts, and bodily sensations you experienced whenever you had an urge to engage in them. (ex. Every time I overate as both a child and as an adult, I felt a deep sense of toxic shame about the way I had been treated).

Next to each compulsive behavior, write some alternatives you could use to replace the unhealthy behavior with a healthy one. (Ex. Rather than overeating, I will go out for a walk until the craving passes. Instead of reaching out to my toxic ex, I will go to a meditation workshop and sit with my feelings. Instead of harming myself, I will reach out to my therapist or close, trustworthy friend).

When in a toxic relationship or friendship, what tends to be your go-to defensive strategies? (Ex. People-pleasing, dissociation, avoidance).

Who were the people you've been in relationships with who are the most similar to your parents? Are you still in contact? If so, what types of thoughts, circumstances, and fears are holding you back from cutting off contact? What is one small step today you can take to detach from them? (Ex. I am still in contact with my abusive friend from high school. What's holding me back from going No Contact is an intense sense of guilt since we grew up together. One small step I can take today is letting her know I won't be available to talk as often.)

What Its Like to Be

A Complex Trauma Survivor
Of Narcissistic Abuse

"Repeated trauma in adult life erodes the structure of the personality already formed, but repeated trauma in childhood forms and deforms the personality. The child trapped in an abusive environment is faced with formidable tasks of adaption. She must find a way to preserve a sense of trust in people who are untrustworthy, safety in a situation that is unsafe, control in a situation that is terrifyingly unpredictable, power in a situation of helplessness. Unable to care for or protect herself, she must compensate for the failures of adult care and protection with the only means at her disposal, an immature system of psychological defenses." – Judith Lewis Herman, *Trauma and Recovery: The Aftermath of Violence – From Domestic Abuse to Political Terror*

Complex trauma is *compounded trauma* and can result in symptoms of Complex PTSD. Survivors of complex trauma endure trauma not only in childhood, but often in adulthood as well. Imagine, if you will, multiple chains of traumas, all of which are connected in some way to each other. The most recent traumas build on earlier ones, reinforcing ancient wounds, maladaptive belief systems and fear-based physiological responses. These childhood wounds create the foundation of deep-seated toxic shame and self-sabotage for the survivor; each "tiny terror" or larger trauma in adulthood builds upon it, brick by brick, creating an ingrained framework for self-destruction. Even when one wound is excavated, addressed and healed, another trauma that wound was connected to will inevitably unravel in the process.

The complex trauma survivor's life history is layered with chronic trauma as a result of ongoing stressors such as long-term domestic violence, childhood sexual abuse and physical abuse – situations where the individual is held "captive" whether emotionally or physically, feels under the complete control of a perpetrator or multiple perpetrators, and develops a perceived inability to escape the threatening situation.

Yet complex trauma isn't just caused by physical abuse; traumas such as severe verbal and emotional abuse in childhood have the potential to wreak havoc on one's sense of self and navigation in the world. According to trauma therapist Pete Walker, "The genesis of complex PTSD is most often associated with extended periods of ongoing physical and/or sexual abuse in childhood. My observations, however, convince me that ongoing extremes of verbal and/or emotional abuse also cause it."

Complex Trauma and Complex PTSD

Trauma expert Dr. Judith Herman notes that those who suffer from Complex Trauma can experience disruptions in the following areas in addition to the regular symptoms of PTSD:

Emotional Regulation.

Complex trauma survivors can struggle with overwhelming feelings of depression, chronic feelings of emptiness, suicidal ideation as well as extreme rage due to the severity and breadth of the traumas experienced. They can struggle with impulse control, self-harm and battle debilitating anxiety as well. Since present-day triggers can send them into emotional flashbacks, in which they encounter the same sense of powerlessness and emotional states of childhood, it can be very difficult for complex trauma survivors to mindfully manage their emotions.

Consciousness.

Those who have endured complex trauma may relive traumatic events, feel disassociated from the trauma, their bodies, the world and/or have problems with accessing their memories of the trauma. This is not surprising, since we know that trauma interferes with parts of the brain which deal with learning, decision-making and memory.

Survivors can endure nightmares of the traumatic event which incorporate both the visceral and emotional aspects of the event. Complex trauma survivors can endure not only visual flashbacks of the trauma but also "emotional flashbacks" which cause them to regress back to the emotional states of hopelessness where they first encountered the original wounds (Walker, 2013).

Self-Perception.

Survivors carry a sense of toxic shame, helplessness and a feeling of "separateness" from others, of being different and defective due to the trauma. They also bear the burden of guilt and negative self-talk that does not belong to them; Pete Walker (2013) calls this the "inner critic," an ongoing inner dialogue of self-blame, self-hatred and a need for perfectionism that evolved from the survivor being punished and conditioned to believe that his or her needs did not matter.

As he writes, "In extremely rejecting families, the child eventually comes to believe that even her normal needs, preferences, feelings and boundaries are dangerous imperfections – justifiable reasons for punishment and/or abandonment." Children who experience abuse in early childhood have a difficult time distinguishing between the abuser's actions and words and reality. A child who is told that the abuse is their fault repeatedly will come to believe in and internalize their lack of worth without question."

Distorted Perceptions of the Perpetrator.

Understandably, complex trauma survivors have an ambivalent relationship to their perpetrators. The 'trauma bond,' a bond created by intense emotional experiences and a threat to the victim's life (whether a physical or psychological threat) has been forged so that the victim could survive the circumstances of the abuse. As a result, they might defend or protect their abusers due to being trauma bonded to them and minimize or rationalize the abuse. They may also become excessively preoccupied with their abusers to the extent of seeking revenge.

They may become obsessed with what the abuser is doing in an attempt to regain a sense of control. They may also assign the abuser complete power and control over their lives by catering their careers, their lifestyles and social lives around the abuser.

Relations with Others.

Complex trauma survivors can become socially withdrawn and self-isolate due to the abuse or become overly invested in toxic relationships early on as a source of self-worth. Since they never develop a sense of safety, they distrust others while simultaneously searching for a "rescuer" who can finally give them the unconditional positive regard they were robbed of in childhood.

One's System of Meanings.

It is disturbingly easy to lose hope as a complex trauma survivor. When you've been re-violated time and time again, it is difficult *not* to lose faith and not to develop a sense of hopelessness which can interfere with a sense of meaning or belief in a bigger picture. Life may feel meaningless to a survivor who has never been shown proper care, affection or authentic connection. One's whole worldview is changed.

Narcissistic Abuse and Complex Trauma

Survivors of narcissistic abuse in childhood, who are later retraumatized by narcissistic or sociopathic predators in adulthood, can also show symptoms of complex trauma.

Imagine the daughter of a narcissistic father as an example. She grows up chronically violated and abused at home, perhaps bullied by her peers as well. Her burgeoning low self-esteem, disruptions in identity and problems with emotional regulation causes her to live a life filled with terror. This is a terror that is stored in the body and literally shapes her brain. It is also what makes her brain extra vulnerable and susceptible to the effects of trauma in adulthood.

Being verbally, emotionally and sometimes even physically beaten down, the child of a narcissistic parent learns that there is no safe place for her in the world. The symptoms of trauma emerge: disassociation to survive and escape her day-to-day existence, addictions that cause her to self-sabotage, maybe even self-harm to cope with the pain of being unloved, neglected and mistreated.

Her pervasive sense of worthlessness and toxic shame, as well as subconscious programming, then cause her to become more easily attached to emotional predators in adulthood.

In her repeated search for a rescuer, she instead finds those who chronically diminish her just like her earliest abusers. Of course, her resilience, adept skill set in adapting to chaotic environments and ability to "bounce back" was also birthed in early childhood. This is also seen as an "asset" to toxic partners because it means she will be more likely to stay within the abuse cycle in order to attempt to make things "work."

She then suffers not just from early childhood trauma, but from multiple re-victimizations in adulthood until, with the right support, she addresses her core wounds and begins to break the cycle step by step. Before she can break the cycle, she must first give herself the space and time to recover. A break from establishing new relationships is often essential during this time; No Contact (or Low Contact from her abusers in more complicated situations such as co-parenting) is also vital to the healing journey, to prevent compounding any existing traumas.

The Journey to Healing as a Complex Trauma Survivor

As the complex trauma survivor gives herself (or himself) time to disrupt dysfunctional patterns, she begins to develop a healthier sense of boundaries, a more grounded sense of self, and severs ties with toxic people. She receives counseling to address her triggers, symptoms of complex trauma and begins processing some of the original traumas. She grieves for the childhood she never had; she grieves the traumatic losses which reenacted her childhood wounds. She starts to recognize that the abuse was not her fault. She takes care of the inner child who needed nurturing all along. She begins to 'reprogram' the beliefs which underlie her sense of unworthiness and shame. Once she understands why her life has been one emotional roller coaster after the other, the path to recovery becomes much clearer.

This is just one example out of many of what being a complex trauma survivor can look like, but it is a powerful one that illustrates just how damaging early childhood abuse and complex trauma can be on the mind, body and psyche. Recovery from complex trauma is intense, challenging and frightening – but it is also liberating and empowering.

Complex trauma survivors carry with them a lifetime's worth of bullying regardless of how old they may be. Survivors of chronic narcissistic abuse especially can face the challenge of attempting to address wounds which may be primarily psychological rather than physical, but just as damaging.

The life experiences of complex trauma survivors have given them a great deal of resilience as well as opportunities to obtain more coping mechanisms than most. Yet their struggles are undeniable, pervasive and require intervention by professional support. A network consisting of a trauma-informed professional who understands complex trauma, a survivor community to supplement the professional support and diverse healing modalities which target both the mind and the body can be absolute life-savers for the survivor of complex trauma.

For a survivor who feels his or her voice was continually silenced and discounted, there is potential for immense healing and growth when one finally speaks and is validated.

References

Herman, Judith Lewis. Trauma and Recovery: the Aftermath of Abuse – from Domestic Violence to Political Terror. Basic Books, 1997.

National Center for PTSD. Complex PTSD. 1 Jan. 2007, www.ptsd.va.gov/professional/ptsd-overview/complex-ptsd.asp. Accessed 1 Oct. 2017.

Staggs, Sara. Complex Post-Traumatic Stress Disorder. 17 July 2016, psychcentral.com/lib/complex-post-traumatic-stress-disorder/. Accessed 1 Oct. 2017.

Stines, Sharie. What Is Trauma Bonding? 23 Oct. 2015, pro.psychcentral.com/recovery-expert/2015/10/what-is-trauma-bonding/. Accessed 2 Oct. 2017.

Van der Kolk, Bessel. The Body Keeps the Score: Brain, Mind, and Body in the Healing of Trauma. New York, Penguin Books, 2015.

Van der Kolk, Bessel. Childhood Trauma Leads to Brains Wired for Fear. 3 Feb. 2015, sideeffectspublicmedia.org/post/childhood-trauma-leads-brains-wired-fear. Accessed 1 Oct. 2017

Walker, Pete. Complex PTSD: from Surviving to Thriving. Lafayette, CA, Azure Coyote, 2013.

Walker, Pete. Frequently Asked Questions About Complex PTSD. Dec. 2013, pete-walker.com/fAQsComplexPTSD.html. Accessed 1 Oct. 2017.

Walker, Pete. Shrinking the Inner Critic in Complex PTSD. Dec. 2013, www.pete-walker.com/shrinkingInnerCritic.htm. Accessed 2 Oct. 2017.

Survey Says:

Adult Children of Narcissists Describe the Symptoms and Aftermath of Childhood Abuse

"I constantly second guess my evaluation of situations, and my responses to them. I can't seem to trust my own sense of reality. I am constantly panicking about having made the right decision, and I look to others to validate my perceptions and actions. I have held several jobs, each one good, but I am always finding a reason to quit. I am afraid people will see that I am not really as capable as they think. Like a promotion would reveal me as a fake, an impostor, because I couldn't really be smart/good, etc." — **Amanda, Upstate New York**

"Feeling lost and loveless. I tried to commit suicide several times when I was a teenager. Most of the time, my mother never knew. Until one day, I had a serious suicide attempt. My cousin found me and brought me to the hospital. My mother checked me out of the psychiatric hospital after I had my stomach pumped and I was okay to be transported to the psychiatric hospital. She checked me out the same day I had attempted suicide. She couldn't have her daughter in the hospital because I may have exposed her if I had stayed." — **Anne, Massachusetts**

"I am extremely self-critical. I was sexually abused and I think it stunted my maturity and development. I had no interest in boys until I was 14, and I was still playing with dolls at age 12. I could block my world out and go into this imaginary one. I hate conflict and confronting people. Often, I don't know what it is I truly want. I overcommit myself. Realized I don't really know myself, who I am, what my interests are. I am terrible at managing finances - maybe because I was deprived of having what were basics for others. I am terrible at self-care. I exhibit avoidance. I get overwhelmed easily. I have moments of loneliness and depression. Also, anxiety." — **Rachel, St. Louis, Missouri**

"I am a massive empath. I am constantly getting involved with narcissists and other Cluster B people." — **Isabella, California**

"Drug use and self-destructive behaviors." — **Andrea, Tampa, FL**

"Constant sadness and suicidal ideation due to unhealthy anger. Chronic depressive anxiety and recently, Dissociative Identity Disorder when overwhelmed. I've been in clinical psychiatric care for thirteen years, plus I've had a regression after a seventeen-year break." — **Ken**

"Being blind to abusive behaviors because they've been normal since pre-verbal stages. Not knowing better. Addiction to chaos. Believing chaos means things are going well. Believing that my desirability sexually is a determinant of my worthiness and lovability." — **Marsha, British Columbia, Canada**

"Some things appear contradictory, but they aren't. I get angry when someone tells me what to do or how to feel but I struggle until today with daring to express that anger. Same for people: if I like someone, I tend to trust (or better: want to trust!) too easily and overshare. But there are phases of isolation, too, and in general I do not really trust anyone. My C-PTSD is self-diagnosed. In Germany, it isn't an official diagnosis at all.

Other contradictions. You can be a perfectionist that always pushes yourself inside and still self-sabotage or the overachieving part of you is just inside, screaming at you while you are far too exhausted and depressive to move. This ambivalence, this inner conflict, this disunity is one of my main problems. I am always between wanting more from life and at the same time wanting nothing at all. There is literally always resistance in me regarding everything I want and need to do. The higher the pressure, the less voluntary my actions, and the stronger the resistance." — **Hanna**

"Codependency. Being too generous with my time and effort and ideas. Trying to save the world. Overwhelmed with political and environmental issues. Addiction to being busy with small tasks (dopamine addiction). Living a small life with little to no pleasure: no vacations, no luxuries, no dining out, etc." — **Chris H.**

"I have always thought something was very wrong with me as I have had a lot of difficulty dealing with close relationships over the years. I think I was too trusting, I had no idea what boundaries were or how to hold them. My mother was the narcissist, and any relationship I was in and went to her with questions about, she told me it was my fault. So, I just always assumed it was. I went on to marry a covert narcissist who was not verbally abusive like my mother was. He was more emotionally and psychologically abusive, so I really did not realize the problems he had since they were so hidden.

To make matters worse, my stepfather was physically violent toward my mother, so I could recognize physically violent and verbally abusive behavior but I just assumed the underhanded stuff were my own issues. So, I stayed married much longer than I should have. Ruminating thoughts about my marriage and childhood are almost constant on my mind. It can get really exhausting to the point where I need to get back into therapy.

Sometimes when I am criticizing myself, it is in her voice. I just recently realized this, and it is very spooky. I am a serial overachiever. If I am not productive at any point during the day, I am putting myself down. I had no idea what self-care was until maybe a year ago and I still struggle with doing nice things for myself. For example, if I take a day to just watch movies, which is really rare, I feel like a complete failure at the end of the day. I feel like I do not know how to relax. Rejection of any kind is crippling for me." — **C. from New Vienna, Ohio**

"The severity of neglect and alienation combined with intense smear campaigning has left me completely unable to make a single friend in my lifetime and I have never had any personal support. I have never experienced a positive relationship and pretty much all of my social memories make me feel nauseous. I have seizures when I get excited, either positively or negatively. I feel like everyone is pretty much brainwashed against me and committed to misunderstanding me or preying on me in one way or another... because that is literally what has happened with 99% of my acquaintances." – **Kristi from Bozeman, Montana**

"Always feeling second best." — **Kara, Canada**

"Feeling unworthy of love, especially romantic love. I have always struggled with feeling like my life doesn't belong to me, even after taking several crucial steps in adulthood to take control - like moving away, choosing my own career, dating who I want, etc. Despite being so adroit at taking care of others, I never thought I could do it alone, so all my life I searched for a man to do it *with* me or *for* me which never really worked out. Emotional and physical intimacy are difficult, and the mental abuse has always been harder to handle than the physical." — **Nadia, West Palm Beach, FL**

"I've become quite misanthropic to be honest. I was the total opposite as a child. I used to be a people-pleaser to the extreme. Now I've become the opposite. I've cut myself off from everyone apart from my husband." — **Clare, UK**

"Total inability to feel any joy - although I wouldn't consider myself depressed at all. I like and appreciate life and count my many blessings. But that purely physical "buzz" feeling of relaxation, joy and peace in happy moments has eluded me for many years now." — **Harriett, London**

"I am currently single. I am afraid to date because of the damage inflicted by my last narcissistic relationship, which was just as bad as my relationship with my mother. Due to dealing with narcissistic abuse for so long, I realized that every partner (dating or engagement) that I dealt with was a narcissist. They exhibited the same traits as my mother.

I ultimately stayed in these toxic relationships because I was trying to fix them or help them in the sense of a mother helping their child. My role with my mother was ultimately where I was the caregiver and she took everything. I assumed the same caregiver role in my relationships. I don't trust men. I have just begun to love myself. I used to blame myself for everything that has occurred in my life without looking at my experiences as a lesson to help me become the woman I am today." — **Clover S. Scott, Saint Rose, Louisiana**

"Pathological dissociation. Recognized it only recently - any stress, ever so insignificant - gets me into an alternative state of mind. It messes up learning, decision-making, and it distorts reality. Sometimes my state of mind is very stubborn, and it is very difficult to ground oneself and get out of it." — **Michael, Ekateringburg, Russia**

"My blind trust shifted 180 degrees after an extremely abusive relationship at age 50. Now I don't trust anyone. I *had* anxiety after the most recent abuse, and I believe I was misdiagnosed with Generalized Anxiety Disorder. I had never experienced anxiety or panic attacks prior to the recent abuse. I believe the condition was PTSD or CPTSD, but it is now in full remission. I suffered depression from teenage years due to my narcissistic parent, as did she and another sibling. My mindfulness practice now prevents me from spiraling into depression. I have a fear of abandonment. I also have a sense of not belonging anywhere and the fear of not being loved by anyone." — Margot MacCallum, Australia

"Flashbacks, panic attacks, several health issues. I have nobody I can talk to completely. A lot of people do not understand how CPTSD can affect you. It is just me and my dog. I am trying, really trying. It feels like just surviving the day takes all the energy in the world. I also moved to another country, and have struggled with getting a job, or launching my business.

I went from a C-level Executive in TV, overachiever and workaholic, to struggling to do basic tasks like eat and take a shower. I have come a long way, and I am trying to get back on my feet. But, some days, the frame of reference is completely lost, and I have devastating thoughts, feelings, flashbacks. Some days, I feel disconnected and unable to feel any kind of pleasure, joy or purpose. I have issues with my sexuality after the trauma bonding (I have been hyper-sexual since a very young age). I have identity issues. I would give anything for a hug. I have so much bottled up inside. I feel like I am disposable, that nothing makes sense anymore." – Melissa, Los Angeles, CA

"I have had to empower myself because of the lifelong injuries. It is hard to explain the distinction I feel between being mentally ill and mentally and emotionally injured. The hypervigilance only began when I realized what I was dealing with, beginning with a series of triggers in 2015 which woke me up to the lifelong abuse. I have suffered enormous grief since December of 2016. Absolutely debilitating. Flashbacks, emotional flashbacks, no help, no money, being in captivity - losing all the friends because they are narcissists. Realizing that I was a sex slave from birth until 2007. But, I am an artist. My career was sabotaged by many others. I have always made art regardless of that, and now I do it in secret, so to speak, because my husband will make certain that I do not succeed. I have a project that I pray I will one day be supported for fulfilling." — Nadine

"Never trusting my own memory." — Rae, Chicago, Illinois

"I go nuts when someone tries to tell me who I am! Thank god my addiction to exercise was healthy compared to all the other options. Self-harm in the form of self-sabotaging myself of good in my life (the 'deserving' button has been annihilated.) I find it very difficult to plan a day, as I never know how I will feel, if I will be able to function. I tend to dissociate easily. My main emotion is overwhelm.

To this day, I still have body memories, massive anxiety and panic attacks sometimes which seemingly come out of thin air! I believe this is due to the fact that the abuse started in infancy when I was preverbal and unable to make any sense of my life. I have a very delicate nervous system. Because of the complex PTSD, some nights I awaken every 20 minutes when a plane flies over the house, with massive chest pain and panic. This is a very dangerous situation as it is slowly breaking down my heart.

I have always had issues around self-care, as it was my job to caretake her and the whole family, I learned to put myself dead last, which extended to relationships, jobs and even with my own family. I can't make a decision to save my life!

Alice Miller says that the worst tragedy for a survivor is in learning to not trust themselves, their own feelings, and their own sense of reality. This comes about through massive gaslighting, and it totally messes with a person's sense of their own identity! Self-doubt and second-guessing oneself is the worst. This also plays into a survivor's total lack of ability to make a decision - about anything! When you can't trust yourself, you cannot truly live. When you can't trust yourself, how can you know who to trust? It's like navigating without a compass." — **Crystal, Burbank, CA**

"Inability to take care of my health properly to the extent of having chronic illnesses." — **Mike, Chicago, Illinois**

"The issues I have come from both parents. I have had two marriages and a long-term relationship of 22 years that I just ended 2 years ago. I attract narcissists. All three men I've been involved with were narcissists and I cleared out three friends in the beginning of the year. I have struggled with depression and anxiety my whole life. I had a breakdown in my late thirties. I have struggled with suicidal ideation

and have longed to die. I have night terrors but never remember what they are about. I did have the trauma bonding until my mother died."
— **Leslie, Australia**

"Trauma bonding with a partner as an adult." — **Annie, Minnesota**

"Difficulty bonding with my own child, trouble forming friendships."
— **Rebecca, UK**

"I trauma-bonded with a man I was in a relationship with; when it ended, I shut down for more than a year. I know that this had its roots in my relationship with my narcissistic mother. I was diagnosed with *aspects* of BPD, though not a true, full diagnosis. I learned to overcome those behaviors with DBT. Mostly. I never had children because I didn't want to turn out to be my mother.

My childhood, adolescence, and most of my adulthood was spent wondering what the meaning of life was and how it could be so painful. It's not like that now - there are moments of pain, bad experiences, but I am able to process through them. But back then, I did NOT want to live... and I didn't want to do that to anyone else. All of those emotions were due to my mother's treatment of me. Due to the lack of love, I felt worthless in this world." — **Anastasia Vishnevsky, Eau Claire, WI**

"As a borderline, I have been completely textbook, according to Gunderson's and Kreisman's books." — **Nadia**

"I realized that I have a fear of authoritative male figures. If I think I have done some something wrong at work, I am afraid to tell my male boss or other male colleagues. I am only slowly realizing that there will not be the backlash that I would get from my father." — **Samantha**

"Since I just found out that this is the problem, I have just stopped everything. I don't leave my home. I don't talk to anyone and don't want to. I had 3 strokes and developed malignant hypertension over the last 22 months, after my father died, which they made a nightmare for me - they kept me from him. I don't know if that's self-sabotage, but I just can't handle anything at all." — **Lisa D., Lexington, Kentucky**

"My narcissistic dad was a compulsive overeater. Food was weird in my house growing up - I think I wanted to overeat to be like my dad and my mom was always trying to reign us in, but not in an active or helpful way as she was an enabler. Even now, I struggle not to eat to suppress feelings. I was diagnosed with Graves' disease, an autoimmune thyroid disease, in my mid-20s, and I often wonder if that was connected with the way I was raised.

My narcissistic dad pushed me to become a lawyer and to go to law school; I did those things but lasted as a lawyer less than a year. It was a career I was wildly ill-suited for. I have bounced around, career-wise, quite a bit since then, and often wonder where I would have landed had I been allowed to choose for myself. I am unable to relax fully and keep thinking about my parents and how my decision to go very low contact is making them feel. I feel guilty sometimes." — **Annie, New England**

"Relationships with toxic people with a "poor picker." Despair." — **PJ**

"Dissociation, seizures, flashbacks, physical ailments. I sometimes suffer from dissociation to the point where I lose small amounts of time. I also find myself saying and doing things that feel like I am a little girl, but I can't stop talking like one. I have "my own" voice inside my head asking "why are you doing this? Stop!" I have no control over this." — **Tanya**

"Recurrent episodes of severe depression. I have had a panic disorder since I was 11 years old, which my narcissistic mother convinced me and the doctors was asthma so I took asthma medications for 20 years until the whole brainwashing cracked open during therapy." — **Megan**

"I am frightened a lot and overprotective of my child. It's like fighting an addiction. Even years down the road, I still have 'cravings' - the patterned response of wanting to 'try hard' to build a relationship with my mother. Like recovery, I know that absolute abstinence is the easiest method." — **Dallas, Ontario, Canada**

"I don't remember correlating nightmares to the abuse, but during therapy, much was processed through my dreams and occasional nightmares. I have been reading about CPTSD. This term was either not around or not used during my therapy history, but it seems to fit." — **Cindy, Evansville, Indiana**

"Trauma bonding in personal relationships. I have been involved in two abusive relationships. I struggle with feelings of worthlessness. I have been fighting to find my voice my whole life. I still struggle with guilt when I use it today. My instincts and old patterns tell me any feeling I may have or using my voice makes me selfish. I overly give of myself and I am still confused about my own identity. Self-doubt, negative self-talk, self-sabotage are all still part of my life at age 44." — **Susie J., Georgia**

"I have a dissociative disorder and Avoidant Personality Disorder. I struggle with severe self-isolation." — **Stephanie, Netherlands**

"I have obsessive thoughts, especially in relation to relationships I've had with narcissistic, addicted, and emotionally unavailable men. I have insomnia, co-dependency, and trauma bonds with narcissistic men. I used to obsess about my weight but now I have a healthy body image. I used to never speak up for myself but that has changed too. I turned 39 in October. I tend to isolate a lot as I feel safe in my hermit pad with my 2 cats. I need a lot of alone time to recharge and reflect but I'm working on keeping a better balance in this area, and to reach out so I can connect to healthier people." — **E. Fox**

"Not feeling able to speak my mind (too sensitive!). Getting "upset" too easily (only way anyone will listen). Self-doubt. Grieving for my sad childhood." — **S. from Montreal, Canada**

"I have the sort of perfectionism and overachieving expectations that prevent me from even starting - if that makes sense. I was diagnosed with avoidant personality disorder. I've also been diagnosed with "high functioning, inward directed" BPD but feel in some ways the Avoidant Personality Disorder saved me from BPD being worse.

I have an incredibly addictive personality (have loads of issues related to dysfunctional dopamine - restless leg syndrome, ADHD, depression, masochism, etc.) which I thankfully recognized early on, so I avoided addictive substances. Since my son has become a teenager, I am pretty much plagued by flashbacks and ruminations over the abuse, mostly from my mom." — **Ahnya**

"After no history of mental health issues, at the age of 40, my husband was made redundant from his job of 28 years and I was being bullied by my new manager at a job I'd had for 10 years. My eldest was being bullied at school too (he's on the autistic spectrum). I had a breakdown. I was put on antidepressants and referred for counseling. I was given the diagnosis of depression and anxiety. After months of therapy, I was told I had Complex PTSD.

I was then referred to a psychologist who diagnosed me with Complex PTSD and Borderline Personality Disorder (BPD was only diagnosed in the last 6 months). I am also under a psychiatrist who has added medications to help me sleep. I have been unable to work since September 2016.

I cried when it was my mom's birthday in May as I felt sorry for her, knowing she was all alone. My feeling is that nobody deserves to be alone. She may have mental health issues and she made her choices - now she has to live with the consequences.

I long for the caring, nurturing mum I should have had, but I also despise the evil piece of humanity I was given. If I lived alone and didn't have my two boys, I know 100% that if she knocked on my door saying she was desperate, I'd let her in in a heartbeat. I hate myself for being so messed up. It's not that I want to kill myself, it's more that I wish I'd never been born in the first place." — **Alison, Essex, UK**

"I am 29 and have never been in a relationship. I thank my lucky stars for this. As I grow and bloom at a rapid rate now that I am coming to terms with my narcissist-soaked past, the quality of people that are coming into my life is a lot higher. I am working through all of the above the only way I know how.

I suffer from guilt as my parents are souls that are beyond lost. I cannot help them, but if I try, I know they certainly will bring me down with them." — **Aleesha**

"I have not healed. I struggle to be able to afford therapy and medication. I suffer from major depressive disorder and feel emotionally overwhelmed most of the time. I have no self-confidence and low self-esteem. I am an underachiever. I am in the same career as my narcissistic father. I was bullied into studying law at the time and now I am 43 and stuck in a career I don't enjoy at all but have nothing else to fall back on. I feel stuck and helpless. I have raised my children opposite to what I was taught by my father, which might have caused other problems." — **Leoni, Cape Town, South Africa**

"Feelings of shame, never being good enough. I hold a lot of fear inside so I have made my world quite small, scared of most things, especially anything medical. I am an awful people-pleaser! I know I am essentially a lovely person, kind and compassionate, and hardworking, but I have difficulty believing in myself and connecting inside with that person. I suffered from anxiety and clinical depression for years. However, since walking away from my whole family five years ago, I haven't had the above symptoms. Occasionally I suffer with bouts of anxiety, but nothing compared to when they were in my life." — **Lou West, Sussex, UK**

"I had to take three years to complete a two-year college degree, because of concentration issues, depression and trouble doing projects. I could not handle the interpersonal conflict at work and have a very patchy work history. I stopped working at about 30 years old. I am now 50.

My partner supports me, or I would have killed myself. I was finally approved for USA SSA disability at age 46. I have work problems, but I would not call it self-sabotage. My father raged and was physically violent, but he was not physically abusive. He damaged things in front of us, but did not hit us, as long as we "behaved."

It took until almost 46 years old to diagnose my Complex PTSD, because there was no physical abuse or sexual abuse. I could not identify symptoms, because this is just how I have lived all of my life. My mother, step-father and older brother worked together against me. We all appeared "perfect" in public. I am even hypervigilant in dreams, so I wake before the bad part of a nightmare happens." — **Slater**

"Low self-esteem. Suicidal thoughts. Depression. I have no relationship with siblings because she brainwashed them, triangulated them into me being the bad person." — **Jennifer, Virginia**

"Social anxiety, depression, being frightened of change. I have a terrible time defending myself or saying no. I have very shaky boundaries. I am not even sure what a boundary is. Predatory people know how to play me like a fiddle. It is so hard to know how my life has been affected by being raised this way. Since at my foundation I believed that I was defective and a mistake, every decision was based on that. I still struggle with this. I am very awkward, introverted and afraid of everything, so it's very hard to make friends or even have a conversation with someone unfamiliar.

Predatory people seem to be attracted to me and I've had two long friendships which turned out to be shams. I can see that now. I did well in school, so perhaps I could have gone further than administrative work, but emotionally, I was not suited to be a professional.

My young adulthood was consumed with flashbacks - I seemed to be in one long, paralyzing flashback. I am much happier now, although not where I want to be yet. I understand now that my mother was not normal and very dangerous to me. Back then, I was so confused, guilty, shameful, frightened that when I tried to defend myself and she would lose her mind, I just backed down. I had to learn all about NPD to really begin healing and accept that I was not defective. What a surprise it was to discover that there was a name for what my mother was. I still get immobilizing flashbacks and feel small and helpless, but at least now I know what is happening now and I can do something about it. Before, it was just my reality. I have so many more options now.

For several years after my mother died, I suffered intense guilt believing that I was such a terrible daughter and I was begging for forgiveness. I am really angry that I was twisted in such a way and not loved and raised properly. It's like I am in a box I can't get out of. I'll never know who I was supposed to be, and I'll probably always feel like a little girl. I am self-destructive also. I drink too much because I like being free of my emotions and myself actually. It's so hard to imagine me as a whole, confident, worthy person. I crave approval and affection." — **Cealie, Queens, NY**

"Autoimmune disorders which I believe are from a semi-broken spirit. Hashimoto's disease and rheumatoid arthritis too." — **Hortense, Austin, Texas**

"Shame but not blame. I was constantly ashamed and wanted to be invisible." — **Pachamama**

"I was married to a doctor who persuaded me to quit college and get married. He then began a ten-year marriage of not wanting to look at my body because it made him sick to his stomach. I should have been enormously successful as a designer, but always chose my kids and their schedule instead of putting myself first. I put myself last and still do. After my daughter died of a heart arrhythmia in 1999, a beautiful girl working at Whole Foods in San Diego and attending San Diego State, I had so much love that had nowhere to go." — **Diane, Scottsdale, Arizona**

"The abuse was severe. I have CPTSD... I am messed up! I know it and I admit it freely to myself. I married a narcissist who abused me, hospitalized me twice, and even poisoned me. When I woke up in the ER that night, I realized that he tried to kill me. He physically and sexually abused my children. He is a monster, but no different than my mother. I have so much guilt for the abuse by their father that I put my children through all because of the abuse that I suffered at the hands of my mother. The cycle is so hard to stop. Seeing the narcissistic abuser is the first step, but it came too late for my children.

I have pseudo-seizures, too. I have nausea and vomiting and lose weight too easily." — **Celtic Accomplishments from Tampa, Florida**

"I've been diagnosed with bipolar 2 and ADHD. While there are other family members with various mental illnesses (such as autism, schizophrenia, and bipolar disorder), it's hard to say whether or not my diagnosis is due to early childhood trauma. I have more trouble letting go of the connection with my enabling father. I always think one day he'll wake up and save me! It's been 58 years. It's so deeply wired in me that it's hard to catch so I can change the pattern." — **Janet**

"Self-harm. Getting into romantic relationships with abusive partners and re-living the original abuse dynamic. Not following my own path in life until I finally went No Contact with her. Not having boundaries because I never learned to develop them, and I still have to work on that. Being afraid to stand up for myself for fear of retaliation and abuse.

At one point, I was diagnosed with Agoraphobia due to the abuse and the resultant C-PTSD. As a result of the abuse, I have, historically, had very unhealthy and unproductive coping skills. At age 48, I am still learning healthy and appropriate coping skills. Up until recently, I carried a great deal of suppressed anger/rage because of the abuse. Until almost 6 years ago, I was in a very unhealthy codependent relationship with my narcissistic mother, which was very detrimental to me, but I didn't understand that dynamic for all the years prior and did not know how to break free of it." — **Morgan, Austin, Texas**

"Sometimes I would bang my head on a wall and contemplate not staying on the planet. I was fortunate the episodes were not often. My first toxic marriage was terrifying. I had hypertension. I could not face the reality of my toxic first marriage and 'Pollyannaed' my way through." — **Paula**

"Still experience hypervigilance, perfectionism and overachieving now at age 70. However, it has considerably weakened since the regression therapy and my own inner work therapy." — **Marie**

"I am highly sensitive and very empathic. Probably so by nature, but I am certain I have also been trained by my mother to pay special attention to her mood of the day, and what to do to earn her attention and approval." — **Ellen C.**

"A pattern of toxic relationships with men. I had major long-term relationships marked by pain and angst. Two divorces. Trauma bonding and fantasy bonding. A very toxic relationship with my father and an unstable relationship with my brother. I had depression and PTSD but I no longer suffer from the symptoms. I have done a lot to recover from depression and anxiety. This includes meditation practices, yoga, and regular walks with my adorable dog. I do still see a very supportive and kind therapist too." — **Cynthia, New Mexico**

"I had severe PMS for 12 years until diagnosed at age 26. I was told the chances of me surviving it were slim to none, it was that bad. I was hospitalized several times for depression, and spent eight weeks in a mental hospital, diagnosed falsely with manic depression. I was also diagnosed as a binge alcoholic. I have no doubt my PMS was a result of being sexually abused, and my mother refusing to save me, and in fact, effectively silencing me for 30+ years.

Being able to support myself and have money has also been affected. I know I'm very good at what I do, but have not been able to translate that into making a living. I also have a really big problem reacting around angry people - I freeze and cannot speak. I became severely ill with Adrenal Fatigue after my father's death. I know I have to stay away from family if I want to survive. Your book helped me more than I can say." — **Kim**

"Rage attacks on kids was what caused me to work on myself. I was in so much denial before then. My husband had an affair and I absolutely fell apart. Low self-esteem and toxic levels of codependency." — **Aurora, San Francisco, California**

"Not feeling good enough and feeling like a refugee in my own life. Decades ago in a very abusive marriage, my then shrink labeled me with a diagnosis of "hysterical" which was a misdiagnosis. He didn't know about any abuse and I chose not to tell him for fear of not being believed as I trained in psychiatry and knew how women are controlled by untrue labels. Years later, the diagnosis was corrected to complex PTSD along with my history of multiple abuse violations and losses, especially my children. Hysteria was refuted at last and shows how unreliable psychiatry can be." — **Polly Magena**

"Due to the childhood narcissistic abuse, I was subconsciously conditioned to seek out narcissists for relationships. I have experienced narcissistic friendships and I had a 23-year marriage with a narcissist. Due to perfectionism symptomology caused by the abuse and then solely MY ability to direct it to wellness and positive growth, I earned a MS in Marriage and Family Therapy and I specialize in Narcissistic Abuse Recovery, Psychological Abuse Recovery, C-PTSD Recovery, Attachment Injuries, Trauma Recovery Therapy, and Gestalt Therapy." — **Joytree5, California**

"Codependency." — **IL**

"Panic attacks because I've been triggered by a smell or a place or the color of a shirt or the sound of a man's voice being similar to my father's or males being direct and authoritative. Inability to sleep well. Inability to focus for any length of time. Body dysmorphia, obsessing over my calorie intake and exercise regimen. Indecisiveness especially if there are too many choices - anxiety over choosing the wrong thing.

I've been diagnosed with anxiety and panic disorder and take medication to manage it. I am the oldest. My middle sister was the scapegoat and our younger brother was the golden child. I was terrified of men but at the same time had the insatiable need to have their attention. I thought that I could not get love unless the sex was good, so I became very good at it. And I never trusted anyone who complimented me on any other parts of my character.

To date all of my relationships, including several bosses and multiple family members (uncles and cousins) fit the description of malignant narcissist, sociopaths. I am currently 48 years old and just escaped from my last and final narcissistic relationship. Synchronicity brought me to a therapist who had experience and knowledge about this and with her help and the help of books like yours and a community of survivors, I am finally a self-care warrior learning to practice radical self-love." — **Melissa, Florida**

"I was in a relationship with an emotional psychopath for two years and I believe my childhood trauma enabled me to fall for it." — **Jenny**

"I am too compassionate. Too forgiving. Too generous. Too understanding. Too tolerant." — **The Dandelion Girl, North Chesterfield, VA**

"Inability to self-motivate. Feeling I will fail. I have been diagnosed with lupus believed to be caused by acute stress. Symptoms in my youth were ignored as I was told I was overreacting and making them up by my covert narcissistic mother. She was "insulted" I could be sick as it reflected badly on *her*. She was a nurse. So, I continued to ignore all symptoms for a further 20 years until I was finally diagnosed.

I feel wary of people who are nice to me. But at the same time, I overshare. I have conflicting emotions. I feel love is conditional. I struggle to identify my emotions. I struggle to regulate my emotions. I second-guess my decisions which often leads to inaction. I struggle to identify what I like and need. I tend to go along with the decisions of others. I feel my needs and feelings don't matter or that they are wrong." — **MJ, Victoria, Australia**

"Getting better every day, thanks to people like you." — **Sue, San Diego**

"I still struggle with generalized anxiety disorder and obsessive thinking and guilt. I think about what I've done wrong and how to make things right even though I know that I haven't done anything wrong." — **Angela, Nevada**

"I put everyone's needs above my own. I always agreed to everything my husband said as I needed to please them. I needed to feel loved. But they were both like her. Now I am learning to love myself. I am finding new hobbies. I have no contact with my ex-husband now as my youngest is 18. It's great. I am a survivor and I'm working on myself. I love being single. I felt a few of these things in my life but not now. I am 46. I've survived a narcissistic mother, sister, and two husbands and a son. I was left with my youngest son who is empathic and a lot like me. I am currently building my inner circle up. It's hard as I do not trust easily. I have learned to depend on myself and no one else. This was sad at first but now I feel empowered by it." — **Alyta from Newcastle, Tyne, UK**

"Anxiety - whenever he does try to contact me or whenever I return to my childhood home. Also, anxious thoughts of whether he's angry enough to kill me, my mom or my sister." — **Melanie, Toronto, Ontario**

"Addiction." — Amber Loganville, GA

"Trauma bonding before going full no contact." — **Nicole Francesca, United Kingdom**

"Emotionally stunted, hypersexuality." — **Jestine, Champaign, IL**

"I don't trust people. It takes a lot for me to trust them. I am still leery that they will find a way to turn the tables and make something my fault when it's not." — **Jen, MN**

"Difficulty holding boundaries and respecting my own needs. Denying my own needs, not recognizing them...because I was conditioned that my needs are really wants and that I cannot have what I want and do not deserve what I want. It has been two years since I decided to stop hiding the abuse and stop protecting the abuser. Now I make my choices based on my own survival and best interests - as best I can." — **Linda**

"All of my long-term relationships have been wrong for me, in one way or another. I have struggled with anxiety about always being alone, and as a result I have allowed myself to get involved in relationships that weren't right for me just to avoid being alone. As time has progressed, I have made more serious errors in judgment, culminating with my last long-term relationship which was with a man who was most definitely a narcissist and who totally ruined me - emotionally, physically, and financially. I was with him for nine years. I have spent the last three years in recovery from him.

I know that if my mother was still alive, I would still be enmeshed in our unhealthy relationship. I loved her deeply, despite the abuse. I also had that deep-seated conviction that I was somehow responsible for keeping it all together, and despite years of therapy I still struggle with that to this day. In some ways, her death was a great relief to me. Which, I also feel a great deal of guilt and shame about." — **Chaosraines, Northern California**

"Teeth grinding, body armoring, insomnia, isolating. I ingested a whole bottle of aspirin at 13, and was given the silent treatment for two weeks after. I hide money, and possessions, for fear of them being taken from me. I parented my children in a fearful way, with the worry that they would be taken from me." — **Angela**

"Always expecting to be rejected or left when I displease my significant other." — **Nancy, Texas**

"A very difficult time with people. I have a huge fear of rejection and of abandonment. I am way too much of a people-pleaser and gave myself little regard. I was treated as Bipolar from 30 until 58 when I realized I was suffering from Complex PTSD, not Bipolar disorder. I tried to kill myself two times. I've realized that the narcissist embedded seeds in me to kill myself because she was always trying to destroy me. My thinking is that since she let me know how worthless I was, my ego took her at her word and tried to destroy the worthless thing that was me. I felt it would never get better and I would always be worthless." — **Susie**

"Chronic shame. I feel guilty when I am successful or prosperous. I feel I am being punished by life for going no contact and abandoning my mother. I am unable to identify who I am or who I want to be, and what I want out of life. I have trauma-bonding with abusive men similar to my parents. I have experienced traumatic work environments that recreated my family dynamics, including bullying and mobbing, especially abusive bosses." — **Karla, Los Angeles, CA**

"Dating unavailable men my entire life. I'm 55." — **Tense, Texas**

"I was told that I was codependent. I am constantly so hard on myself. I never think I am skinny enough, smart enough, pretty enough for the "right" people to love and admire. I am incredibly insecure in most things I do in life...whether it's job hunting, raising my children, talking to people. I have a terrible habit of nail-biting which I believe is linked to my insecurities about men. I attract, and have been attracted to, narcissistic men my whole life. Fortunately, now my radar is fine-tuned and I can see the bad guys coming from a mile away." — **MissyM, Chicago, IL**

"Physiological symptoms when I am in tense or confrontational situations. I experience a racing heart, shaking hands, shortness of breath, stomachaches. My brain feels like it's shutting down and I unable to think straight." — **Elda Sarid**

"Refused to listen and trust my real friends, who still are beside me today despite everything. PTSD. I have been left with medicated anxiety and depression, but I live with this in peace, and I now know how to be when I have those days I just can't face, they are lessening too. All I can say is I no longer sit in Plato's cave watching the shadows of life wishing I could be free. I am free now and alive and living, but it wasn't easy breaking the chains of being a slave to a narcissistic father." — **JoJo, Suffolk, UK**

What Therapists Have to Say

About Childhood Narcissistic Abuse

I asked therapists and life coaches who have a wealth of experiences working adult children of narcissistic parents to share their insights and tips about what they saw as the most common struggles among their clients. Here is what they had to say.

In your professional experience, what are some of the most common struggles (personal, professional and health wise) you see among adult children of toxic/narcissistic parents? Is there any advice you would give to adult children of narcissists on their journey to healing?

From Allison Hutson, MA, LPC[13]

"I specialize in complex childhood trauma working with children, adolescents, and adults. My main client population consists of adult survivors of familial abuse. Common struggles I see among adult children of toxic parents are the following: difficulties holding boundaries. They experience chronic toxicity from intimate relationships, friendships, and workplaces. Guilt and shame are extremely intense with this population.

Moderate to severe anxiety and depression are also results of toxic/narcissistic parents. Negative cognitive belief systems are interwoven into all aspects of their lives - resulting in low self-worth, hopelessness, PTSD, and often suicidal ideation, including passive ideation. This population does not conceptualize or even perceive safe and unsafe people accurately having internalized a misconstrued concept from their parents of what a loving healthy relationship is. Adult children of narcissistic parents often end up in manipulative and abusive relationships. This population frequently functions in chaos.

On healing and recovery: I always encourage clients to take the time to heal and gain a better educational framework to help them re-enter future relationships in a preventative manner. I work on helping them define and understand safe and unsafe people as well as what their boundaries need to be. I also help them identify negative cognitive beliefs they have developed from others since childhood.

Children of narcissistic parents become susceptible to other abusive interpersonal interactions, which increase their vulnerability to filter experiences negatively. Rebuilding an identity for themselves is a large part of their healing and transformation. I encourage clients at the beginning of their journey to give themselves permission to grieve. Critical to the healing process is properly assigning the blame that has been unjustly shifted onto them their entire life.

Find a support system, even if that is only your therapist for a while, until you can identify a healthy support system. But the most critical advice I could give is this: please, find a therapist who specializes in trauma and/or narcissistic abuse. Finding the right therapist is critical to your healing. The wrong therapist will never understand your true experience and will potentially do more harm through invalidation or superficial interventions."

From Lea Voigt, MA, CSAT-C[14]

"I work with adult children of narcissistic parents individually and I also co-facilitate women's groups for adult children of narcissistic parents. The common struggles I see are: mistrust, perfectionism, addiction, fear of abandonment, an anxious-preoccupied attachment style, approval-seeking, people-pleasing, poor boundaries, and codependency. There is often a pattern of choosing relationships similar to the relationship with the toxic parent.

On healing and recovery: I advise adult children of narcissists to educate yourself on narcissism, find a therapist who specializes in children of personality-disordered parents, attend ACA groups or another 12-step program (and actually work through the program), join a women's or men's group, learn about betrayal bonds (Patrick Carnes), learn about the specific negative programming you picked up throughout your life and come to understand and believe these messages are lies."

From Pamela Morris, Ph.D, Psychologist

"Adult children of narcissists struggle with low self-esteem and feeling as if they don't fit in. I find that they are indecisive as they have lost the ability to trust themselves. They have very little confidence. Many of my clients are empaths and are overly sensitive to criticism. They settle for unhealthy relationships. Many have some form of PTSD having suffered from abuse. Their main strength is resilience.

On healing and recovery: I would advise them to educate themselves on the traits of narcissism, engage in self-care techniques, and, in cases where it is warranted, to go no contact with the abusive parent."

From Melissa Pudney, Certified Life Coach

"Although it is not my specialty, the amount of NPD survivors coming to me for help is on the rise. My specialty is breaking negative cycles and changing habits as well as PTSD, stress, anxiety, panic attacks etc. Adult children of narcissists can struggle from lack of self-esteem, difficulty making decisions, co-dependency issues, and financial problems. They may have extreme weight gain or loss, addiction issues (drugs, alcohol, food, sex etc.), depression, anxiety, PTSD, panic attacks, flashbacks, migraines. Lack of direction (especially in their career), financial instability, toxic friendships or workplaces."

From Linda Parsons, Psychotherapist

"Because they do not understand gaslighting, a lot of clients feel they are going crazy. Clients feel frustrated that nobody understands the psychological abuse and the mental and emotional torture they are experiencing by their abusive partners. It is because their partners are so charming when they are interviewed by the social workers who have no experience whatsoever with NPD."

From Nova Gibson, Managing Director and Counselor of Brighter Outlook Counseling[15]

"I specialize in working with victims of narcissistic abuse and see adult child victims of narcissistic abuse approximately two times a week. Their struggles relate to their incredibly low self-esteem, feelings of obligation to the abusive parent, guilt around their feelings of ambivalence or hatred of toxic parent, and guilt over not being willing to accommodate that parent. Adult children of narcissists are extremely defensive, and they seek out the toxicity they became familiar with as a child. Any healthy relationship can seem boring due to the lack of toxic intensity. They feel immense shame, develop a resilience for trauma, and they minimize the trauma. I advise adult children of narcissists to seek advice and support from other victims who understand. They should go no contact from the toxic parent as biology does not give anyone the right to abuse you. Therapy with a counselor experienced in working with adult children of narcissists is also important."

From Paul S. Brandt, MS, LCSW[16]

"Dependent personality, avoidant personality, low self-esteem, chronic caregivers, poor personal boundaries. Many have a parent or parents who are intrusive in their lives."

From Lilian Ing, MA, Clinical Psychologist and Therapist[17]

"Adult children of narcissists can struggle with the parenting of their own children, attachment, boundary setting, discipline, romantic relationships, abusive work relationships, depression, and anxiety."

From Rebecca Johnson, M.S., LMHC[18]

"It's extremely difficult to unlearn the negative beliefs that the abusive parent has planted. Lack of family/friend support. Cognitive dissonance. Feeling like they are the crazy one. Feeling unworthy of real love. PTSD, anxiety. I feel that validation is the biggest need for children of narcissists. As in, "This was real, this did happen, no matter how others see my parent, they abused me!""

Part Two

Relationships and Love for Adult Children of Narcissists

Essays on how adult children of narcissists operate in relationships in adulthood and how they "love differently."

7 Things People Don't Realize

You're Doing Because You Were Raised By A Narcissist

Being the child of narcissistic parents is one of the most heartbreaking and traumatizing things a person can go through. Not only are you required to survive a war zone in childhood, but you are also left with life-long consequences that extend far into adulthood. Here are seven things you might be doing as a result:

(1) Apologizing more than you have to, even if no apology is needed.

Children of narcissistic parents tend to become fluent in saying "sorry" – even for just their very existence. It's because they've been taught by their parents that they are a burden. This is especially true for female victims who are also socialized to be people-pleasing and accommodating. It takes time to unlearn this behavior and learn to only apologize for actual transgressions rather than any perceived burdensomeness.

When evaluating whether to apologize, ask yourself: Was I the cause of this in any way? If not, replace your "sorry" with "That's unfortunate" instead. You *could* be "sorry" that the circumstances are what they are, but if you are not personally responsible, you have no reason to apologize. And if the event in question was the fault of someone else, let them carry the burden – lift the weight off your shoulders completely.

Remember that there are many people in this world who don't even have the courtesy to apologize to you for *their* wrongdoings – so the last thing you want to do is overextend yourself by apologizing for things you didn't even do wrong.

(2) Hesitating to say no, because it might displease others.

As a child, you were conditioned to obey your toxic parents even at the expense of your own welfare and basic needs. You were punished and abused when you did refuse to comply to their demands. Saying "yes" was a vital part of your survival as a helpless child who did all he or she could to ensure that their parent did not abandon them.

Now, as an adult, saying no is a part of having healthy boundaries. However, it can feel absolutely intimidating at first. The key is to checking in with yourself about why you're fearful of saying no, preparing for any potential consequences, and allowing yourself to feel the discomfort – all while still sticking to what you know to be true.

Ask yourself on a daily basis, "Am I doing this to please someone else, or because I really want to do this?" It's okay to evaluate whether someone has invested in you in the way they want you to reciprocate and go from there. *If you're the only one giving while they're taking, it's an unequal relationship and there's bound to be a power imbalance.* There are some things you may not be able to avoid doing, but this is still a healthy start to reconnecting to your authentic desires.

(3) Doubting your own perceptions and second-guessing your intuition.

Although we're highly sensitive and intuitive, we've also been gaslighted most of our lives by abusers into thinking otherwise. We tend to underestimate our own emotions and instincts while overvaluing the comfort of others. This can lead us into some very dangerous situations like abusive friendships, relationships, work environments, or shady business deals.

There are some simple questions you can start asking yourself if you want to understand whether the problem is you or them. Does everyone make you feel this uncomfortable, or is it mainly this person who sets off the inner "smoke alarm"? Have you noticed similar toxic behaviors in this person as you've experienced with your parents? Would you ever treat anyone the way this person is treating you? And if not, would you feel uncomfortable witnessing them treating someone else in a similar manner?

These questions can help you to reconnect with your basic rights, to see the situation from multiple perspectives. For example, often as children of narcissists we tend to prioritize the suffering of others over our own, so the last question helps to distance ourselves and recognize when mistreatment is occurring because we see how awful the situation would feel to someone else other than just ourselves. It makes us realize that it's okay to verify when someone is being a straight up asshole – and that it has nothing to do with you and everything to do with *them* as human beings.

(4) Checking in constantly about how someone else feels about you without tending to how *you* really feel about the person.

Since you were raised in a chaotic, unstable environment, it makes sense that you're fearful of situations where you're likely to encounter the possibility of change. As a result, you're always on the lookout as to whether something has shifted or changed. You're always questioning the status of your most intimate relationships. You don't have a firm grasp on how others feel about you, so, as a result, you try to take back control by micromanaging your relationships.

The healthier route would be to step back and reevaluate whether the people in your life you're so desperately attempting to cling onto even deserve a seat at *your* table. Do *they* deserve your energy and efforts? Sometimes, we're so consumed with how others perceive us that we forget to honor how we feel about them.

We forget to give ourselves permission to dislike someone, to address conflict, to confront, or even just to acknowledge when someone has reached epic levels of douchebaggery. A fun way to counter this people-pleasing behavior is to create a mantra for yourself: "Are they a douche?" If so, so be it! Acknowledge the reality rather than bending over backwards trying to rework your perception of toxic people into something more socially acceptable. Some people really are just horrible people, and that's okay – that doesn't mean you have to tolerate them.

And even if they are trustworthy friends or partners, they are not the arbiter of your self-worth or your right to be loved. This can be terrifying to consider for someone raised to be dependent on the validation of others, but we can and will survive with or without them or their approval. Some people rightfully need to be cut out of our lives, while others will provide a source of safety and support. The key is discerning the difference and taking concrete actions to ensure that our support system is healthy and nourishing, and not another reenactment of the toxic family dynamics we've experienced.

(5) Picking up on micro-signals of abandonment or displeasure.

Children of narcissists become hyper-aware and attuned to microexpressions, gestures, changes in tone of voice that signal abandonment or displeasure. They *had* to become aware of these to survive and navigate sudden changes in their environment. They needed to know when their parent's next rage attack was about to begin or what they could "do" to avoid being punished.

As an adult, you're highly intuitive about the motives of others as well as their true emotions. You can catch subtle shifts in someone's emotions or your surrounding environment. This gift of intuition can be used wisely to navigate social interactions, but it can also be overwhelming. Sometimes, this hyperfocus detracts from owning your agency in detaching from the person and instead causes you to become obsessed with pleasing them. Rather than focusing too much on these, try taking note of such changes without becoming enmeshed in the other person's feelings.

(6) Taking your time to trust.

As a child you were violated, emotionally or even physically abused. Your trust was taken advantage of, time and time again. It is no wonder you have a hard time letting people in. That doesn't make you wrong – this is simply a testament to the trauma of your experience.

In many cases, slowing down and taking the time to trust is a good thing – it means you are aware that there are emotional predators who could take advantage of your kindness. You might take months to disclose personal information (or seconds, if you have more porous boundaries where you're oversharing). You might feel hypervigilant when you notice red flags. It's okay to know that trust has to be earned – and to trust *yourself*, first and foremost.

There are trustworthy people out there, you just have to be willing to see people for who they truly are, not who you want them to be or who they pretend to be.

(7) Having a problematic relationship with uncomfortable emotions like pain and rage: either repressing them completely or allowing them to consume you.

Children of narcissists are chronically emotionally invalidated from a very early age. They are conditioned to believe that their emotions don't matter or that their emotions make them defective. They learn to suppress their anger and stifle their hurt. Owning their "dark side" (or what they perceive to be dark) can be frightening.

As a result, they may bury their true emotions for a lifetime, eventually "snap" or become easily overwhelmed with bottled up emotions because they never learned how to healthily process, channel and heal these emotions from the onset. Children of narcissists can be straight up scary when their real emotions are finally allowed to come to the surface – I say this in half-jest, knowing how overwhelming it can be when you were raised to feel like having emotions were pathological. Developing a healthier relationship to your emotions – and a better outlet for them (such as writing, meditating, counseling, exercising) can be life-changing.

Learning to identify and validate all of your emotions – without necessarily acting maladaptively on them – can be vital to exercising your basic human rights and implementing your boundaries. It's important to learn how to constructively stand up for yourself – and it is especially important as the child of a narcissist, when nobody stood up for you.

The Powerful Effect

of Love Bombing and Intermittent Reinforcement on Children of Narcissists

What is love bombing?

Love bombing is a process of grooming in which a predator uses flattery, praise and the promise of a supreme alliance to fulfill their own agendas. By love bombing their victims, abusers are able to persuade their targets to fulfill their requests and desires. Love bombing is not only a tool used by covert manipulators to exploit their victims, it is also used in cults to ensure loyalty to the cult leader. In fact, there is much overlap between the behavior of cults and the abuse cycle of an abuser and his or her victim.

While *anyone* can be the victim of love bombing, it has an especially powerful effect on children of narcissistic parents, because they have already been subconsciously programmed to seek approval, engage in people-pleasing habits and look for external validation as a way to survive their psychologically turbulent childhoods.

When children of narcissists meet emotional predators in adulthood, they are especially susceptible to becoming ensnared in the web of a malignant narcissist.

Love Bombing and Intermittent Reinforcement Work Together to Create an Environment of Uncertainty, Coercion, and Control

In a relationship with a pathological predator, love bombing is combined with **intermittent reinforcement** to create a sense of instability and longing in the victim. Intermittent reinforcement (in the context of psychological abuse) is a pattern of cruel, callous treatment mixed in with periodic affection. The abuser hands out "rewards" such as affection, a compliment, or gifts sporadically and unpredictably throughout the abuse cycle. This causes the victim to perpetually seek their approval while settling for the crumbs of their occasional positive behavior.

As author Adylen Birch writes, "Creating fear of losing the relationship – and then relieving it periodically with episodes of love and attention – is the perfect manipulation." Much like the way a gambler at a slot machine becomes addicted to playing the game for a potential win despite the risk of major loss, a victim in the abuse cycle can become attached to the idea of getting a return on their "investment" in the relationship despite the toll it takes on their well-being.

Intermittent reinforcement also affects our feelings towards our perpetrators, paradoxically bonding us more deeply to them and causing us to perceive their rare positive behaviors in an amplified way. Dr. Carver describes this as the "small kindness perception." As he notes in his article, "Love and Stockholm Syndrome":

> "In threatening and survival situations, we look for evidence of hope – a small sign that the situation may improve. When an abuser/controller shows the victim some small kindness, even though it is to the abusers benefit as well, the victim interprets that small kindness as a positive trait of the captor...In relationships with abusers, a birthday card, a gift (usually provided after a period of abuse), or a special treat are interpreted as not only positive, but evidence that the abuser is not "all bad" and may at some time correct his/her

behavior. Abusers and controllers are often given positive credit for *not* abusing their partner, when the partner would have normally been subjected to verbal or physical abuse in a certain situation."

Targets of emotional and psychological violence seek the love bombing that was so nourishing in the idealization phase, even as they are now being devalued and discarded by their abusers. This is not surprising, since love bombing, intermittent reinforcement and the effects of trauma work together to strengthen an intense trauma bond between target and abuser.

There are three ways adult children of narcissists, who grow up scapegoated and diminished, are vulnerable to the tactics of love bombing. I discuss them below, as well as some "immunity methods" to resist these manipulation tactics.

1. While hypercriticism puts us on the defensive, love-bombing disarms us initially. It mirrors our deepest desires to be wanted, desired, loved, cared for, heard and seen for who we truly are, down to every little nuance and quirk.

When we are love bombed, there is an immediate sense of belonging and of kinship, something that is very attractive to children of narcissists, who feel very much like outcasts in their families as well as society.

Narcissists and sociopaths are very good at "hooking" us by pointing out our desirable physical attributes, personality traits, and/or accomplishments that deep down we want admired and recognized. At the same time, they fixate on those traits to further their own agenda, not because they actually care to know us deeply. They dig deep when they have to in order to get what they want (praise in return, sex, money, a place to live, etc.), but their affection for us is often short-lived and transient, escalating to contempt and envy should we ever threaten their sense of control over us. As Dr. Floyd (2013) writes:

"Love bombing is an extreme example of something that turns out to be relatively common—something I call "toxic affection." If affection is the expression of love and fondness, then toxic affection is any such expression that has an ulterior motive. Perhaps I say I love you because I really do, and I want you to know that. Or, perhaps I say it only because I want to sleep with you, want to borrow money from you, or just want you to say it back to me. Using affection as a form of persuasion is often successful for the same reason that love bombing is: we want and need to be loved."

Immunity method

Seek internal validation for those traits that you've been love bombed with in the past. It's not that you don't embody what the predator has flattered you with, but that you no longer need to depend on them for your sole source of self-esteem. Surround yourself with healthy people who recognize, rather than exploit, those qualities in you. Genuine compliments are given freely, without a need for you to do something in return or to be a certain way for a person. Be alert to over-the-top flattery and unwarranted praise merged with a request. Even if the praise does seem warranted, just be aware that *some* (but certainly not all) praise has a hidden purpose.

2. Since children of narcissists are often triangulated by their parents, pitted against their own siblings, they fall for predators who make them feel special and unique.

This is the type of attention that children of narcissists always craved to receive in childhood and they get plenty of validation from an emotional predator that grooms them. Yet they later become retraumatized by these same manipulators when they are "triangulated" with former or new harem members and lovers. This causes targets of malignant narcissists to feel even more diminished and lacking, never feeling quite "enough" and feeling like they have to compete with others in order to be seen as important.

Immunity method

Pinpoint what makes you irreplaceable and resist comparing yourself to others negatively. Remember that you may be seeing an abuser's new shiny target or someone they triangulated you with fresh eyes, and you are unaware of what makes you truly beautiful and outstanding. Look at yourself with fresh eyes instead – if you were an outsider looking in, what amazing traits, talents and qualities would you notice about yourself? What makes you special and unique?

Cultivate an authentic relationship with what makes you stand out and embrace visibility in areas where you may have previously hidden yourself to avoid the spotlight for fear of punishment or reprisal. Bring in healthier social feedback when needed to brainstorm what those areas could be. When you have a deep inner knowing that no one could ever replace you, you don't find it necessary for someone else to make you feel that way.

You can then become much more selective about who you let into your life. Manipulative, toxic people can no longer gain easy access by just being charming or sweet – they have to show up and be there for you in real ways in order for you to take them seriously.

3. We mistake superficial alliances for deep, meaningful, and once-in-a-lifetime connections.

Children of narcissists are forced to navigate the world alone and become their own rugged heroes. We tend to our own wounds, our own scraped knees and emotional voids due to the necessity for survival. With no supportive caretakers to mend our aches in either childhood or adulthood, we find solace in even the most superficial of connections, holding onto them for indications that we have finally found a "home" for our tattered hearts and weary souls.

As author Peg Streep writes in "Why Unloved Daughters Fall for Narcissists," we often don't notice the red flags as much as we do the potential for connection:

> "Because you're so hungry for love and connection—and still trying to fill the hole in your heart left by an unloving mother—you're likely not to notice how he amps the volume and drama. You stay focused on the make-up sex and the warm feelings of reassurance you feel when he tells you not to worry."

Unfortunately, the fast-forwarding nature of the type of relationship that has love-bombing, mixed with the intense chemistry of finally being noticed and seen, makes for a rather addictive biochemical and psychological cocktail. We become addicted to the attention because we mistake it for authentic connection.

Immunity method

Differentiate between connection and flattery early on to avoid investing in people who may not have your best interests at heart. Assess which relationships and friendships in your life have the capacity to grow into deeper alliances and which ones fall short of authentic partnership and true compatibility. The former usually takes some time to build and is built over time with someone who is trustworthy, consistent, transparent and reliable. The latter is often a quick fix or sleight of hand, a magic show followed by a disappearing act.

Flattery, even if it is based on truly amazing qualities you might have, rarely lasts long-term. Connection, on the other hand, is built on a solid foundation – not just on empty compliments, but on genuine rapport, support, and intimacy. It involves two individuals who *both* share parts of themselves with vulnerability, along with a respect for personal boundaries and reciprocity. Connection, not crumbs, is what nourishes you long-term. Remember that you are truly worthy and deserving of nothing less.

References

Birch, A. (2016, December 18). The Most Powerful Motivator on the Planet ~ Intermittent Reinforcement. Retrieved July 31, 2017, from http://psychopathsandlove.com/intermittent-reinforcement/

Carver, J. M. (2011). Love and Stockholm Syndrome: The mystery of loving an abuser. Retrieved July 31, 2017, from http://drjoecarver.makeswebsites.com/clients/49355/File/love_and_stockholm_syndrome.html

Floyd, K. (2013, October 14). Beware of toxic affection. Retrieved July 31, 2017, from https://www.psychologytoday.com/blog/affectionado/201310/beware-toxic-affection

Streep, P. (2016, September). Why unloved daughters fall for narcissists. Retrieved July 31, 2017, from https://blogs.psychcentral.com/knotted/2016/09/why-unloved-daughters-fall-for-narcissists/

Thompson, L. (2016, March). When family is a cult (Part One). Retrieved July 31, 2017, from https://blogs.psychcentral.com/narcissism/2016/03/when-family-is-a-cult-pt-1/

10 Ways Children of Narcissists

Love Differently

"I am currently single. I am afraid to date because of the damage of my last narcissistic relationship, which was just as bad as my relationship with my mother. I don't trust men. I have just begun to love myself. I used to blame myself for everything that has occurred in my life without looking at my experiences as a lesson to help me become the woman I am today." – **Clover, Survivor from Saint Rose, Louisiana**

1. We trust too easily and we don't trust enough.
The children of narcissists are taught that they live in a frightening world – one where love is rarely unconditional. In the early stages of healing, the sight of healthy love and affection always looks slightly suspect to us. On the other hand, the sight of toxic love is all too familiar and feels like a comfort zone. We trust in the monsters disguised as saviors far more easily than we do those who offer us a stable version of love.

Dangerous people represent the same challenges that we underwent in early childhood, so to our subconscious, they ironically feel a lot less frightening. The trick is not to trust too easily or not trusting at all: the balance is found in trusting ourselves. Until we've learned to grieve and heal our core wounds from childhood, we won't be able to trust our inner voice. We'll continue to ignore the instincts that could save our lives or pre-judge someone who may want the best for us; that is why healing is so essential on our journey to self-love and love.

2. We deeply desire commitment, but we also fear it like the plague.

Outwardly, we seem to be the types in search of long-term commitment. Some of us may even have a habit of settling just for the sake of settling down; long-term relationships can provide an odd sense of comfort to someone who has always felt alienated, especially by their own flesh and blood. However, deep down, we also have an intense fear of commitment, especially when it comes to committing to a person who may actually truly care for us. The prospect of a stable partner represents a "forever" that is frightening.

Due to the enmeshed and dysfunctional family we grew up in, commitment to us signifies another person having complete control over us and our emotions. As a result, we tend to defend our freedom whenever we feel it might be challenged and can withdraw when things get too intense. On one hand, this is good when it comes to weeding out those who were just trying to fast-forward us into a shady arrangement anyway. On the other, it can also put a damper on a healthier longer-term relationship when things always feel at a standstill.

3. We are hyper-attuned – to everything.

Changes in tone? Check. Micro-shifts in facial expressions? Noted. Gestures that contradict spoken words? Documented. We are emotional private investigators that are highly attuned to changes in our environment. We *had to be* in order to survive our childhood – we had to be on the lookout for whenever our parents were about to verbally, emotionally or even physically harm us. Due to this, we are highly sensitive and intuitive to the needs of others, but we are also constantly on the lookout for what's about to come.

This hyperactive attunement in childhood abuse survivors has even been confirmed by research. It comes in handy when analyzing situations, picking up on someone else's hidden emotions and predicting someone's behavior, but it can help to take a step back from overanalyzing and also see the bigger picture every once in a while. In other words, it's important to tune back to ourselves, what we're feeling and how we can best take care of ourselves in that particular situation. We cannot control the actions of others, but we *can* control which relationships we continue to pursue and how we reclaim our power from toxic ones.

4. We can be 'swallowed whole' by the person we love; we make excellent caretakers, but we have to work on becoming better boundary-makers.

Remember that hyper-attunement? Well, it comes in handy for being caretakers but not so much when it comes to maintaining boundaries. We learned to cater to the needs of our toxic parents at a very young age in order to survive. Many of us even took on parent roles. This means our boundaries are porous and need extra work and maintenance.

Otherwise, we can be swallowed whole by whoever we're dating or in a relationship with. Their needs can become our fixation, often at the expense of our own. This can be especially dangerous if we're dating another narcissistic person in adulthood. Learning that we have basic needs and rights seems like a rudimentary step, but it's actually one of the most important milestones children of narcissistic parents can achieve.

5. We're always waiting for the other shoe to drop.

Since the remnants of our childhood tend to lead to destructive cycles in adulthood, it's not often that we meet someone who embodies what love and respect look like. On the rare occasion that we find consistency in a partner or even a friend, it can initially scare the hell out of us.

What does it mean to have someone believe in us and support us without a hidden agenda? We don't know, so in the early stages of healing, we might unconsciously find ways to sabotage that connection before it even has a chance to begin.

For a long time, our mentality might be, "what can't come near us can't hurt us." This is natural for someone who had to endure multiple violations even before they became adults. It can also be a protective barrier against predators who are drawn to our empathy and resilience. Unfortunately, when taken too far in some contexts, it means we lose out on opportunities for true intimacy along the way. During the healing journey, children of narcissists can heal their fear of intimacy once they begin getting to know and trust themselves first.

6. We become easily enmeshed with toxic people.

Due to our past experiences of abuse, we tend to become attached to toxic people and chaotic situations in early adulthood in a more intense way because they bring up past wounds while also cementing new ones. We internalized verbal and emotional abuse as a twisted sense of "normal" in childhood, so it's no wonder that we rationalize toxic behavior in adulthood. Anyone can be the victim of a predator, but as a childhood abuse survivor, people who envy or belittle us seem like a natural fit because this type of pain-pleasure dynamic is all we've ever experienced.

Children of narcissistic parents may find that they have unwittingly become tethered to *numerous* toxic people throughout their lives. We have to do a LOT of emotional house-cleaning to detach from these toxic relationships once we reach adulthood. It is crucial to clear that space for healthier relationships to enter and to breathe fresher air away from the constant toxicity.

7. We are fiercely independent.

While we're taking care of everyone else's needs, we give little mind to who's taking care of ours. The thing about children of narcissists is that they learn to fend for themselves early on, to strategically navigate a psychological war zone. Children of narcissists are fighters, so at the end of the day, they don't really need anyone to do anything for them – or so they believe.

Independence is a powerful trait, but it's also wise to balance it out with the ability to ask for help and to look for reciprocity in relationships. Do not allow your independence to deprive you of the love and affection you deserve and give freely to others, especially to those who are undeserving of your time, energy and efforts. You are not an emotional punching bag or sponge. You are your own person and you are also deserving of having someone care for you in return should you need it.

Many children of narcissists tend to get into one-sided friendships or relationships where they get drained by the other person without getting any benefits in return. They give, give, give without getting because they've convinced themselves they don't need anyone to do anything for them. This endless 'giving' is usually rooted in a deeply painful feeling of never being quite enough and having to work hard to receive love. Children of narcissists are conditioned to become givers by their parents and they grow up with the belief that no one should be there for *them*.

They must learn to ask for and be receptive to receiving the same type of love and attention they're so used to giving to others.

8. We are afraid of being seen, so we either become too visible by oversharing or disappear altogether by withdrawing.

Sometimes, children of narcissists have a tendency to overshare in the early stages of healing in the hopes that someone will see their pain and come rescue them. They put themselves out there to find that rescuer – only to find that the toxic types pretending to do the "rescuing" are only there to feed on their wounds and exploit their vulnerabilities.

However, once they become their own saviors, children of narcissists tend to vacillate in the other direction – they tend to close themselves off so no one can hurt them. If we are vulnerable with you, it's because we want you to see us for who we really are and accept it. We crave that intimacy. But we take a huge risk in this, because for us, being visible was always akin to being punished and degraded. So be gentle with the child of a narcissistic parent – they're disclosing things at a slower rate than most because they are trying to protect themselves from annihilation.

9. Despite it all, we are magnanimous with our love.

Children of narcissists are remarkable – in their strength, in their resilience and in their capacity to love despite everything they've been through. When we grow accustomed to the safety of someone truly safe, we give it our all and our all is a whole lot of love that we never received ourselves. If that isn't a beautiful feat, I don't know what is.

Just give us time and space to adjust to this sense of safety as a new normal. When we have reached an optimal stage of healing, we love fiercely, with intention, with passion, and with special care because we deeply know what it's like to be unloved – and we never want anyone else to go through what we did.

5 Powerful Healing Benefits

Of Being Single After An Abusive Childhood

After the ending of a toxic relationship, survivors may be tempted to fill the void and avoid confronting their pain by reentering another relationship quickly. Sometimes, survivors are able to find an empathic, caring partner shortly after the ending of their abusive relationship. **Unfortunately, what happens more often than not is that they end up with another emotional predator who resembles the same one they just left, retriggering and cementing the same abandonment wounds that they attempted to escape in the first place.**

Or, because they haven't taken the time to address their wounding and become self-reliant, they unconsciously push away any healthy partners that come their way.

For any abuse survivor, taking the time to be single (whether or not you plan to have another relationship in the future) is crucial to the healing journey. For childhood abuse survivors who have a pattern of entering unhealthy relationships, it is essential to have a period of being single to help interrupt and break the cycle of abuse. This hiatus from dating and relationships can change the course of your life and bring forth a healthier, renewed sense of self.

Since society places such an unhealthy emphasis on overvaluing relationships at the expense of one's self-care, it is important to recognize how *healthy* being single can be, especially for a trauma survivor. In fact, research has shown that single people can be just as happy as their coupled counterparts (DePaulo, 2007; Grime et al., 2015).

Here are five healing benefits of being single to keep in mind:

1. It allows you to create a new normal.

As we know, children who grow up in abusive households literally have their brains rewired and are prone to engaging in a trauma repetition cycle which deepens existing wounds in adulthood. Those who have been in a long-term abusive relationship, whether emotional or physical, can also suffer from symptoms of PTSD or Complex PTSD. Without proper intervention and treatment, abuse survivors come to normalize verbal, emotional, psychological and sometimes even physical abuse as part of love. Without healing the wounds from childhood and examining any maladaptive beliefs, behaviors or boundaries, abuse survivors risk continually becoming attached to toxic partners throughout their lifetime without pause.

Being single for a period of time mitigates some of this risk by allowing you to carve out space and time exclusively devoted to you and your healing, without exacerbating those wounds. In conjunction with No Contact or Low Contact when co-parenting with your abuser, it is a necessary time to create psychological separation from your abuser. It enables you to create a new normal of peace, stability, and independence that will serve you well – whether or not you decide to get into another relationship in the future.

2. It compels you to have higher standards.

Confronting your own loneliness can be difficult, especially if you suffered from isolation during the abuse cycle. Yet as you begin to heal from the abuse, consult support networks and mental health professionals, you begin to feel less lonely, far more validated and much more comfortable being by yourself.

In fact, you may even welcome the peace and the quiet after such a tumultuous relationship filled with traumatic highs and lows. A long reprieve from the toxicity of abuse can teach you exactly what you deserved and were worthy of, all along. It can teach you to appreciate silence as sacred. You are finally granted the space for much needed reflection and hibernation.

After you have grown accustomed to being on your own, standing on your own two feet and becoming self-reliant, you begin to enjoy your own company. This self-reliance is vital to building emotional health and resilience (Ryan, 2016). You learn how to go on adventures, engage in self-development and indulge in your own self-care without compromises and without the need for a partner.

The longer you spend time alone, the more likely you'll develop a higher standard for who you allow into your life. This is because you are creating such an enriching and emotionally satisfying life that you desire only people who *add* to your experiences rather than detract from them. You'll nurture relationships with people who support and uplift you and cut ties more easily with those that belittle or berate you. This is a great way to filter out toxic friendships as well.

3. It gives you the space to grieve the complex emotions that arise – without taking your experiences out on anyone else.

It is important to remember that when you have been abused, your brain and your body are still reeling from the trauma. Just because the abusive relationship has ended does not mean that the effects of trauma will automatically dissipate. It takes time, effort and often the help of a validating professional to repair any harmful beliefs that you internalized as a result of the abuse, and for your body to return to baseline levels of safety and stability (Van der Kolk, 2016).

You may still be dealing with emotions of anger, sadness, anxiety and even conflicting feelings about your abuser. You might suffer from flashbacks, nightmares, depression, a critical inner voice, toxic shame and self-sabotage (Walker, 2011). The intense trauma bonds that have formed with your abuser need time to heal and be properly severed (Stines, 2016).

Jumping back into dating or into another relationship bears the risk of amplifying these emotions and dumping salt on these wounds. Taking a hiatus from dating can grant you the freedom to honor your emotions and take the time to validate, express and process them in a healthy way. Working with a trauma-informed therapist is a great way to address your triggers in a safe space.

4. Instead of investing in another relationship, you get to invest in yourself.

Abuse survivors are well acquainted with putting a great deal of investment in a toxic relationship with little to no positive return. However, investing in yourself is quite different because it will always be worth it. When you invest in living on your own, you get the experience of a lifetime, perhaps one you might not have again if you plan to have a steady relationship in the future (Ryan, 2016). When you invest in your dreams, education, goals, career, self-care, it will always pay off because you are enriching your own life experience, wisdom and opportunities for success and joy. You learn that you are "whole" on your own and you are far less likely to settle for anyone who isn't similarly self-motivated.

As researcher Dr. DePaulo (2013) astutely notes:

"We hear all about how single people are supposedly at risk for becoming lonely, but little about the creative, intellectual, and emotional potential of solitude... We are told that single people do not have the *intimacy* that married people find in their partners, but hear only crickets about the genuine attachment relationships that single people have with the most important people in their lives. Missing from the stacks of journal articles is any sustained attention to the risks of intensive coupling—investing all of your emotional and relationship stock into just one person, "The One"—or to the resilience offered by the networks of friends and family that so many single people maintain."

Being single opens you up to infinite possibilities for self-exploration and self-advancement without sacrificing your time or energy on anyone else. You have more time to exercise, do yoga, try meditation, travel, experiment with new hobbies and interests, make new friends, do things on your bucket list and integrate different aspects of your personality that may have felt stifled in the abusive relationship. Whether you're blissed out on a yoga mat or launching your dream business, there is no greater way to spend your time and energy than investing in someone who will always appreciate and benefit from it: you.

5. You develop an improved immunity to abusive tactics.

There is no guarantee that you won't encounter another toxic or abusive person in your lifetime. Even experts on this topic can still be duped by predatory types. However, as you begin to heal your wounds, develop better boundaries and learn more about covert manipulation, you also learn to trust your inner voice. As you find validation from trauma-informed professionals and survivor communities, you realize that you never have to discount another gut instinct or abandon your own needs for the sake of maintaining a relationship.

You become confident that you can fulfill your own emotional needs and manage your emotions without the need for anyone to validate your self-worth. This is an exquisite life skill to have that will serve you well throughout your entire life, whether single or with a partner. It will allow you to become less susceptible to tactics such as love-bombing (because you already have high self-esteem, over the top flattery just won't cut it for you; you'll require a genuine connection), triangulation (you will resist comparing yourself to others because you know how to self-validate), and gaslighting (because you've learned to trust your own instincts). The projections of others won't rattle you to the core as they once did; you'll take them as signals to move on from toxic people and only own what is yours alone.

Perhaps your journey won't be perfect, but it will be much more authentic and liberating. You'll learn that you are the only one who can save yourself. Most importantly of all, being single will give you the time you need to recover, evaluate what you truly desire and make your dreams come to life.

Narcissistic Mothers and Fathers

Essays on the characteristics and
behaviors of narcissistic mothers and fathers.

8 Traits of The Narcissistic Mother

Our mothers are the foundation of our first attachment to the world. As infants, we learn by her example how to bond with others. We derive our initial sense of our self-worth from how she cares for us, nurtures us, protects and shields us from harm.

A mother's capacity to provide us with a healthy attachment, to tune into our emotions, validate our pain, and meet our basic needs has a fundamental impact on our development, attachment styles, and emotional regulation (Brumariu & Kerns, 2010). When this initial attachment is instead tarnished by psychological violence, it can leave scars that can take a lifetime to heal.

A toxic, narcissistic mother sets up her daughters and sons for inevitable danger due to the nature of her disorder. Her insatiable need for control, excessive sense of entitlement, stunning lack of empathy, tendency towards interpersonal exploitation, and constant need for attention overrides the welfare of her children.

Not only does she fail to protect us early on from the terrors of the outside world, she becomes the *source* of our terror. Rather than affection, we are exposed to unhealthy enmeshment, chronic rage, and egregious boundary-breaking. Narcissistic parenting distorts our self-perception; instead of being given the building blocks of a healthy self-esteem, we internalize a nagging inner critic and a perpetual sense of self-doubt.

The narcissistic mother's rapid shift in emotions, her ever-conditional "love," her constant shaming tactics and her ruthless comparisons terrorize us, creating a persistent sense of anxiety where safety and security should be.

Not all toxic mothers are narcissistically *disordered*; some are toxic because they are the victims of long-time domestic violence where they've been unable to protect their children from witnessing abuse. Sometimes, they are the enablers of their abusive husbands, turning a blind eye because they're trauma bonded or unwilling to intervene. Others are toxic because they are addicts, histrionically inclined, emotionally unstable, or unhealed as a result of undergoing narcissistic abuse or severe trauma themselves.

However, what toxic parents *all* have in common is the inability to provide their children a safe, nurturing, and loving environment. If they are narcissistically abusive, they are without empathy and sometimes even conscience. This type of ruthless behavior has a damaging impact on our early development as well as the way we navigate the world as adults.

The narcissistic mother engages in the following emotionally abusive behaviors:

1. She chronically shames her children. Shaming is a tactic the narcissistic mother uses to ensure that her children never develop a stable sense of identity or self-esteem – to ensure that they never grow independent enough outside of seeking her validation or approval. She shames her children for not accomplishing enough academically, socially, professionally and personally. She shames them for their choice of career, partner, friends, lifestyle, their manner of dress, their personality, their preferences – all of these and more come under the scrutiny of the narcissistic mother. She shames her children for acting with any sense of agency because it threatens *her* sense of control and power. By doing so, she instills in them a sense of never being good enough, no matter what they achieve.

2. She sets up damaging comparisons among her children as well as their peers. Like any narcissist, the narcissistic mother engages in "triangulation" – manufacturing triangles among her children and even their peers. She destructively compares her children to their peers, teaching them that they fall short in terms of looks, personality, obedient behavior, and accomplishments. She unfairly pits two or more siblings against one another, always asking, "Why can't you be more like your sister or your brother?" She stirs up competition, drama, and chaos. She might make one child a golden child (doting upon them excessively) while making the other a scapegoat, blaming them for even being born. This form of devaluation can leave a painful imprint; it causes her children to compare themselves to others as a way to evaluate their self-worth. It causes the scapegoated children to feel like a burden while teaching her "golden" children the same excessive sense of entitlement she possesses.

3. She treats her children as extensions of her. The narcissistic mother micromanages and exerts an excessive level of control over the way her children act and look to the public. Her children are objects and must be pristine and polished in every way, lest *their* actions or appearance "taint" her own. Though she criticizes them and treats them with contempt behind closed doors, in public, she shows her children off as if they were prized possessions. She brags about how little Timmy always gets straight A's and how her darling Stacy is the prettiest little girl in town. Yet behind closed doors, she is pouncing on Timmy with reprimands about what he has yet to accomplish and picking on Stacy's weight.

4. She competes with her children, disrupts their transition to adulthood and crosses sexual boundaries. It is common for narcissistic mothers to compete with their children, especially their own daughters. The narcissistic mother is likely to overvalue her own looks and sexual prowess. Female narcissists exhibit internalized misogyny and often view other females as competition. The daughter is thus looked upon with fury, jealousy, and envy – her own offspring is viewed as a threat.

As a result, she may devalue her daughter's appearance, criticize her body and shame her. On the other hand, some narcissistic mothers will objectify their daughters and demand physical perfection. She may expose her daughters to inappropriate discussions about sex or flaunt her body, emphasizing the value of appearances. She might teach her daughters and sons that a woman derives value from her body and her ability to please men sexually. If the narcissistic mother has histrionic tendencies, she may even seduce the friends of her children to demonstrate her superiority over her younger competition.

In other cultures where sexuality is far more restricted, the narcissistic mother may instead attempt to stifle her daughter's burgeoning sexuality and punish her for being anything less than abstinent. She may fail to provide her daughters with the proper education concerning sex and their growing bodies.

5. An obsession with the external, at the expense of her child's needs. To the narcissistic mother, appearances are everything. She may construct the false image of being a sweet, loving and charitable person to others all while gossiping about others, engaging in petty one-upping and abusing her children emotionally, physically or even sexually. She enjoys the social status of being a mother without doing the actual maternal work.

She shows off her children without properly tending to their basic emotional and psychological needs. To her, how things look is far more important than how they actually *are.* Depending on her social class, the narcissistic mother may enlist the help of others to care for her children around the clock while neglecting to give her children affection or attention when they are around, treating them as nuisances rather than as human beings. She may even be callous and cold to the point where she refuses to touch her children altogether.

6. Engages in horrific boundary-breaking. At the other end of the spectrum, the narcissistic mother may become so enmeshed with her children and overbearing that she engages in covert emotional incest. She makes her children the center of the world and responsible for fulfilling *her* emotional needs.

Rather than taking on the responsibilities of being an authority figure and parent, she "parentifies" her own children, making them feel obligated to cater to her arbitrary desires and expectations. She violates her children's basic needs for privacy and autonomy, demanding to know every facet of their lives. She might enter their rooms without knocking, read their diaries, and interrogate them constantly about their friends or romantic partners.

Much like the narcissistic father (which we'll discuss after this chapter), she keeps her children in a state of perpetual childhood by punishing them for growing up – whether that means moving out of the house, getting married, going on a date or becoming aware of their sexuality.

7. Becomes enraged at any perceived threat to her superiority. The narcissistic mother is not unlike any other narcissist in that she feels entitled to have her way and endures narcissistic injury when this sense of superiority is questioned or threatened in any way. As a result, her emotions tend to be a psychological rollercoaster from start to finish. From the sudden outbursts of rage when you "fail" to obey her demands to the abrupt love-bombing which occurs when she needs something from her children, there is little consistency in a household with a narcissistic mother. Her children walk on eggshells every day, fearful of encountering their mother's rage, punishment, and hysterical outbursts.

8. Emotionally invalidates, guilt-trips and gaslights her children. A child's reactions to her narcissistic mother's abuse are frequently met with invalidation, shaming and further gaslighting. The narcissistic mother views her children with contempt and treats them as if they were disposable.

The narcissistic mother lacks empathy for the feelings of her children and fails to consider their basic needs. A narcissistic mother is prone to telling her children that the abuse never occurred. It is common for the narcissistic mother to claim that her child is being "oversensitive" or "overreacting" when they call out horrendous acts of psychological violence. The narcissistic mother may also engage in a pity ploy every time she is being held accountable for her actions. She may fake emotional upset or even sudden illness in an attempt to garner sympathy to avoid taking responsibility, taking on the role of the victim even though she remains the abuser.

The narcissistic mother has no qualms about using her emotional outbursts to control and manipulate her children, yet when her children express their emotions, she invalidates them completely. She redirects the focus to her needs and guilt-trips her children at every sign of perceived disobedience. She provokes her children and is sadistically pleased when her put-downs and insults have staying power.

Empathic mothers are attuned to the emotional welfare of their children; narcissistic mothers represent a perversion of the maternal instinct.

How A Narcissistic Mother Affects Us In Adulthood

Our mother is our earliest role model for attachment, bonding, prosocial behavior, and our relationships with other females. Having a narcissistic mother can lead us to the following symptoms as a result of the behaviors she displayed:

We feel insecure, anxious and lack confidence in our relationships or friendships (especially friendships with other females).

Our narcissistic mothers taught us that relationships with others are meant to be one-sided, parasitic affairs, where we are meant to serve the needs of others. Thus, we become perpetually anxious about pleasing our romantic partners or friends at the expense of our own needs. We may withdraw from intimacy as a result of anxiety, mistrust and hypervigilance about the motives of others. We may even establish friendships with narcissistic females because they remind us of our toxic mothers and we're subconsciously seeking to heal that core relationship. Sons of narcissistic mothers may gravitate towards female partners who exhibit controlling and overbearing attitudes, a damsel-in-distress façade, or have other narcissistic tendencies.

We are prone to being gaslighted in our adult relationships.

The narcissistic mother teaches her children that their thoughts and feelings are illegitimate. In adulthood, we learn to swallow our feelings of unease around dangerous people. We become susceptible to the gaslighting of abusive and toxic friends, partners, acquaintances, colleagues and bosses. We learn to distrust our own intuition and betray our inner voice.

We suffer from chronic feelings of emptiness and lack a core sense of self-worth.

Our narcissistic mother failed to mirror to us that core sense of self-love that every developing child needs and desires. Rather than teaching us to love ourselves, she taught us vanity, self-absorption, selfishness, and a propensity to chase external validation. As a result, we feel "empty" of the nourishment that children who grew up in a healthy family received. We may fill that sense of emptiness with various addictions, unhealthy relationships, overeating, indiscriminate sexual promiscuity, overachieving, and other self-sabotaging behaviors which fail to fulfill us in the long-term. Daughters of narcissistic mothers may become especially hypersexual or hyper-conservative if their mother modeled inappropriate sexual behavior in front of them.

We have a propensity for people-pleasing and perfectionism.

The moving goalposts of the narcissistic mother habituated us to become overachievers and perfectionists. We tend to compare ourselves to others and strive to be the best. We forget to actually celebrate our accomplishments even when we do establish a high level of achievement and success. We try so hard to become accomplished, to win societal approval, and to please the outside world that we forget how to unconditionally love and approve of ourselves.

We feel emotionally off-balance or unstable.

Narcissistic mothers teach us that our emotions are our enemies. Rather than validating them or teaching us how to cope with them in a healthy way, we instead become emotionally stunted and repressed in fear of the punishment and reprisal we experienced whenever we expressed our emotions. This repression can lead to outbursts after years of being silenced or mental breakdowns.

We have a venomous inner critic.

The hypercriticism of the narcissistic mother leads to the growth of a venomous inner critic that attempts to hold us back in every endeavor. We perceive ourselves through our mother's eyes and it can take a great deal of inner work to overcome this negative programming.

Narcissistic mothers create the original wounding and blueprint for our relationships, our self-esteem and the ways we perceive our value in the world.

In order to heal from a narcissistic mother, similar modalities which are used to heal from the narcissistic father can be used. This is discussed in the next set of essays.

Daddy Issues:

Daughters of Narcissistic Fathers

Much has been written about the dynamics between narcissistic mothers and daughters, but less has been explored about the daughters of narcissistic fathers. How do young women raised by toxic male authority figures later navigate the world? How do they come to see themselves and their relationships? Daughters of narcissistic fathers face all the common challenges of having an unempathetic, cruel and abusive parent, but along with these they may also encounter unique triggers and obstacles on the path to their healing journey.

Here are five common challenges daughters of narcissistic fathers experience and tips on how to overcome them on the healing journey. Sons of narcissistic fathers as well as daughters of narcissistic mothers may also be able to relate to these.

Part 1: Our Desire for Danger

Daughters of narcissistic fathers are drawn to dangerous people and situations which on the surface appear to be harmless. This tendency was birthed from being conditioned by their father's own Jekyll and Hyde behavior.

The grandiose self-image and reputation of their fathers rarely matched the coldness and indifference behind closed doors, habituating their children to accept interpersonal danger as the norm. Narcissists are masters of impression management and the charismatic narcissistic father is no different. As the daughter of a narcissistic father, you may have noticed that your father prioritized his reputation in the community above the happiness or wellbeing of you and your family members (Banschick, 2013).

Your father was most likely known as generous, friendly and exceptionally charming to all those who knew him in public; yet behind closed doors, he was verbally, emotionally and/or physically abusive to his spouse and children. This is not uncommon in households with a narcissistic parent; their 'false self' is rarely a match for the true self within the realm of the family unit.

As a result, daughters of narcissistic fathers are likely to have been silenced should they ever have attempted to speak out against the abuse or speak ill of the father within the household or in public.

Combined with gender roles and expectations for young women to be quiet, demure and polite, daughters of narcissistic fathers may have been conditioned to adapt to danger rather than to protect themselves from it.

That is why dangerous situations and people with a Jekyll and Hyde personality – people who are rarely consistent in their character or integrity – feel like an oddly familiar unsafe comfort zone to daughters of narcissistic fathers in adulthood.

What to do:

Validate and acknowledge the experiences you had with your narcissistic parent and don't allow the opinions of others detract from the reality of the abuse you experienced.

It is common for survivors of *any* form of abuse to doubt and question themselves about the horrific violations they experienced.

This is especially true when their abuser is a loved figure in the community or projects a charitable and loving image to the world.

They may have also experienced an enormous amount of gaslighting from their abusers, enabling family members, or friends of the family. Survivors of narcissistic abuse tend to 'gaslight' themselves into believing their experiences were not valid, due to the reputation of their abusers.

If the abuse is taking a severe toll on your mental health and well-being, consider limiting contact with your narcissistic parent to only holidays and special occasions. Limited contact enables you to take your power back, as you can control the frequency with which you interact with the parent and walk away from potentially threatening situations before they escalate.

Some survivors find that their particular situation warrants going No Contact with their abusive parents; if that is the case, know that you do not have to feel guilty or ashamed. **You have every right to protect yourself from dangerous people, even if they share your DNA.**

Learn constructive ways to self-validate. Journal or speak with a counselor about the abuse you endured to reconnect with its reality. Confer with validating family members or friends who were also recipients of the abuse and do not minimize it. Honor what you experienced and recognize that you did not deserve it, in any shape, way or form.

Find ways to give yourself the emotional nourishment you needed but didn't receive in childhood. Re-parent yourself with the soothing words, actions as well as acts of radical self-care that can combat some of the destructive conditioning you may have faced in your childhood (Cooney, 2017; Markham, 2014). Connect with your inner child through visualization, meditation and self-soothing whenever you're in emotional distress (Jenner, 2016). We will talk more about specific healing modalities in Part 3 of this series as well as the chapters on re-parenting here and the more extensive healing modalities here.

Identify and consider limiting contact with any people you currently have in your life who also have a 'false self' that do not align with their true ones.

Often when we've been raised by a father figure like this, we tend to gravitate towards people who feed us empty words and false promises, or who are also emotionally unavailable. No wonder: our early role models for relationships also lacked emotional depth and an inability to connect with us emotionally.

We can become "tone-deaf" to verbal and emotional abuse as well (Streep, 2016). That is why it is important to recognize any toxic patterns of communication we may also be tolerating from our other family members, friends, acquaintances and dating partners and to set firmer boundaries that honor how we deserve to be treated.

Finally, ensure that you're in touch with your authentic self – honor all of the facets of your identity that make you who you are. Know that you don't need to hide your true self from others and that you don't have to follow in your narcissistic father's footsteps in excessively depending on external validation.

Self-validation and connecting with your true self are key on the healing journey.

We may not be able to change the narcissistic parent, but we *can* take steps to ensure that we ourselves are living authentic lives and not modeling the parent's destructive ways of behaving and relating to the world.

Part 2: The Perpetual Childhood

Daughters of narcissistic fathers are devalued, shamed, objectified and controlled, leading to feelings of always being "out" of control. This can be due to the fact that affection stopped once daughters reached puberty or it may have overstepped boundaries.

It is common for parents and teenagers to be engaged in a power struggle especially when it comes to the teenager dating or entering relationships. Yet with a narcissistic father, the devaluation is excessive and immense during this stage.

This is especially true if there was idealization (putting you on a pedestal, doting on you) involved in the beginning. Perhaps your father *did* show affection and care towards you when you were a toddler or a young child because you were easier to control. However, the tender hugs right after he came home from work or the sweet praise may have come to an abrupt halt as you reached puberty and he found himself confronting a teenager who was not as easy policed.

For some daughters, affection was never present at all; the narcissistic father may have refused to touch or even care for the infant child and emotionally neglected the daughter throughout her life span.

Perhaps the narcissistic father chose one daughter as a golden child to spoil and dote upon, while assigning another daughter the role of the scapegoat, barely interacting with her at all, or even going so far as to shun her from his attention altogether.

Affection or no affection, the narcissistic father's lack of boundaries can take a disturbing turn. As some daughters of narcissistic fathers can attest to, becoming aware of one's sexuality and entering relationships can be a huge 'trigger' for the narcissistic father's need to micromanage his children.

The narcissistic father believes he 'owns' his children and your burgeoning sense of independence – as well as your interactions with those who challenge his power and authority – can cause him severe narcissistic injury and rage.

To the narcissistic father, no one is 'good enough' for his 'little girl' but this belief has even deeper and darker implications – he has a need to ensure that his daughter stays in a state of *perpetual childhood* so that she is easier to control.

Her sexuality and interest in boys (or girls) as an adolescent challenge this and compels him to police and shame her in unhealthy ways. He may have instilled in his daughter an overreliance on his approval that can be difficult to break away from.

The narcissistic father may have engaged in covert emotional incest that 'parentified' his daughter so that she felt that he was the only 'partner' she could turn to (Weiss, 2015). If he struggled with addiction issues, he may have assigned her the role of caretaker or even more disturbingly, in the absence of a mother in the household, a surrogate 'wife' figure.

He might have substituted emotional connection with financial 'generosity' and control, teaching her that in order to be loved she had to also be 'bought' – and that, whoever did 'purchase' her was entitled to her.

Or, if he had a son, he might have bragged about his sexual exploits and taught his son to follow in his footsteps while holding a sexual double standard for his daughter, who he demanded be kept sexually 'pure.'

There are many ways that this form of sexual micromanaging can manifest, but rest assured: all of them can deplete the child a sense of security and independence when growing up.

According to Dr. Karyl McBride (2011), in the most extreme scenarios, a malignant narcissistic father can even cross over to sexual abuse and violence. This is because narcissistic fathers have no boundaries in the ways they see their children. They see them as objects to fulfill their needs, as extensions of themselves, rather than individual human beings.

By degrading or devaluing them sexually, they maintain control over their daughters (or their sons) in ways that are damaging beyond words.

How to deal:

Track the journey from idealization to devaluation. Was there a certain point where your narcissistic father stopped idealizing you or was there always devaluation and abuse? Learning the 'trigger point' can be helpful to reducing the cognitive dissonance that arises when we've been raised by these types of toxic individuals.

As we identify that the point when we were devalued was also when we were becoming independent of the narcissistic parent, we understand that it was not our fault in any shape or form.

We may have felt ashamed or even engaged in self-blame as a result of the abuse, without realizing that this had more to do with the toxic parent's deficiencies and malignant traits rather than any of our own perceived shortcomings.

Recognize faulty and negative feedback as attempts to control you. It's helpful to begin to deconstruct and reframe any criticism we received during this time as illegitimate nonsense meant to keep us from becoming our authentic selves and from establishing relationships that would have facilitated our transition into adulthood.

Replace negative feedback and distortions with healthier self-talk that challenge the inner critic – harness the power of positive affirmations, pattern 'interrupting' thoughts and behaviors that redirect you from your inner critic, and remodel the ways you've been speaking to yourself (Martin, 2016; Roe, 2015). Bring the power and agency back to you.

Gain mastery over your body and sexual agency. As daughters of narcissistic fathers, our sexuality may have been stifled, eroded or misused to serve the narcissistic father's needs. It's time to regain mastery over our bodies and our sexuality.

Some ways of doing this might include:

- Reconnecting with a spiritual sense of sexuality that enables us to see our sexuality as sacred rather than shameful.

- Experimenting with self-pleasure and/or greater emotional intimacy in our relationships to increase feelings of safety and trust.

- Working with a trauma-informed counselor to unravel any deep-seated core beliefs or triggers that may be holding us back from embracing our sexuality and finding fulfillment in physical intimacy.

Narcissistic fathers excessively try to maintain power and control over their daughters. It is essential that daughters of toxic parents take their power back, emotionally, financially, sexually, and psychologically on the journey to healing.

Part 3: Trauma Repetition and Toxic Men

Daughters of narcissistic daughters are drawn to narcissistic men or women in adulthood. Due to the first blueprint for romantic relationships being molded by their toxic fathers, daughters of narcissistic fathers run the risk of engaging in a trauma repetition cycle and ending up in unhealthy relationships or friendships in adulthood.

Daughters of narcissistic fathers may find themselves being retraumatized by predators who are very similar to their first male 'role model.' **This is not their fault:** *anyone* **can be targeted by a malignant narcissist regardless of their trauma history and anyone can be affected by the effects of trauma.** Yet it is important to consider that childhood abuse survivors may be especially vulnerable to grandiose, narcissistic types not only due to their deeper core wounds and beliefs, but also the narcissist's own predatory behavior.

Toxic narcissistic types tend to find a great deal of narcissistic supply in those who have empathy, compassion and resources, as well as psychological resilience built up from trauma (Frankenhuis & de Weerth, 2013). **The resilience of survivors** may, at first glance, seem like an odd trait to pinpoint in this context, but it is actually one that the abusive narcissist depends on in the abuse cycle.

Consider that the children of narcissists may not have learned how to implement appropriate boundaries, but they learned how to survive while subjected to extreme duress. These essential skills of survival might have been necessary in childhood to avoid the threat of emotional and/or physical harm, but in adult relationships, they become the very factors that can make us susceptible to predators in adulthood.

How Resilience Plays a Factor in the Trauma Repetition Cycle

That is why daughters of narcissists who have been 'primed' for abuse may find themselves encountering one predator after another without understanding why. They blame themselves for staying or getting into these relationships, not realizing that two of their greatest strengths – the ability to be resilient and their empathy for others – are being unfairly exploited in a dangerous power play.

Daughters of narcissistic fathers can fall prey to exploitation in adulthood because they learned early on how to be caretakers, adept problem-solvers and multi-taskers: they learned how to juggle detecting threats in their environment while responding to them in a way that mitigated danger. They are extremely competent at performing emotional labor for others as well as picking up on nonverbal cues that signal potential threat or abandonment.

In an abusive relationship, this gets translated into people-pleasing, walking perpetually on eggshells and an entrenched sense of powerlessness. In a healthy relationship, with healthier boundaries and an expectation of emotional reciprocity, daughters of narcissists have much to offer their partners. Their maturity, emotional generosity and attentiveness to their partner's needs can be assets in a healthy relationship, *after* they have developed a healthy sense of self and worked to heal their core wounds. In an abusive one with a malignant narcissist, however, her willingness to see her partner's perspective and meet his needs gets taken advantage of and used against her.

What may be surprising for others to learn is that it is not just her vulnerability that makes her a target; it is also her resilience. The more resilient the daughter of a narcissist is from the violations of her childhood, the more likely she will 'bounce back' after incidents of abuse, and continue to try to 'fix' or solve the problems of the abusive relationship, much like she did in her early childhood.

She will avoid the threats of confrontation and conflict, leaving her open to the far greater danger of being in a long-term toxic relationship that depletes and drains her. This is especially pertinent to consider since abusive types will test the boundaries of their victims continually throughout the relationship to ensure that the victim grows accustomed to the abuse over time.

How to address this:

Heal your subconscious wounding through mind-body techniques and alternative remedies. A great deal of our behavior is actually driven by the subconscious mind; that is why talk therapy alone often does not do justice in healing significant trauma or deeply destructive, ingrained beliefs (Lipton, 2016).

It is also important to note that trauma is often stored in the level of the body; its imprint is left on parts of the brain that do not have as much access to the more rational parts of our brain and thus cannot be healed 'cognitively' (Tippet & Kolk, 2017).

That is why in addition to traditional therapy, survivors may benefit from EMDR, EFT, hypnotherapy, trauma-focused yoga, Reiki healing, aromatherapy, sound bath therapy as well as a daily meditation practice and exercise regimen to 'cleanse' the subconscious wounding that may be tethering them to these abusive partners or friends. You can learn more about these specific healing modalities in the later essay, "Healing Modalities for Adult Children of Narcissists."

Speak with a mental health professional to find the therapies that best suit your unique needs or triggers; remember that there is no 'one size fits all' healing path for survivors. What may work for one survivor may not work for you, but as you experiment with different modalities, you might just find the right healing 'package' to meet your wounds.

Rework existing narratives and modify your behavior accordingly. Psychologists and sociologists believe we construct narratives out of our life experiences to give our lives and identities shape and meaning (McAdams, 2006). Bring any destructive narratives and beliefs you have about yourself, your relationships and the world to the surface – and dismantle them.

You may unravel these through the healing modalities we discussed and you might also discover these by delving into past patterns of feeling, thinking and behaving. How do you speak to yourself and treat yourself on a daily basis? What sort of behaviors do you tend to tolerate or rationalize? How do you feel when navigating the world? What is your personal life story and identity story?

If you have a pattern of getting involved with emotionally unavailable partners, for example, you might be acting out from the childhood trauma of encountering emotional unavailability from the only father figure you ever knew. You may have a running narrative of never feeling like you belonged and never being 'good enough' for a healthy and loving relationship.

Gently replace these narratives with more empowering affirmations to regain your sense of safety in the world as well as your sacred boundaries for future relationships. A healthier rewriting of the narrative might look something like, **"I am and always will be enough. Just because I was traumatized doesn't mean it was my fault. I, of all people, deserve healthy and safe relationships. I am a survivor who can break the pattern."**

Then, begin to reinforce these new beliefs and cement them by engaging in small steps that communicate to yourself that you are paving a new path to freedom from old beliefs. For example, limiting contact with toxic people in your life can be one small step to prove to yourself that you are committed to your new belief that you can trust your instincts about toxic people and newfound willpower to stay away from them.

Creating a **"sacred boundaries"** list and brainstorming a plan for implementing healthier boundaries can also be helpful to this process. For a list of guidelines for fairness and intimacy, check out trauma therapist Pete Walker's Human Bill of Rights.

Seek more positive male role models. Due to their upbringing, daughters of narcissistic fathers may have been conditioned to feel as if males are potentially dangerous or emotionally bankrupt in some way. This might act as a filter or even drive a confirmation bias where they end up meeting more and more dangerous men that prove their core beliefs about men and masculinity right – a form of **trauma reenactment** to attempt to resolve past childhood wounds (van der Kolk, 1989).

Unfortunately, in a world that is steeped in violence against women – from sexual assault to brutal honor killings – we may have also internalized this sense of danger culturally as well – for very legitimate reasons.

It's not about getting rid of this very valid fear of meeting dangerous men, but gently inviting the idea of safer men into the narrative. It's important to recognize that there *are* 'safe' men in the world even in the midst of oppression – men who wouldn't dream of deliberately hurting or terrorizing you.

These are the men who are *truly* attractive and desirable – even if your early childhood programming (through no fault of your own) made you feel more drawn to danger on a subconscious and biochemical level. So begin to take notice of these men who provide an alternative narrative – one of empathy and compassion. Even if these role models are public figures rather than anyone you personally know, start to think about the kinder, gentler and protective males you have met, encountered or heard about in your life's journey.

Branch out – they could be your neighbors, your classmates, a teacher who influenced you, a local community leader, an author, a social activist, an old boyfriend or a male friend...the possibilities are endless.

Think about the men in your life who have worked hard to evolve and have emotionally comforted and validated you in the past. If you have a validating male therapist, you may want to also consider him as a role model for what positive 'masculinity' represents.

By recognizing and identifying healthier models, you can also pinpoint the qualities, characteristics and behaviors of what an empathic, compassionate mate or friend would look like for the future. You may also want to compile a list of what your ideal partner would be like. What sort of values, beliefs and behaviors would he engage in? What would his true nature – not his persona - be like?

While daughters of narcissistic fathers can have a history of complex trauma and trauma repetition, the cycle can and will be broken. The strong will and resilience of survivors can serve them well when it comes to utilizing the necessary healing modalities, resources and self-compassion it takes to heal themselves and future generations.

Part 4: People-Pleasing and Validation Seeking

Daughters of narcissistic fathers (as well as mothers) tend to become people-pleasers with porous boundaries in adulthood.

As a result of the neglect and abuse, daughters of narcissistic parents can suffer from boundaries which are too porous or severely rigid, either shutting out the outside world completely due to distrust or catering to everyone else's needs while excluding their own.

For those who turn to people-pleasing, consider that daughters of narcissists witnessed their charismatic father constantly search for external validation from society and his local communities while abandoning any attempts at authentic familial connections. As a result, they developed a core belief system that validation is best found in the external world rather than from within, fearing the vulnerability it takes to be their true selves in the world.

Due to this, daughters of narcissistic parents might be prone to modeling that same behavior and chasing after external validation – whether it be through wealth, status, prestige, or emotionally shallow relationships.

These people-pleasing habits also stem from their *relationship dynamic* with their narcissistic fathers; they may have constantly tried to please him and meet his arbitrary standards in an effort to gain affection, love or approval, to no avail.

In households with extreme abuse, the struggle to please the narcissistic parent may have been in an effort to survive. The narcissistic rage of this type of toxic parent "trains" and conditions their children to meet the needs of others to avoid anger, disappointment or verbal, emotional or even physical abuse. Thus, daughters of narcissistic fathers (or any type of narcissistic caretaker for that matter) are accustomed to walking perpetually on eggshells to keep the peace and to have their basic needs (such as physical safety, food, shelter, clothing) met.

In his discussion of the four F types that arise from trauma, trauma therapist Pete Walker (2013) notes that people-pleasing tendencies tend to be associated with the 'Fawn' type of defensive structure, where for the trauma survivor, "the price of admission to any relationship is the forfeiture of all their needs, rights, preferences and boundaries."

This 'fawning' trauma type can lend itself to self-sabotage and self-harm. In "25 Things You Do When You've Experienced Childhood Emotional Abuse," survivors open up about how these self-defeating behaviors in childhood translate to the betrayal of one's own needs in adulthood – ranging from apologizing when we've done nothing wrong to demonstrating excessive levels of perfectionism.

It doesn't help that the very traits of people-pleasing can also be exacerbated by gender roles and stereotypes. As Sharon Martin, LCSW (2016), notes in her article, "How Women Can Overcome People-Pleasing and Perfectionism," women in society are more likely to be socialized as caretakers and to be more passive about their own needs. Social and cultural influences, combined with the abuse of a narcissistic parent, can be a lethal combination for cultivating boundaries and authenticity.

How to break the spell:

Identify your people-pleasing habits as well as your authentic desires. Getting in touch with what we really need, think and desire is a very basic but essential step to getting closer to honoring our authentic selves. Brainstorm the ways in which you've been people-pleasing, whether it be in friendships, relationships, the workplace or everyday life. In what ways have you been silencing who you really are, whether in the personality you projected to the outside world or the dreams you're currently pursuing? What are some steps you can to take to cultivate the parts of yourself you've been hiding from the world because you feel they wouldn't meet society's approval?

Engage in alternate or positive rebellion on a daily basis to challenge your fears of breaking the mold. You may have been 'acting out' your trauma in ways you did not realize – through passive-aggressive methods to get your needs met (such as people-pleasing or being overly sweet to dangerous people) or repressing your anger towards others and directing it back to yourself through negative self-talk and toxic shame.

It's time to turn the tables and find constructive ways to 'rebel' against what you've been through. See this list of tips for alternate rebellion, which can help you to reconnect to the sides of yourself that you may have been stifling.

Work on your boundaries in every area of your life. As the child of a narcissist, your boundaries may have been trampled upon and eroded on a daily basis. Our lack of boundaries, combined with our empathy and compassion for others, can signify to predators that we will cater to their needs at the expense of our own and break our own boundaries to win their validation.

Check out this worksheet on how to create personal boundaries and also be sure to check out my exercise on creating boundaries in dating in Part Five of this book. If you're struggling with envisioning what your boundaries might look like, you may also want to read author Natalie Lue's list of 12 Core Boundaries to Live By in Life, Dating and Relationships.

Look within – often. Get in touch with your inner voice, the one you might have neglected or pushed aside as you struggled to validate yourself through others.

Great ways to do so are through: (1) meditations geared to help you hone in on your intuition such as this one by Joe Treacy to connect with your higher self, (2) journaling about your authentic feelings, desires and beginning a dialogue with what Elisabeth Corey, MSW, calls the inner parts of yourself in an uncensored way and (3) learning to love and accept the aspects of yourself you may have devalued due to the opinions of others.

Find ways to validate yourself as a human being worthy of the same love and consideration as anyone else, regardless of any flaws or shortcomings. It is, in fact, those same things that you decry about yourself that make you an interesting and well-rounded person; don't sacrifice your true attributes to become a replica of who you think you should be.

Becoming who you truly are and leaning into the power of your own vulnerability and authenticity, will help you to build more meaningful relationships, as well as more intimate ones that your narcissistic father wasn't capable of building.

Part 5: Self-Sabotage

Daughters of narcissistic fathers develop a fragmented sense of self and engage in self-sabotage.

Daughters of narcissistic fathers tend to be subjected to hypercriticism and high standards that they are rarely able to 'fulfill' no matter how hard they try. As a result, they can turn to self-sabotaging behaviors and struggle with a stable sense of identity and confidence.

Daughters of narcissistic fathers have their sense of self eroded and annihilated in childhood. The daughter of a narcissist can develop a fragmented identity made out of the very parts the narcissistic father strove to erase as well as the parts he 'installed' within her through cruel insults, belittling remarks and a hyperfocus on her flaws to make her doubt her abilities, assets and capacities.

She is taught to second-guess herself at every turn and to excessively scrutinize herself in her talents, her appearance, her potential, and her aspirations. She is also 'programmed' to self-destruct in relationships and sometimes even her own goals because she does not develop the sense of worthiness early on that prevents her from reenacting the same traumas she endured in childhood.

If you are the daughter of a narcissistic parent, you were rarely celebrated for who you truly were and what you could accomplish; instead, you were forced to meet impossible, arbitrary and ever-shifting goal posts that instilled in you a pervasive sense of worthlessness.

The hypercriticism and denigration of the narcissistic father has long-lasting effects. It is part of the larger dynamic of psychological maltreatment, which puts children at greater risk for depression, suicidality and PTSD, among other issues such as substance abuse problems, anxiety disorders and attachment problems (LaBier, 2014). A recent study (Spinazzola, 2014) showed that children who suffered psychological abuse showed similar and at times even worse mental health problems than those who suffered physical or sexual abuse.

Psychological violence overlaps with the covert, insidious tactics that narcissistic parents use to chronically shame, degrade and belittle their children. **The critical voice of the narcissistic parent that the daughter grows up with as a child soon forms an automatic 'Inner Critic' that plays like a record in the back of her mind as that child transitions into adulthood (Walker, 2013).** Daughters of narcissistic fathers are prone to blaming themselves and may even struggle with self-sabotage, negative self-talk, self-blame as well as various methods of self-harm in adulthood.

It is no surprise that narcissistic parents exploit the accomplishments of their children only to bolster their own egos; anything the narcissistic father praised about you, he tended to do in the presence of a witness. Yet in private, he may have been controlling and abusive towards you.

He may have trampled upon your dreams, your goals, and aspirations, especially if they were not ones he wanted to see you achieving. Or, even if you did follow in his footsteps and expectations, he may have still made you felt as if you were falling short of his standards – never quite being 'good enough' to meet any arbitrary criteria he threw your way.

As a result, daughters of narcissistic fathers can fall into defeatist attitudes about accomplishing goals. They may even go the other route entirely and develop an excessive perfectionism that drives them to be number one at all cost.

Their drive towards an illusion of perfection can easily turn into an unhealthy obsession that affects their mental health as well as self-esteem.

How to thrive:

Get real with yourself about which dreams are yours and which ones are derived from the expectations of your narcissistic father.

Did you go to medical school just to please your toxic parent, even though your heart, mind, body and soul ached to be a musician or artist? Did you abandon your dream of becoming a professional dancer just because your narcissistic father pushed you to go to law school? Make a list of aspirations you were never allowed to pursue due to the influence of your toxic parent, as well as any ideologies or beliefs they imposed upon you that you no longer wish to follow. It's never too late to pursue your authentic calling, even if it means re-engaging in your passions on the side.

Start to celebrate your accomplishments, instead of minimizing them.

Daughters of any type of narcissistic parent are used to being criticized at every turn and subjected to moving goal posts that make pleasing their parents impossible. It's time to start validating what you've accomplished so far in your life – whether it be success in your relationships, career, self-development or all three.

Start recalling the compliments others have given you and instead of dismissing them, begin to integrate them into your own self-perception. Maybe you really are a successful person as your friend says, even though your narcissistic father always berated you for not achieving this or that.

Maybe you really are deserving of a healthy relationship, like your counselor told you. Take pride in the beautiful things others celebrate in you and take note of what *you* are proud of as well! They all come together to cultivate a healthier self-image.

Release the idea that you have to be perfect in order to be good enough.

Consider that there are children who grow up in nourishing and validating family environments where their imperfect selves are still unconditionally loved and respected. Just because we may have had the misfortune to be raised in a different environment does not mean we deserved anything less.

Cultivate a sense of being 'enough' just as you are: use positive affirmations, do self-love and self-compassion meditations such as these on a weekly basis, develop a healthy, accepting relationship with your inner child, engage in loving mirror work, and connect back to a sense of faith or sacred spirituality that reminds you of the divine human being you are.

You have a right to be cherished, loved, seen and heard just like any other imperfect human being in this world.

Never equate the narcissistic abuse of a parent with your level of self-worth. You are truly worthy, with or without the approval of anyone else.

References

PART 1

Banschick, M. (2013, March 13). The Narcissistic Father. Retrieved from https://www.psychologytoday.com/blog/the-intelligent-divorce/201303/the-narcissistic-father

Cooney, L. (2017). How to Re-Parent Yourself. Retrieved May 19, 2017, from http://drlisacooney.com/how-to-re-parent-yourself/

Jenner, N. (2016, December 28). Re-parenting your inner child. Retrieved May 25, 2017, from https://boundariesofthesoul.com/2013/05/23/re-parenting-your-inner-child/

Markham, L. (2014, January 19). Committing to Radical Self-Care. Retrieved from https://www.psychologytoday.com/blog/peaceful-parents-happy-kids/201401/committing-radical-self-care

Streep, P. (2016, September). Why Unloved Daughters Fall for Narcissists. Retrieved May 19, 2017. From https://blogs.psychcentral.com/knotted/2016/09/why-unloved-daughters-fall-for-narcissists/

PART 2

HealthyPlace (2017). Positive Sex Play for Sexual Abuse Survivors – Abuse – Sex. Retrieved May 19, 2017, from https://www.healthyplace.com/sex/abuse/positive-sex-play-for-sexual-abuse-survivors/

Martin, B. (2016, July 17). Challenging Negative Self-Talk. Retrieved May 25, 2017, from https://psychcentral.com/lib/challenging-negative-self-talk/

McBride, K. (2011, March 25). Child Sexual Abuse and Narcissism. Retrieved May 19, 2017, from https://www.psychologytoday.com/blog/the-legacy-distorted-love/201103/child-sexual-abuse-and-narcissism

McBride, K. (2013). *Will I ever be good enough?: Healing the daughters of narcissistic mothers*. New York: Atria Paperback.

Piatt, J. (2016, February 28). 11 Steps To Sacred Sex. Retrieved from https://www.mindbodygreen.com/0-23995/11-steps-to-sacred-sex.html

Roe, H. (2015, September 03). Why a pattern interrupt is just what you need. Retrieved from http://www.huffingtonpost.com/helen-roe/why-a-pattern-interrupt-i_b_8075800.html

Weiss, R. (2015, October 13). Understanding Covert Incest: An Interview with Kenneth Adams. Retrieved from https://www.psychologytoday.com/blog/love-and-sex-in-the-digital-age/201510/understanding-covert-incest-interview-kenneth-adams

PART 3

Frankenhuis, W. E., & de Weerth, C. (2013). Does early-life exposure to stress shape or impair cognition? Current Directions in Psychological Science, 22, 407-412.

Kolk, B. V. (1989). The compulsion to repeat the trauma. *Psychiatric Clinics of North America, 12*(2), 381-411. Retrieved May 19, 2017, from http://www.cirp.org/library/psych/vanderkolk/

Lipton, B. H. (2016). *The biology of belief: Unleashing the power of consciousness, matter & miracles*. Carlsbad, CA: Hay House.

McAdams, D. P. (2006). *The stories we live by: Personal myths and the making of the self.* New York: The Guilford Press.

Tippet, K., & Kolk, B. V. (2017, March 9). Bessel van der Kolk – How Trauma Lodges in the Body. Retrieved May 19, 2017, from https://onbeing.org/programs/bessel-van-der-kolk-how-trauma-lodges-in-the-body/

PART 4

Brown, B. (2010, June). *The power of vulnerability.* Speech presented at TEDxHouston, Houston. Retrieved June 10, 2017, from https://www.ted.com/talks/brene_brown_on_vulnerability

Corey, E. (2017, June 08). Beating Trauma by working through our Inner Parts, with Elisabeth Corey. Retrieved from https://www.survivingmypast.net/beating-trauma-by-working-through-our-inner-parts-with-elisabeth-corey/

Martin, S. (2016, November 24). How women can overcome perfectionism and people-pleasing. Retrieved June 10, 2017, from https://blogs.psychcentral.com/imperfect/2016/11/overcomin g-people-pleasing-perfectionism/

Virzi, J. (2017, June 8). 25 Things You Do as an Adult When You've Experienced Childhood Emotional Abuse. Retrieved June 10, 2017, from https://themighty.com/2017/06/childhood-emotional-abuse-adult-habits/

Walker, P. (2013). The 4Fs: A trauma typology in Complex Ptsd. Retrieved June 10, 2017, from http://www.pete-walker.com/fourFs_TraumaTypologyComplexPTSD.htm

PART 5

A., & Spinazzola, J. (2014, October 8). Childhood psychological abuse as harmful as sexual or physical abuse. Retrieved June 18, 2017, from http://www.apa.org/news/press/releases/2014/10/psychologic al-abuse.aspx

LaBier, D. (2014, December 15). Childhood psychological abuse has long-lasting impact. Retrieved from http://www.huffingtonpost.com/douglas-labier/childhood-psychological-a_b_6301538.html

Walker, P. (2013). *Complex PTSD: From surviving to thriving: A guide and map for recovering from childhood trauma.* Lafayette, CA: Azure Coyote.

Part Four

Healing and Re-Parenting the Inner Child

Exercises and healing modalities for adult children of narcissists to aid in recovery.

Cutting the Emotional Umbilical Cord:

Going No Contact or Low Contact With Toxic Parents

"I let go of the guilty feeling of her "being my mother." I realized that by keeping in regular contact with her, I was caring more for her than myself. It can be extremely toxic and I needed to heal. I have always put myself last. I've always sacrificed my own needs for others. It was time to stop." – **Susie J, Survivor from Georgia**

Before you can get to true healing, you have to cut the emotional umbilical cord that we talked about at the beginning of this book. So many survivors ask me how it is possible to go no contact when the narcissist in your life is a parent. I agree that it is very difficult to go full No Contact with a parent. However, my answer is: why do you feel it is impossible to cut or lessen contact with someone who deliberately harms and abuses you, just because they share your DNA? Family does not always have to be biological. Some of the best "families" consist of life-long friendships with people who do not share our genetics but do share our common values.

I do understand the plight of keeping in contact with elderly and sick parents. There is always fear, obligation and guilt involved when it comes to any form of abusive relationship. Even the most toxic parents can still pull at the heartstrings of their empathic children when they are ill. Evaluate where you are right now and do what you can to minimize contact if possible, even if you can't go No Contact.

There are also cases of child abuse so severe that they warrant no contact whatsoever: no phone calls, no visits, not even the passing on of messages through a third party or carrier pigeon. Each set of circumstances is different and will call for a different response. If you are able to go No Contact and feel it is absolutely necessary due to the abuse you endured, you should make the right decision for you and any family members who may be harmed by the influence of your toxic parents.

If you're in a situation where you want to go Low Contact instead, there are some general guidelines that can help:

1. Establish the parameters of contact and stick to them.

What does Low Contact with your abusive parents look like to you? This truly depends on your unique circumstances. If you were raised in a toxic household where holidays were the only happy times, perhaps you do want to spend holidays with your family and limit contact only to special occasions and holiday get-togethers. If, however, the holidays were always a source of extreme stress and abuse, you may want to limit contact to a yearly visit during non-holiday times. Perhaps you want contact to consist only of occasional phone calls with a visit in the case of medical emergencies. Perhaps you're the primary caretaker for an elderly narcissistic parent and the only way to minimize contact is to take a day off and share your responsibilities with a sibling. Whatever the circumstances may be, cater your Low Contact protocol to them to make things convenient and emotionally safe for you. Make it clear that you won't tolerate bullying or guilt-tripping in response and that the alternative is no visitation at all.

2. Cut off interactions that are becoming abusive before they escalate.

Regardless of whether you're paying your toxic parents a visit or catching up with them on a phone call, promise yourself that in any cases of abusive behavior, you end the interaction right away. Hang up the phone, get a cab to take you home, or call a friend to pick you up. Bring a "witness" or supportive friend with you on visits if you think it will help. Always have a "safety plan" which allows you to exit situations where you feel threatened, unsafe or suspect the abuse will escalate.

It's important to end the interaction as soon as soon as it becomes dangerous to you – don't pause, follow your instincts. If you need to "explain" yourself in any way, be straightforward, factual and direct. Remember that you are dealing with a disordered individual who will not be empathic to your emotions. Try not to waste energy explaining your feelings to them. The goal is to exit before the abuse begins. Exercise the "broken record" technique (you can find more communication techniques in the section "Communication Skills for Dealing with Difficult Parents," located in Part 5 of this book). Repeatedly and firmly state, "I will not be spoken to in that manner" when you are met with an abusive remark. Due to the history of abuse, you don't owe your toxic parent an explanation beyond that prior to making an exit. This will not only continually establish healthy boundaries, it will also teach your toxic parent that they will not be able to abuse you any longer without consequences for their behavior.

3. Establish financial independence and freedom.

To fully escape the grasp of your narcissistic parents, it's important to have financial independence and freedom. Having your own home, your own sources of income, your own savings, and your own career are crucial if you want to never have to rely on your toxic parents again. This goes for any abusive relationship – the more financially independent you are, the more likely you will be able to rely only on yourself and leave if the situation is dangerous. If you have any financial ties with your toxic parents – find ways to cut them off sooner than later. You'll be so thankful you did.

4. Relocate if you can.

Low Contact with narcissistic parents can be even more effective if you live far away enough from them that you have an actual justification for not visiting. If you're able to move to a different city or even state, this can give you the time and space you need to work on your own healing without the interference of your narcissistic family members. I understand this is not a possibility for all adult children of narcissistic parents, but if it is an option for you, it is highly worth considering.

5. Make healing a priority.

Speaking of healing, make it a priority while in Low Contact. Let go of the fantasy of having a loving parent and acknowledge the reality of having had an abusive one. Enlist the help of a trauma-informed counselor, preferably one who understands narcissistic personalities and specializes in childhood abuse and trauma. Explore different healing modalities such as EMDR or EFT to begin healing some of the destructive subconscious programming instilled in you by adverse childhood experiences. As you begin to grieve the absence of healthy parents and do the inner work and re-parenting necessary to heal, you will also be able to set firmer boundaries and pursue healthier relationships in the future.

6 Manipulation Tactics of Narcissistic Parents and How To Respond Effectively

There are certain manipulation methods toxic parents engage in to control their children. As adult children of narcissists, it's important to learn how to resist these tactics and set boundaries, especially if we have some form of contact with our parents as adults.

Below, I describe each tactic briefly, offer an example to illustrate how this tactic may be used, and then provide two types of responses.

The first response consists of what you, as an adult child of a narcissist, may have been accustomed to doing in the past to please your parent. Often, even as adults, we tend to "regress" back into emotional flashbacks of childhood which cause us to feel guilt, shame and fear about standing up for ourselves.

The second response is what you will now do as you begin to honor yourself and your self-worth. It will describe how you might set a boundary assertively and stick to that boundary, thus presenting the narcissistic parent with the consequences of their behavior each time they try to mistreat you.

1. EMOTIONAL BLACKMAIL.

The narcissistic parent appears to make a request, but it is really a demand. If you say no, set boundaries, or let them know you'll get back to them later, they will apply increased pressure and threaten consequences to try to get you to acquiesce to them. If you still refuse, they may then punish you with sulking, passive-aggressive statements, or even violence.

Example: Your narcissistic mother may tell you that she would like you to come over on the weekend for a family dinner. All the relatives will be there and they want to see you. Knowing her abusive ways, you tell her you can't make it this weekend because you have a prior engagement. Rather than respecting your wishes, she proceeds to talk about how ungrateful you're being and how all your family members are looking forward to seeing you. You say no, and she hangs up on you and subjects you to the silent treatment for weeks.

What you might have done in the past: In the past, you may have given in to the pressure to please her. You may have subscribed to the idea that you are an ungrateful daughter. You might have reached out to her to try to apologize during her silent treatment and decide to come after all, thus giving into her demands and manipulation.

What you will do in the present: You will use the broken record method to firmly and continually tell her you won't be able to make it, then make an excuse to get off the phone. If she gives you the silent treatment or makes passive aggressive comments, you do not try to win back her favor. Instead, you use the period of silence to engage in self-care, meditate, relax, and you might even momentarily block her number on the weekend so you can have a peaceful one without her interference or attempts to sabotage it.

2. GUILT-TRIPPING.

It is common for narcissistic parents to use FOG (Fear, Obligation, Guilt) on us to evoke the kind of guilt that would cause us to give into their desires, even at the expense of our own basic needs and rights.

Example: Your narcissistic father disapproves of the fact that you're single. He tells you that time is running out to give him grandchildren and that you should marry someone with your same faith and background. He gives you a list of people in his community who he wants you to date. When you tell him you're happy being single, he lashes out in rage and despair, telling you, "So I am going to die without grandchildren? I am getting older and sicker every day – don't you think I want to see my daughter start a family? Is this how you're repaying me for all I've done for you? What will our community think, to see an unmarried woman at your age? It's shameful and disgraceful! You're a disgrace to the family!"

What you might have done in the past: You feel guilty about the fact that you're not living up to your father's expectations. You rethink your choices and start to believe that maybe you should start dating again and look for someone with a similar background, despite the fact that you're not really interested in men from your community. You tell your father that you'll look into the list he provided, even though it makes you feel controlled and helpless.

What you will do in the present: Examine your guilt. Is it really based on any kind of reality? Did you do anything to mistreat, abuse, insult, or harm your father? No, you are simply living your life and are happy being single for now. You have your own preferences for who you want to date and when, and that's perfectly valid. It is your right as an adult to have the relationships you wish and on your own timetable. Your body and your life are your own, and you don't owe anyone children or marriage to keep them happy. When your father mentions the list he wants you to look at, you will tell him firmly that you are not interested in being married right now. You will cut off the interaction immediately and tell him, "I am not interested in being married or dating right now. I am also not interested in being guilted into doing anything I don't want to do. If you don't have anything else to discuss, I am done with this discussion."

3. SHAMING.

Narcissistic, toxic parents shame their children to further belittle and demean them. This is actually quite effective, as research has shown that when someone feels flawed and defective, they tend to be more compliant to the requests of others (Walster, 1965; Gudjonsson and Sigurdsson, 2003).

Example: Your narcissistic mother remarks upon your outfit at Thanksgiving dinner, telling you that it is "too revealing" and that you ought to dress more modestly. She looks at your body with disgust and tries to shame you, despite the fact that you are simply wearing what you normally wear.

What you might have done in the past: You may have regressed back into childhood as a teenager, feeling the toxic shame of when your mother used to scrutinize and criticize your appearance, weight, and body. You remember how it felt as you developed eating disorders and learned to hate your body. Stuck in this feeling of shame, you react by covering yourself, withdrawing into yourself, and staying silent during dinner. After you leave, you engage in some form of self-harm – whether it be drinking, cutting yourself, or even throwing up the food you had during dinner.

What you will do in the present: You will mindfully notice the familiar sense of shame that arises. You will tell yourself, "I am having an emotional flashback." Rather than letting the regression take over your body, you will take a deep breath, sit up straight and tell your mother, "I won't be spoken to or looked at like that. If you have a problem with the way I dress, you'll just have to become accustomed to seeing less of me, because I won't tolerate those types of comments." If she continues to shame you, you can either exit right away or leave early and call a friend to pick you up.

4. COMPARISON AND TRIANGULATION

Narcissistic parents love to compare their children to other siblings or peers in an effort to further diminish them. They want their scapegoated children to fight for their approval and attention. They also want to provoke them into feeling less than.

Example: You get a call from your parents who tell you the news of your cousin getting engaged. Your mother makes a snide comment like, "You know, your cousin Ashley just completed medical school *and* got engaged. What are you doing with *your* life?"

How you might have reacted in the past: This snide remark reminds you of the countless times your narcissistic parents humiliated you in front of your school friends by comparing your test scores and grades to theirs aloud, deliberately making you feel inferior in comparison. You become triggered and attempt to tell your parents all about your accomplishments to try to prove to them that you're surpassing Ashley in other ways. In effect, you've regressed back to your teenage self – trying to get your parent's approval.

How you react in the present: You take a slow, deep breath and notice the sensations in your body. You might notice the tension in your muscles and your instinct to fight back and prove your narcissistic parents wrong. You resist the urge to compete and compare. Instead, you might coolly say something like, "Well, I am happy for Ashley, and I have my own accomplishments to be proud of. Let's talk later, mom." Rather than engaging, you hang up the phone, and write down a list of everything you're proud of achieving to remind yourself that you don't have to feed into the competition in order to shine. You don't have to compare yourself. You have your own things going on. Nor do you have to continue to engage with such a toxic person in order to validate yourself.

5. GASLIGHTING.

Gaslighting is an insidious weapon in the toolbox of a narcissistic parent. It allows the toxic parent to distort reality, deny the reality of the abuse, and make you feel like the toxic one for calling them out.

Example: Your narcissistic father leaves you an abusive voicemail at 3 am in the morning and ten missed calls when you refuse to go out of your way to do something for him. Even though you've explained to him that it's inconvenient for you to do, he persists in punishing you for not complying to his requests. The next day, you call him to confront him about his harassing behavior and he responds by saying, "You're making a mountain out of a molehill. I barely called you last night. You're imagining things."

How you might have reacted in the past: You immediately apologize, feeling guilty about letting him down and agreeing that the number of calls and texts weren't really too much. You begin to doubt yourself and wonder if he even called more than twice. You agree to fulfill his request, even though it will majorly inconvenience you and take away time from your various projects.

How you react in the present: You send your father a text letting him know that his harassing behavior is unacceptable. You temporarily block his number to prevent him from continuing to harass you like this. Or, if you've already reached out to confront him and he gaslights you, you tell him firmly, "That's not what happened and you know it. I have it on my phone. You called me ten times and left a voicemail swearing at me and insulting me. This is unacceptable and I won't stand for it. I am blocking you for now. Goodbye."

6. LOVE-BOMBING AND HOOVERING

When narcissistic parents realize that they are losing control over their children, they will often try to induce a form of abuse amnesia by reaching out to you lovingly. This appeals to what clinical psychologist Lindsay Gibson calls our "healing fantasies" – a fantasy of finally having the caring and compassionate caretaker we always wanted, of having our ideal relationship with our toxic parent. Yet this form of contact is simply another manipulation method known as hoovering. Aptly named after the Hoover vacuum, it is used to suck you back into the traumatic vortex of abuse. This love-bombing brings with it a sudden wave of affection and attention – and it is quite inauthentic since it is used for the sole purpose of further controlling you.

Example: You were recently verbally and emotionally abused by your mother during Thanksgiving and decided to cut off contact. After a month of not contacting your narcissistic mother, you suddenly receive a care package in the mail and a text from her, saying something like, "How are you? Thinking of you. Hope you don't abandon us during Christmas, your grandparents would love to see you and our grandchildren."

How you might have reacted in the past: You feel your heartstrings being pulled at, thinking of how your children might like to see your grandparents for the holidays. Bombarded by constant images of happy families during this vulnerable time, you feel a sense of guilt and obligation to forgive your mother for the antics she pulled on Thanskgiving. You respond to your mother by saying you'll be coming for Christmas after all.

How you will react in the present: You identify this as a Hoover maneuver, knowing full well that your narcissistic mother will drop the kind and caring act as soon as you and your family show up on Christmas. You make alternative plans for the holidays with friends who truly appreciate you. You also call up your grandparents on your own and make arrangements to visit them separately, now knowing that you don't need the permission of your mother or her approval to see those you love.

References

Gibson, L. C. (2015). *Adult children of emotionally immature parents: How to heal from distant, rejecting, or self-involved parents.* Canada: New Harbinger Publications.

Gudjonsson, G. H., & Sigurdsson, J. F. (2003). The Relationship of Compliance with Coping Strategies and Self-Esteem. *European Journal of Psychological Assessment,*19(2), 117-123. doi:10.1027//1015-5759.19.2.117

Walster, E. (1965). The effect of self-esteem on romantic liking. *Journal of Experimental Social Psychology,*1(2), 184-197. doi:10.1016/0022-1031(65)90045-4

Healing and Re-parenting

The Inner Child

Inner child work – the act of tending to our inner child – is an essential part of the road to recovery and of establishing healthy boundaries with ourselves and others. Here are some ways you can "re-parent" the inner child and give yourself the nourishment you always deserved.

I've created a helpful acronym to help you remember the priorities and activities involved in healing and re-parenting your inner child. We will be exploring these in-depth throughout this chapter.

Rectifying negative beliefs

Eradicating subconscious wounding

Parenting the Inner Child

Affirmations

Relational healing

Emotion regulation

Negative self-talk

Telling your story

Identifying the trigger

Needs-based recognition

New Reframing

Emotion validation

Release

Crying

Helping

Integration

Loneliness

Diffusing

Rectifying negative beliefs means uncovering and rewriting the harmful core beliefs you internalized as an abused child. *Eradicating subconscious wounding* requires using diverse healing modalities which target the body and mind to heal core wounds. *Parenting the inner child* refers to self-mothering and self-fathering techniques – the ability to nurture and discipline our inner child in healthier ways – something we did not receive in childhood. *Affirmations* help to reinforce new and healthier, more positive beliefs about ourselves and our self-worth. *Relational healing* is healing through the community – therapists, support groups, friendships - the cornerstone of healing wounds related to attachment and providing the essential "mirroring" back of our divine worth that we did not have in childhood.

Emotion regulation refers to the skill sets we must develop as adult children of narcissists who have grown accustomed to the chaos of living in a war zone – skills such as self-soothing, crisis management, and distress tolerance are essential if we want to be able to navigate everyday life with confidence. *Negative self-talk* reminds us to tackle our Inner Critic, to curb the tides of self-criticism and toxic shame. *Telling your story* refers to the verbal ventilation involved on the healing journey – as we create a cohesive narrative about the traumas we experienced, we can better process the trauma and incorporate it into our life stories.

The "Inner Child" part of the acronym can help you to better assist your Inner Child on the healing journey. When you find a core wound coming to the surface, *identify* the trigger and its origins from childhood. You may find it helpful to ask your Inner Child how old it is as it cries out to you. Then, recognize the *unmet need* that it is carrying and visualize cradling your Inner Child – find a way to meet that need. If, for example, the Inner Child did not get enough healthy praise, give it a *new reframing*, soothing it with the affirmations it deserves.

Give the inner child *emotional validation* – let it know that everything it is feeling is okay, that it did not deserve the abuse it went through. *Release* any trapped emotions by exercising, crying, channeling your grief into art – whatever outlet is appropriate. If the inner child wants to *cry*, let it cry. Stand by the inner child's side and *help* him or her to recognize that they are not alone. You are your inner child's new savior – you are the one that will always be there for him or her. *Integration* reminds us that we are always in the process of putting the fragmented parts of our identity together so we can come back to wholeness – so we can meet our Inner Child in its most powerful state of being.

Address the Inner Child's emotional *loneliness* – the one it has inevitably been struggling with since the very beginning. There are ways to assuage the loneliness that do not involve self-destruction. Find safe communities and be a safety net for your Inner Child. Finally, don't forget to work with a therapist and mind-body healing modalities to *defuse* the atomic bomb that are the triggers to your emotional flashbacks by healing the core wounds at the heart of your pain.

Grieving.

Grieving the loss of a parent who is alive may seem counterintuitive, but when you are the child of a narcissistic parent, you are essentially an emotional orphan. You never received the same form of nurturing, love and comfort that empathic parents could have given you. This leads to a complicated grief in which you have mixed emotions towards the person whose absence you feel acutely.

Trauma therapist Pete Walker, M.A., suggests that there are four processes of grieving:

1) Angering. Many of us are afraid of expressing anger or rage because we're frightened of becoming our abusers. However, being able to express our anger at being unjustly abused and mistreated is an essential component of the healing process and it's a healthy, normal part of being human. I call anger the inner child waking up and fighting back.

You can express your authentic anger and outrage in the presence of a witness such as a therapist before you transition into angering on your own. Walker suggests that we use our anger to halt the Inner Critic.

We can literally say, "No!" or another thought-stopping proclamation whenever the Inner Critic pops up, to redirect the blame and shame to where it belongs, thereby also bringing us out of our state of learned helplessness and embodying a more powerful mindset. We can use our anger not only to neutralize the Inner Critic, but also to stop trauma reenactment in its tracks. When someone who is similar to our abuser comes along, angering helps us to remember that we do have a right to protect ourselves and that we can trust our instincts. Rather than blaming ourselves for someone else's toxic behavior, we're more likely to hold the culprits accountable.

2) Crying. Crying provides a crucial emotional release and helps to promote self-compassion. As John Bradshaw writes, "Scientists have shown that tears actually remove stressful chemicals that build up during emotional upset. The brain will naturally be moved to equilibrium by means of the expression of emotion unless we are taught to inhibit it." If our narcissistic parent tried to shame us about crying, this is our opportunity to figuratively "cradle" ourselves while doing so. Envision holding yourself as a child and being the parent you never had. You can also physically give yourself a hug while crying. Gently soothe yourself and allow yourself to feel the pain without invalidating it, judging it, or shaming yourself for expressing it. Crying and angering can work together to soothe the fear, anxiety and self-abandonment wounds that often come with trauma.

3) Verbal Ventilation. Venting about our uncensored thoughts and feelings through writing, with a witnessing third party or a caring friend, can open the door to acceptance and recovery. It can also help with flashbacks and the brain's tendency to shut down the area of the brain responsible for speech (thereby putting the traumatic experience into words). When we are having a traumatic, emotional flashback, the emotional "right brain" becomes overactivated and the thinking-oriented left-brain becomes under-activated.

According to Walker, "Verbal ventilation, at its most potent, is the therapeutic process of bringing left brain cognition to intense right brain emotional activation. It fosters the recoveree's ability to put words to feelings, and ultimately to accurately interpret and communicate about his various feeling states. When this process is repeated sufficiently, new neural pathways grow that allow the left and right brain to work together so that the individual can actually think and feel at the same time."

4) **Feeling.** Feeling asks us to surrender to the emotional experience – the bodily sensations, the depth of pain, the awareness of our thoughts without attempting to resist them. You must grieve for the childhood you never had as well as the parent who was never there for you. You must validate and observe all of the emotions that may arise – rage towards your narcissistic parent, a confusing love and compassion for your parent, the need for their approval, the excruciating abandonment pain – *all of it.*

Use the Reconnect with Grief exercise in Part 5 of this book to help you better understand and tune into your grief.

Mirror work.

Having a narcissistic parent distorts our self-perception and self-image. We are taught to see ourselves through the toxic parent's eyes. Mirror work gives us the reins to love our perceived imperfections and approve of ourselves – even the parts of ourselves we were taught to hate. Mirror work consists of looking at yourself in the mirror and learning to love and accept the so-called flaws you were made to feel ashamed of. It allows you to cultivate a habit of befriending yourself, cherishing yourself, and loving yourself unconditionally even when things go wrong or when the Inner Critic is on full blast. You'll find that as you do mirror work on a daily basis, you'll be less likely to give into that negative self-talk and more likely to speak to yourself in a gentler, more mindful way.

Here are some creative and fun ways you can do mirror work, even on a busy schedule:

Greet yourself. When you get up in the morning and use the restroom, use that time to greet yourself. Say positive, welcoming things – perhaps even sneak in a greeting you always wish your parents said to you. For example, you might smile at yourself and say, "Hello, beautiful! I hope you have a wonderful day." Or, you could say something like, "Hey there. You're lovely and you deserve the best."

Focus on the good. This is especially helpful for those of us who have been taught to criticize our physical appearance or strive for physical perfection. Look into the mirror and note some physical and emotional qualities you love about yourself. An example might be, "I have such wonderful, kind eyes. I am a very sweet, giving person. I have a warm smile." Don't be shy in "love-bombing" yourself in a healthy way!

Be your own motivational coach. In times of stress, mirror work can be a healthy way to reset, refocus and be mindful. Go to the mirror and say encouraging things to yourself – as if you were speaking to a dear old friend. How would you speak to that friend? Would you criticize? Blame them? Of course not! So speak more kindly to yourself. Tell yourself things like, "I know this is painful, but you're going to get through this. I know how much it hurts. You don't deserve this pain. I love you so much." This is the type of emotional support and validation you deserved in childhood but never received. Now it's time to give it to yourself whenever you're in need.

Tackling the Inner Critic.

Trauma and narcissistic parenting create that venomous inner critic which attempts to "protect" us at every turn by sabotaging us and demeaning us. These can also add onto emotional flashbacks – which are triggering present events that cause us to regress back to the emotional state of the primal childhood wounds. They reawaken and re-cement our fears of abandonment, unworthiness, fear, anxiety and agony. It is important to work with a counselor on tackling both.

Our inner critic may have also been "trained" by the narcissistic parent to compare ourselves needlessly to others. Here are some ideas on how to tackle the inner critic, embrace our irreplaceability and celebrate ourselves:

Use affirmations designed to re-parent and nurture the Inner Child.

Adult children of narcissists may benefit from using affirmations using "you" to direct the type of nurturing language towards themselves that they never received as children as a form of re-parenting.

Visualize yourself as a child. Use a photo to help remind yourself of what you looked like. Then, holding that image mentally in your mind, speak to the child lovingly and gently. Some affirmations you might try:

You are so loved.

I am so happy you were brought into the world.

The world is so lucky to have a treasure like you.

You are so beautiful, brilliant, and worthy.

What a gift you are!

Your personality is so loveable.

You are so loveable.

You are adored.

You are so unique and special to me.

I adore you (speak as if you were a parent nurturing your inner child).

I am so happy you were born.

You deserve the world.

You deserve the absolute best.

The bullies were wrong about you.

You are so funny.

You are so lovely.

You are so kind.

You are so smart.

You are terrific!

You are a champion, yes, you are!

I am so delighted to see you!

You are perfect, just the way you are.

You are doing so great! Keep it up!

Everyone wants you to succeed.

Everyone wants you to be loved.

Everyone wants you to be happy.

Make an epic "love list" or bulletin board containing positive qualities and accomplishments to refer to daily. This will get you in the habit of waking up in the morning with an attitude of being

grateful for all that you are and have, rather than feeling lacking in any way.

What sort of miracles in your life, in your personality and in your abilities could you be missing out on as you waste time demeaning yourself or comparing yourself to another person? This is all about moving forward with the determination to refocus on what *you* do well and to celebrate the most attractive and desirable qualities about yourself. Every day, honor the qualities, traits and attributes that you are proud of – even if the narcissistic parent put them down.

What successes did your narcissistic parents downplay? Reminisce lovingly about them, knowing that the reason they were diminished in the first place was that they evoked the narcissist's pathological envy. What intellectual, spiritual, emotional and physical attributes do you find people most notice about you and are captivated by? Your abusive parent probably tried to exploit these strengths, only to later devalue them so that you wouldn't feel as confident about yourself or your ability to become independent of them.

Now it's your turn to see these qualities again with fresh eyes. What do you see within yourself that you know makes you special and unique? Make an entire list if you have to, about the things you like and love about yourself and your life. Also make another list for your goals, dreams and anything you want to enhance in your life and brainstorm the steps to do so (such as your existing financial success or good health).

Tackle things that you need to breed more confidence in head-on. Use whatever the narcissist diminished you in as motivation or fuel to celebrate, improve or enhance loving that specific part of yourself.

As I mentioned earlier, if you have insecurities about your appearance, do some heavy-duty mirror work each morning and night before going to sleep. Find joy in the various characteristics that make you beautiful and breed acceptance for any perceived flaws.

What you might see as a flaw, another person might see as a treasured part of you. If you find this exercise difficult, start with staring into your own eyes in the mirror and saying, "I love you and I care about you, and goddamnit, I am going to fight for you. You are THAT worth it."

If you struggle with harmful messages about your body, do some yoga to increase appreciation for what your body is capable of rather than engaging in judgments about what it looks like. You will find that when you focus more on appreciating and honoring your body, you'll also begin to treat it more mindfully and everything else you want will fall into place naturally.

According to research, yoga is also helpful for releasing trauma from the body – it's a win-win! You may also want to engage in daily exercise to release endorphins and increase an overall sense of joy and well-being – meeting your fitness goals will just be the icing on the (gluten-free?) cake.

If your narcissistic parent insulted your intuition or intelligence, get mindful and attend a meditation workshop to reconnect with your sacred inner guidance. Pursue any academic or professional goals you put on the back burner – ones that reconnect you with your brilliance. Those are just some ideas for how to use the bullying messages of your abuser to get you moving in a positive direction.

Don't hold back on celebrating yourself – even if the voices of society, your abuser or your own inner critic seems to interfere.

If you normally shy away from complimenting yourself, it's time to heap on some healthy self-appreciation and self-praise. If you're one to belittle or judge everything you do or say, it's time to take a step back and observe the inner critic without engaging the negative self-talk or feeding into it.

You may think that I am asking you to get somewhat "narcissistic" in the process of loving yourself – but don't worry, this is not about being cocky, shallow or self-aggrandizing like the narcissist is prone to being. It's about appreciating yourself more fully and increasing your sense of self-efficacy, power and agency.

It's about recognizing your own desirability (inside and out) and foregoing the dark voices of your abusers and bullies saying otherwise. It's about owning your strength and your ability to validate who you really are, not what the abuser tried to make you out to be. If the voice of your abuser arises and tries to squash your burgeoning confidence, learn how to distinguish that voice from those who truly love and care about you. Check in with yourself and say explicitly,

"That's not what I truly think and feel. That's what the abuser tried to make me believe about myself."

Do something to 'interrupt' the pattern of negative self-talk and get yourself back into the habit of nourishing yourself with empowering affirmations.

Think of hypercritical feedback from the narcissistic parent as criticism from an angry, jealous toddler – it is not valid nor has it been given to you with the best intentions. It is a pathological defense mechanism and has very little to do with your worth or value.

Speak to that voice compassionately at first by thanking it for its feedback and letting it know that while misguided, you realize it's an attempt to protect you from something the parent caused you to fear. For example, if your inner critic is pouncing on you for not being thin enough, tell it, "I understand why you would think in such a critical way, because you've been taught all your life you need to look perfect in order to be loved."

Then, set firm boundaries with the critical inner voice. "But, I think I can speak in a way that's a lot more loving. I am gorgeous in any size and what I was taught as a kid is not okay for me, especially not as an adult."

Pull in feedback from others if you need to. For example, you could say something like, "My best friend loves the way I look, and honestly, I am starting to as well. It feels good to finally start accepting myself!"

Honor however you'd like to tailor the message. You can speak to the voice gently as you would like, or, if you'd prefer a bolder approach, you can also say something in the likes of, "Wow, thanks for the feedback and I get where it's coming from, but I say fuck that! I am totally sexy, right here and now. What I learned as a child was a distortion and I am unsubscribing from these distortions. I want to see myself for who I am, not what my parents said I was."

Realize that feedback from grounded, emotionally stable individuals as well as your own inner voice are the anchors and true testaments to your character and potential. This is all about getting the focus off of the narcissist and onto the magic that is within you.

Pull in some healthy external feedback when you need to and distinguish it from the harsh words of your abuser.

These exercises are all about what you enjoy in yourself, but don't be afraid to also pull in positive feedback from healthier past partners, friends, family members, co-workers and acquaintances about what they cherish and positively regard about you as well. Keep a running document of any and all compliments you've ever received in your life that you can refer to whenever you're feeling especially low or find yourself getting into a space of self-doubt.

Use reverse discourse to create a new reframing.

Reverse discourse is a series of techniques I developed and taught myself to decrease negative ruminations and negative self-talk arising from the Inner Critic and the horrific messages my bullies attempted to instill in me. In the work of Foucault, reverse discourse was discussed as a medium through which power was reclaimed and redirected by challenging the normative discourses of sexuality and gender.

In the way I am using it (or adapting it), creating a reverse discourse involves a reclaiming of power, connotation and values of negative statements wielded at you by toxic people over your lifetime.

This is a method I've adapted and developed from my own real-life experiences. It has put me back in control of the language that has been used against me throughout my lifetime. This is an especially effective technique when you're recovering from verbal abuse.

This is also one of the most helpful techniques I found to release some of the rage I had towards my abusers and the cruel words they said to me. I used the technique to create a powerful reverse discourse that undermined every single abusive thing I had ever heard in my life.

Reverse discourse helped me to become driven, confident and motivated to succeed beyond anyone's expectations. While it takes practice, when you regain control over how you define yourself and the language you use to reframe your reality, toxic people begin to lose their power and you begin to regain your own.

In short, methods of reverse discourse are creative ways you can empower yourself by taking back control of the language your narcissistic parents, as well as any other abusers or bullies have used against you. You can use reverse discourse by (1) "talking back" to your abusers, (2) replacing a word they used to disempower you with a new positive affirmation, and (3) reassigning degrading words with new, positive connotations that serve you.

1) Talking back to the abuser. This is not about literally talking back, it's more about mentally talking back to the ruminations over the abuse in your own mind. When talking back to an abuser, I find it most liberating when I allow myself to be as uncensored as possible when I write these down. It's the only safe space where I know I'll ever get to vent my frustrations freely without consequences. Feel free to unleash your rage onto the page. That's what it's there for, and it sure does beat pursuing literal revenge which could have real-life consequences. Related to this, you may also choose to create lists that outright challenge all the negative declarations toxic people have made about you. Creating this "reverse discourse" means writing down the concrete accomplishments or positive feedback others have given you, to counter snide remarks or abusive comments that you find yourself ruminating over.

If you're stuck, here are some ideas:

Start by turning everything your abuser said onto them.

Did your toxic parent talk about how useless you are? Mentally tell them how useless they have been as a parent and how you, on the other hand, are a valuable human being with gifts and empathy to give to this world.

Did they say you'd never achieve your dreams? Talk back to them and say *just because you haven't achieved yours doesn't mean I won't achieve mine. Big ideas are not suited for small-minded people like you.*

Did they say you weren't smart enough? Tell them you were smart enough to stop spending time with a dummy like them.

Yep, when I said harsh, I meant harsh. Let it out. Be a badass. Stop censoring your own anger. It's not as if your narcissistic parent can hear you, so feel free to express yourself uncensored, to yourself. Connect with your authentic self, your authentic rage and your fighter attitude. So long as you do not act upon any of these thoughts or break No Contact by sending them any part of this new discourse, you're safe to release your anger in a healthy manner. In fact, according to Beverly Engel, LMFT, attempting to stifle your anger while forcing yourself to forgive your abuser too soon actually impedes the healing process.

(2) Word or phrase replacement. For the second component of reverse discourse, you can replace abusive words you've heard with new words or phrases whenever they come up in your mind or you find yourself ruminating over them. How you use this is up to you and your personal needs. Some survivors will find word/phrase replacement jolting, so for them, they might have to start small and begin to use positive words they have an easier time believing in that eventually lead up to the beliefs they want to have for themselves.

A survivor who has been criticized for her appearance by her toxic mother may find more solace in replacing his or her rumination with something small like, "I am imperfect, but imperfection is beautiful," rather than right away saying, "I am so beautiful" without any belief in it. Assess where you're at and what you feel most comfortable saying – don't force yourself into extremes if you're not ready for them.

Other survivors, however, may benefit from extremes. I personally found it helpful to make the new word or phrase as hard-hitting and extreme as possible, because as an abuse survivor, I was used to hearing the other extreme end of the spectrum. For example, if your abuser constantly attacked your intelligence, replace any abusive phrase they've used against you with, "I am smart as hell" or "I am brilliant." It may even be helpful to add an additional phrase that gives back the projection to your abuser – for example, "I am the smart one, you're just sad you aren't," is a great example of how to actively defuse the abuser's power while igniting your own. Whichever way you use this method, make sure that it caters to what you personally feel comfortable with.

This can be an incremental process and there is no right or wrong way to do this method.

(3) Giving previously disempowering words a positive connotation and reframing their meaning. In our society, words like "bitch" have been "taken back" with more positive connotations that refer to being a powerful woman, the most famous example being the new use of the word in Sherry Argov's book, *Why Men Love Bitches*.

There's no rule that says we can't apply the same principle to degrading words. If there is a phrase you need to "remodel" to serve you and feel that you can without being triggered, all the more power to you.

For example, if you're the son of a narcissistic father who emasculated you by saying, "You're not a real man, you're too sensitive," and this thought keeps popping into your head, try remodeling this. You might mentally talk back to him by saying, "If being a real man means using violence or abuse, sure, I am not your definition of what it means to be a real man. I am even better." It's powerful to recognize that while words can be destructive, they can also be taken back, reconstructed, rewritten and remodeled to revive your power.

Remember, only use these methods in ways that empower you and only if they make you comfortable. Do not actually use this to communicate with the parent; we talk about more effective communication strategies here and here. Reverse discourse is all about interrupting your usual thought patterns, taking back control over the language being wielded against you, and reframing words to serve your healing journey. It's not about embracing the abuse, but rather, reclaiming your power from it.

Reprogramming the Negative Inner Critic

Some ideas might be:

Engaging in a daily habit of positive affirmations customized to your unique needs and triggers. This is especially helpful when your abuser's voice comes up. You may want to record these affirmations in your own voice and play them back (or have a trusted, loving friend do these for you). If you have severe anxiety over hardcore affirmations, start small. Maybe you don't start with "I am beautiful," but begin with "Everyone has beauty and I have beauty in me too." instead. Do whatever it takes to make the affirmation believable to you before moving onto bigger and better confirmations of your value.

You can also listen to pre-recorded affirmations for a specific purpose online – everything from enhancing confidence to feeling beautiful. Here are some affirmation exercises you may find useful:

Ultimate Confidence and Inner Strength

Clear Negative Blocks – Remove Subconscious Limiting Beliefs/Negativity/Blockages

Self-Love Affirmations: "I am Beautiful"

Affirmations for Health, Wealth, Happiness and Abundance

A weekly meditation practice (best to do this on a day you are most vulnerable to cravings to break No Contact) to help you listen to and observe your train of thoughts rather than become increasingly reactive to them. Mindfully approaching these cravings or ruminations can help to ease the 'addictive' pull we often develop to keeping tabs on an abusive family member or ex. This addiction is formed by the trauma bond and needs time, space, effort and practice in order to heal.

Emotional Freedom Technique, EMDR and/or hypnotherapy to clear negative thought patterns and target subconscious beliefs from the trauma that we may not even be aware of that are holding us back. Learn more about these healing modalities in the chapter Healing Modalities for Adult Children of Narcissists.

Self-soothing through inner child visualization and progressive muscle relaxation meditations.

Self-soothing is a critical tool for children of narcissists. Visualization meditations which include imagery of beautiful places of nature can be crucial to our ability to self-soothe, inducing states of peacefulness and relaxation in times of distress. Visualization can also be used to "overwrite" some of our painful experiences. We can meditate by visualizing soothing our inner child, protecting it, nourishing it and feeding it the love that it always deserved. Progressive muscle relaxation meditations can also be helpful for trauma survivors who are used to storing the trauma in their bodies and "tightening up" like a form of armor. They can help to ease our bodies and help us to become more mindful of when we're carrying tension and toxic stress. Combining these two modalities of healing can help us to locate where the trauma is stored in our bodies and be mindful of these areas when we're visualizing a safe space for our inner child.

Here are some meditations to get you started:

Inner Child Meditation Healing Guided Self-Love Meditation
Progressive Muscle Relaxation
Hypnosis for Meeting Your Inner Child
Safe Place Visualization
15 Minute Guided Imagery Meditation Exercise
Inner Child Meditation for Codependency, Lack of Self-Love and Negative Programming

Trauma-focused therapies such as DBT or EMDR. As I explore more in-depth in my section on diverse healing modalities, Dialectical behavioral therapy is a therapy for highly sensitive and vulnerable populations, such as those who have experienced abuse in childhood. DBT is an evidence-based treatment for those who struggle with chronic suicidal ideation, self-harm and extreme emotions. Combining Eastern mindfulness techniques with cognitive-behavioral methods, this unique and comprehensive treatment has been proven especially effective and teaches you skill sets in emotional regulation, impulse control and interpersonal effectiveness.

DBT can be helpful for children of narcissists who might have problems with emotional regulation as a result of the abuse they endured. EMDR is another trauma-focused therapy that can help you alleviate the effects of flashbacks and ruminating thoughts from unprocessed childhood traumas.

Practice mindfulness techniques and meditation. Meditation targets the same areas of the brain affected by trauma. Meditation can also help with self-compassion, emotion regulation and impulse control. Find a daily practice that works for you. Even five minutes of focusing on your breath can help. Meditation can also help you to mindfully connect with your Inner Child. Read more about meditation in my section on healing modalities here.

Surround your external environment with positive reminders of your worth. It's easy for adult children of narcissists to become burdened by a world that makes them feel "not good enough." Have safe spaces where you are reminded that you are enough. Dress up your room with vision boards, positive affirmations, photographs of yourself, your accomplishments (photos of milestones, diplomas, trophies), beautiful memories and cherished vacations. Create a corner or even a room dedicated to meditation. Build a space in your house for your inner child to play – fill it with coloring books, your favorite stuffed animals, music you loved to listen to as a kid, special treats and stickers.

Journaling. As we spoke about before, trauma therapist Pete Walker notes that "verbal ventilation" and "angering" are helpful ways to process the complicated grief of childhood abuse. Journaling is an excellent way to put your uncensored thoughts and feelings to the page without the interference of your toxic parent. You no longer have to carry the guilt and shame of how you really feel. It is all valid. Even if you feel hatred and rage towards your parent, know that this is a result of the hostility and abuse you experienced from them. Write down what hurt you and "talk back" to your abusive parent. Let them know it was not okay. Remind yourself of what you deserved.

Create a sacred boundaries list. Children of narcissists have trouble maintaining boundaries - not just with their abusive parents but with their friends, their colleagues, and even themselves. Write out a sacred boundaries list of what you will not tolerate in all types of relationships. These are behaviors that are deal-breakers. For example, one sacred boundary of yours might be, "I will not be spoken to in a condescending manner." Also apply that sacred boundary to your negative self-talk. When that Inner Critic inevitably pops up, tell it, "I know you're trying to protect me and thank you for that, but there are better ways. I will not be spoken to and will not speak to myself in a condescending manner." You can learn more about boundaries in dating in this exercise.

Solitude: take time to be alone and repair your body. The risk of trauma repetition is high for adult children of narcissists. If you have a pattern of getting into unhealthy or toxic relationships and friendships, it may be time for a physical break from dating and relationships. Your body is so accustomed to the dangerous highs and lows of childhood that it needs time to repair itself and return to the baseline levels of safety it should have always experienced.

Many children of narcissists don't feel safe with their own thoughts and feelings. They feel as if they always "need" to be in a relationship or that they always have to be doing things for others. Take time out to do things for yourself. Date yourself for a while; take yourself out to beautiful, quiet places and engage in solitary activities. Or, if you'd like some company, you can always opt for classes in dancing, cycling, yoga, meditation, and spiritual workshops which allow for a more internal focus in a community setting.

Take some time out every day to just be yourself and grow accustomed to listening to yourself and how you feel and think about things. This cultivates a habit of authenticity. This can be daunting at first because we have so much anxiety and negativity from the past and we would prefer not to be alone with how we really feel. Yet if we don't take this time for ourselves, we will inevitably suffer the consequences. Read about this more in-depth in the essay, "5 Powerful Healing Benefits Of Being Single After An Abusive Childhood."

Eradicate subconscious wounding that says you're not enough and cultivate new seeds of self-worth. Many (but not all) survivors who have been in unhealthy, abusive relationships in adulthood also come from unhealthy family dynamics. Childhood is where many survivors first learn to dim their own light.

Survivors of childhood abuse by narcissistic parents are usually pitted against a sibling or a group of siblings growing up. Your parents may have tried to "bury" your gifts because they were abusive narcissists and wanted to see you fail. They knew your potential, but they worked hard to stifle it to meet their own selfish agendas.

That being said, there are a variety of circumstances that can lead to a child growing up believing that he or she is not meant to shine. Maybe you always had a more athletic brother or a "prettier" sister (at least from society's perspective or your narcissistic parent's claims). Perhaps you had a best friend that tended to outshine you in social circles. It's possible you were bullied or were made to feel invisible by toxic teachers who paid more attention to their favorite students. You may have also endured complex trauma and were the victim of *all of these* scenarios and more.

Whatever your situation was growing up, even if it was a healthy and happy childhood where you were nourished and supported by others outside of your parents, there may still be beliefs lingering about not being good enough – whether it is from the influence of society, culture or childhood programming. Identifying these experiences and the *associated beliefs* that came with them can go a long way in tackling any wounding that is being reinforced when triangulation is used as a method to provoke or further diminish you.

After you've identified the ways in which you have been brought down in the past, ask yourself the following questions and explore:

In what ways can I embrace my visibility? For example, is there a dream you've been holding off on pursuing due to self-doubt or sabotage from your abusive parent or partners? Now is the time to start working on or rebuilding that dream to make it come to life, bigger and brighter than ever – it represents an authentic desire you're meant to fulfill.

What parts of myself and what gifts have I resisted showcasing as a way to hide myself the way I've been taught to hide? We were taught to minimize our talents and desirable traits due to the pathological envy of the narcissist and their put-downs, as well as any childhood programming. Perhaps you're an incredible artist and your abuser told you negative things about your potential for achieving your dreams because it took the spotlight off of *them*. Now it's time to embrace those again and remember the gifts that made us who we truly were before the abusive relationship.

What ways has being invisible protected me from what I've been taught to fear (such as criticism) and how can I cultivate the type of confidence that allows me to overcome those fears? Childhood abuse survivors can learn to fear success of any kind due to being punished for daring to succeed by their abusive caretakers.

Similarly, survivors of narcissistic abuse who are re-traumatized in adulthood can be taught that with success comes punishment via the callous put-downs of their intimate partners whenever they were daring to achieve something that enabled them to become independent of the narcissist. You may have developed an extreme fear of 'displaying' who you are as a person and the things that make you truly special. Beneath this fear is an underlying need to protect yourself.

Perhaps your five-year-old self still fears being noticed by others because your abusive mother taught you weren't worthy of being acknowledged or instilled a deep fear in you about the dangers of being too pretty or smart. Or maybe your 23-year-old self is still reeling from that abusive father who told you that you were too 'damaged' to find a worthy partner – this is a common fear these toxic types try to convince their partners of in order to hold them back from pursuing healthier relationships.

Suppressing or acting on these fears might have been a go-to coping mechanism for you, but now it's time to unravel these fears and invite curiosity about what they are protecting you from as well as what they're preventing you from obtaining. These lingering fears may come with protective intentions, but they are ultimately holding you back from what is meant to flourish within you.

How can I rise above the people who tried to keep me behind the curtain, when I really deserved my chance in the spotlight too? If you find yourself fearing criticism or envy from others as a result of outshining them, remember that *everyone* deserves recognition – and that there's plenty of it to go around. Unlike predatory narcissists, survivors of abuse know deep down that they don't ever have to rob someone else of their light in order to be seen.

We can celebrate the accomplishments of others as well as our own – in fact, we take special joy in it. So why not extend that same courtesy of being happy for others to ourselves? We don't have to be made to feel ashamed or guilty about being proud of who we are. What are more ways you can allow yourself to be in the spotlight and truly enjoy yourself? For example, your abuser may have pushed you to be quiet in social groups whenever you were with them so you wouldn't get attention from anyone else – now is the perfect time to relearn how to speak out and show off your personality.

Here's a truth-bomb for the people-pleasers out there: you're allowed to take up space and own that space without apologies.

You're allowed to speak your voice. You're allowed to be beautiful (or handsome) inside and out, brilliant, worthy, valuable, seen and heard. You're allowed to be successful and be proud of yourself in a healthy way. You're allowed to accept compliments. You're allowed to compliment yourself. You're allowed to set boundaries and say "no" when you mean no and say "yes" to the things your heart and soul say "hell yes" to. You're allowed to realize that your toxic, abusive parent who put you through this mess is just another incredibly flawed (and dysfunctional) human being who has no say on your worth or abilities. You're allowed to see the people your parents tried to pit you against in childhood as other flawed human beings who are not worth any of your time, energy or competition.

Yep, you heard me. You never have to compete with anyone to prove that you're worthy of love – and a healthy parent would never want a child who they truly love and cherish to feel like they're competing with anybody anyway. Narcissists want us to compete for their love and attention but what we're pulled in to fight for is ultimately meaningless, as narcissists don't even have the capacity to love anyone in a healthy manner.

Let the narcissistic parent get the consolatory prize: having to make others who are willing to compete for their attention – while *you* move onto bigger and better things. Your biggest prize is your new life of freedom and a path back to your true, authentic self – and, if you're looking for it, an open space for *true, authentic* love to enter your life – the kind with empathy, compassion and respect. The kind that is so deliciously *appreciative* of everything that makes you so beautiful and worthy.

Minimize unnecessary comparisons and reprogram negative self-talk. One of the most damaging lies we can learn from narcissistic parents or partners is that we have to compete with others in order to prove our worth. Whether it be the golden child or the new source of supply, victims of narcissistic abuse are made to feel deficient and worthless by the toxic, destructive conditioning of the relationship. They begin to compare themselves to others as a form of self-sabotage, continuing the abuse even after the relationship has ended.

If we spent our lives comparing ourselves to every person we came across or focusing on every time we were rejected, we would drive ourselves certifiably insane. Similarly, the last thing we want to be doing on our journey to healing is to make unnecessary comparisons to someone a toxic person has triangulated us with.

Narcissistic abusers are masters of triangulating us with people who may be very different from us – this is done intentionally to provoke a sense of unease and self-questioning about qualities we may "lack." Yet what you have to remember is that when you've gone No Contact, you will probably at some point get re-idealized by the narcissistic parent while they devalue and triangulate other members of the family who are more under their control.

No one is exempt from their devaluation – not even the golden child at some point. Sometimes your narcissistic parent will start to compare the golden child sibling to *you* – talking nonsense about how this sibling (you) did this or that and suddenly putting you back on the pedestal to use you as an example for further manipulation.

They don't discriminate on who they criticize and for what – they're looking to feed off of the emotional reactions they get with *all* of their sources of supply and they will continue the same cycle of triangulation with other adult children or relatives as well.

Given that the toxic parent's behavior extends to the entire family unit at some point, we have to embrace the truth that the problem was never us. It was them. We were always deserving of the love, care, respect, consideration and empathy that healthy parents give their children. We are not a burden. We are a gift. We are perfect and worthy of approval in all of our imperfections. We are not lacking in any shape, way or form. We are "full" of the very things we need.

We are absolutely sufficient and "enough" in what we have now, because within that unique brand of quirks, flaws, strengths – is exactly who we are and who we need to be. We are already whole and we need to work on the negative self-talk and inner critic that may pounce to detract from our own wholeness.

Breaking the triangle and integrating wholeness.

You might be catching on that this part of the journey is not about the toxic family triangle itself but the core wounds it reveals and learning how to navigate the pathway to deeper, richer self-love. Don't get me wrong – triangulation hurts no matter what sort of wounding you may have, because no matter what insecurities you have, triangulation is still abuse. It is a form of devaluation from a toxic person that no one should *ever* have to go through. Narcissistic abuse erodes our identity, our self-esteem and threatens to destroy the dreams we're meant to fulfill. As survivors heal, triangulation comes up as a common way they've been dehumanized and traumatized.

However, as you begin to work on core wounds, self-sabotaging beliefs and any issues with self-confidence in conjunction with No Contact, you'll find that your emotional resonance with the narcissist's ploys is not as heightened as before. You're able to move on a bit more quickly rather than tethering yourself to comparisons or creating new ones in your mind. On some level, even subconsciously, we feel trapped to remain within the toxic triangle because we have forgotten to honor our wholeness and we're still attached to the abuser through traumatic bonding.

Regardless of whichever context you might be facing triangulation, it's important to remember and honor that wholeness. Comparing ourselves is a dishonor to the very things that make us who we are. If you have a need to constantly compare yourself to the people your abuser pitted you against, why not compare yourself to who you used to be in your abusive childhood or to a healthy role model that you aspire to be more like?

Now that you've paved the path to freedom, you're probably stronger, more resilient, and more determined to succeed. You've grown a great deal since the abuse. You've survived the worst moments of your life and are now on your way to thriving. Don't allow the narcissist's attempts to make you feel less than detract you from the independence you've worked so hard to achieve. Hoovering and triangulation are ploys that are deliberately staged to get you off of your journey to freedom and right back into the narcissist's trap. Instead, "reverse triangulate" the narcissist with a new support network, a new flourishing life and a new sense of confidence that births your revolution and victory after abuse.

Healing Modalities

for Adult Children of Narcissists

Traditional Healing Modalities

Internal Family Systems Therapy

This type of therapy is quite useful for complex trauma survivors who struggle with disparate inner parts of themselves which arose from childhood trauma. It helps to pull the client towards the identification of these parts, communication with these parts and greater overall integration. Family therapist and creator of the Internal Systems Model, Dr. Richard Schwartz, developed this approach when he realized from his experiences in working with dysfunctional families that the communication among family members was not unlike the interactions we had with our own inner "parts."

Imagine, if you will, an entire system of parts living within your psyche. Each "family member" or inner part has a role to play, and many of them developed out of the need for survival. If there is no communication or unhealthy communication among these parts, they can act out their defenses destructively.

In internal family systems therapy, you are guided to identify three common types of parts below and work with them to effectively manage your emotions and coping skills. The key is not to try to control these parts as they arise in therapy, but to become curious about them, their roles, intentions, functions, and how they may have developed. These parts all serve a purpose and it is usually far more effective to honor how they have "served" you (even if their methods were maladaptive), validate the wounds they're operating from, and communicate ways in which you can use healthier coping mechanisms.

Exiles – These are traumatized inner parts which include emotions, memories, and sensations from the past. As children, we were often shamed, humiliated and intimidated into silence and fear by our toxic and abusive parents. Exile inner parts contain these vulnerable parts and are usually protected by our "managers" and to some extent "firefighters" to avoid exposing that vulnerability to our consciousness. Our "exile" parts may come up and overwhelm us, for example, when our fear of abandonment is triggered. We may regress into childhood and react in ways to the perceived threat of abandonment that are not in alignment with our true selves or adult self.

Managers – Managers keep control of the vulnerability of our inner parts by overachieving, being critical or controlling, or finding preventative ways to avoid vulnerability or triggers in the first place. According to Dr. Schwartz, "After working with a large number of clients, some patterns began to appear. Most clients had parts that tried to keep them functional and safe. These parts tried to maintain control of their inner and outer environments by, for example, keeping them from getting too close or dependent on others, criticizing their appearance or performance to make them look or act better, and focusing on taking care of others rather than their own needs. These parts seemed to be in protective, managerial roles and therefore are called managers."

Firefighters – These parts are the defenders, acting out through addictions and self-harming behaviors which "douse out" the fire or the exiles being triggered. For example, a sexual abuse survivor may go into a triggered state after a first date. She may then choose to cut herself to escape the pain of the overwhelming trigger. Dissociation, self-harm, suicidal ideation, substance abuse and compulsive sex are all examples of common firefighter activities.

The Self

Dr. Schwartz observed that in many of his clients, there was an overarching "Self" that emerged when the inner parts stepped back. This "Self" was present even in the most traumatized of clients who had never had a healthy role model to assist in developing such a self. How could this be? There are many spiritual ideologies which have discussed the existence of an overarching "self" which transcends even the most horrific of traumas – a part of us which is able to lead confidently and calmly regardless of our inner parts and defenses. Schwartz observed that there were eight qualities the true "Self" possessed: calmness, curiosity, clarity, compassion, confidence, creativity, courage, and connectedness.

The work of Internal Family Systems therapy is to help us tap into the Self once we learn to communicate effectively with our inner parts, heal our wounds, and better integrate these parts to create a more functional "family" which exists within us.

To learn more about IFS, be sure to visit Dr. Schwartz's website at www.selfleadership.org[19]

Also be sure to listen to his enlightening lecture series on our different inner parts on Youtube here: Part 1[20], Part 2[21], Part 3[22], Part 4[23].

Cognitive-Behavior Therapy

Cognitive-Behavior Therapy is a form of psychotherapy which targets maladaptive emotions, behaviors, and thoughts. It was developed by Dr. Aaron Beck in the 1960s. It can help survivors to identify any harmful beliefs and thoughts which may be negatively affecting their actions. Clients are assisted in reworking harmful beliefs and acting accordingly based on their new belief systems. For adult children of narcissists, CBT can be especially helpful in identifying cognitive distortions, harmful automatic thoughts, and patterns of behavior we internalized in childhood regarding our self-worth, loveability, and sense of feeling "enough" and "deserving."

To learn more about CBT, visit www.beckinstitute.org[24]. You can also find helpful CBT handouts here:

CBT Worksheets[25]
Specialty Behavioral Health PDFS[26]
Lynn Martin's Cycle of Maladaptive Behavior Client Handouts[27]

Prolonged Exposure Therapy

Prolonged exposure therapy is a specific type of Cognitive Behaviorial therapy used to treat PTSD. The client is asked to gradually face the trauma-related memories and triggers in order to lessen their symptoms. It has four components: (1) education about the symptoms of trauma and the goals of treatment, (2) breathing techniques to manage distress, (3) real world exposure which helps you work on approaching safe situations that you may have avoided due to the fear of being triggered – as treatment goes on, you work towards exposing yourself to more distressing situations and (4) talking through the trauma, which involves addressing the painful memories you have been avoiding. As survivors continue to desensitize themselves to imagining and talking about these avoided memories, the fear of them lessens.

Learn more about Prolonged Exposure Therapy here.[28]

Cognitive Processing Therapy

Much like Prolonged Exposure therapy, Cognitive Processing Therapy involves educating the survivor about their PTSD symptoms. The client is also asked to confront the memories of the trauma they once avoided. However, the emphasis in this type of therapy is on identifying maladaptive thoughts and feelings and then learning skills which help you challenge these cognitive distortions. This type of therapy also enables you to work through changes in beliefs you may have had in your worldview due to the trauma, addressing your old and new beliefs about safety, trust, control, relationships, and self-esteem.

Learn more about and cognitive processing therapy here[29].

EMDR

EMDR (Eye Movement Desensitization and Reprocessing) is a form of therapy where the client is asked to recall traumatic or distressing events while making side-to-side eye movements or hand tapping. It was developed by Dr. Francine Shapiro, who noticed that these eye movements had the effect of alleviating the intense impact of disturbing traumatic memories. Simply put, EMDR allows you to process your trauma without being overwhelmed by your emotional reactions to it.

EMDR is said to help access the traumatic memory network so that new, healthier associations can be formed between traumatic memories and information. Using a complex eight-step process, EMDR can help to better process the traumatic memories in ways that reduce emotional distress and develop new beliefs about the trauma. EMDR targets present, past and future: clients are asked to address the past events which have caused distress as well as the present triggers which evoke the distress. Then, they are asked to incorporate their new beliefs to help better serve them in the future.

Adult children of narcissists may benefit enormously from processing their early childhood traumas with an EMDR therapist, to relieve some of the burden of how intense these traumas can be and their daily impact. This type of therapy may also be used in conjunction with Internal Family Systems model to ensure that a level of safety and integration has been achieved prior.

To learn more about EMDR and find an EMDR therapist, be sure to visit www.emdria.org[30].

Emotional Freedom Technique

Much like acupuncture, Emotional Freedom Technique (EFT) stimulates energy points on the body, but without the invasive use of needles. These energy points are known as "meridian tapping points" and when tapped, they release trapped energy throughout the body. This is a way to clear our old, destructive feelings and beliefs while replacing them with healthier, positive beliefs.

Coupled with positive affirmations, EFT helps to reprogram the ways we think and feel. Since certain emotions are said to reside in specific parts of the body, it is said that EFT allows us to release energetic blocks by allowing electromagnetic energy to flow more freely throughout the body. The affirmations used help to validate the protective mechanism of negative emotions while allowing the client to feel empowered to let them go.

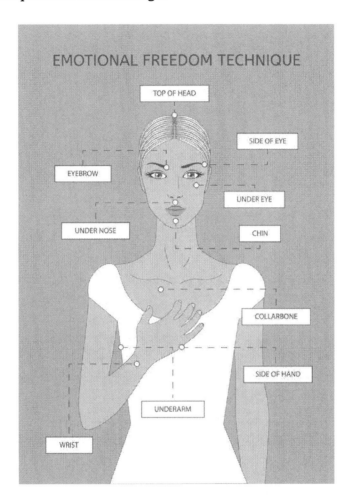

The nine tapping points include:

TH: Top of Head
EB: Eyebrow
SE: Side of the Eye
UE: Under the Eye
UN: Under the Nose
Ch: Chin

CB: Collar Bone
UA: Under the Arm
WR: Wrists

To learn more about EFT, visit https://eft.mercola.com/.

Dialectical Behavior Therapy

Dialectical behavior therapy is an evidence-based therapy developed by Dr. Marsha Linehan designed to help those who are suffering from intense emotions, self-harm and suicidal ideation. Combining both individual and group therapy sessions, DBT can be helpful for adult children of narcissists in both their emotional functioning as well as interpersonal relationships. It focuses on four modules: (1) mindfulness (2) distress tolerance (3) emotion regulation and (4) interpersonal effectiveness. DBT combines cognitive behavioral therapy with Eastern mindfulness techniques. It is traditionally used for patients with Borderline Personality Disorder (although, as you have read previously, many victims with complex PTSD can be misdiagnosed with BPD).

DBT offers a comprehensive mindfulness approach that enables individuals to regulate and cope with their emotions, improve their interpersonal effectiveness skills and stay grounded in the present moment during crises. It is also very practical since DBT group therapy sessions allow you to practice and role-play the skills you've learned – which can help you to better cope with interactions with your toxic parents or other difficult people in your life. The skills of DBT can be taught to anyone and everyone. These skills are also very useful for anyone who struggles with emotion regulation and toxic interpersonal relationships.

To learn more about DBT, read my in-depth article on it here[31].

To find a DBT therapist, visit:

https://behavioraltech.org/resources/find-a-therapist/.

Somatic Experiencing

Created by trauma therapist Peter Levine, somatic experiencing targets the physical symptoms of PTSD. Levine realized that animals are able to effectively respond to danger by noticing, responding and recovering from threat; they use up a great deal of energy to escape the threat successfully, discharging that energy from the body. The body is able to then return to baseline as the nervous system of the animal is reset by physical reactions like running, shaking, or trembling. Humans, however, do not always have the luxury of going through this same cycle when they respond to threat. We may freeze or be unable to flee. As a result, there may be unresolved activation and energy stuck in the body depending on how we respond to the threat and whether we perceive the danger has truly passed.

Somatic experiencing attempts to reset the nervous system. It guides the survivor to become aware of and to release the tension in their body which may be trapped in the aftermath of traumatic events. The primary focus of this therapy are the physiological responses that happen when someone recalls a traumatic event. Trauma becomes so embedded within our bodies that it can affect our body language, our posture, our facial expressions, our tone of voice, as well as our immune system. Sessions may include the incorporation of breathing exercises, dance, physical exercise, voice work, and healing touch.

Read more about somatic experiencing here[32].

Find a somatic therapist here[33].

For more information about somatic experiencing, be sure to read *Waking the Tiger* and *In An Unspoken Voice* by Peter Levine.

CoDA

Not everyone who is a survivor of narcissistic abuse or childhood narcissistic abuse identifies or even meets the criteria for being codependent[34], although childhood abuse can certainly cause us to have codependent tendencies in adulthood. For those who do struggle with codependent tendencies or the effects of trauma-bonding, Codependents Anonymous support groups can be safe places to work towards a healthier sense of self and boundaries in relationships. To read the twelve promises of Co-Dependents Anonymous and find a local CODA meeting near you, go to their website here[35].

Psychosomatic Therapy

Psychosomatic therapy is a holistic approach to healing; it includes a systematic analysis of stress, tension, and discomfort throughout one's body as well as a targeted treatment plan to restore emotional balance to those parts of the body. Techniques can include but are not limited to emotional-release bodywork, breathing techniques, and counseling. Since adult children of narcissists are prone to adverse health outcomes, psychosomatic therapy is a possible treatment to target mind-body healing.

Read more about Psychosomatic Therapy here[36].

Gestalt Therapy

It is common for survivors of narcissistic parents to reenact their past traumas in the present moment. Gestalt therapy is a client-focused form of therapy which centers the focus back to the feelings, thoughts and beliefs which arise whenever past experiences come up. Developed by therapist Fritz Perls, gestalt therapy is based on the idea that self-awareness of present choices and their connections to the past can help to alleviate issues with depression, anxiety, and relationships. Gestalt therapists often redirect you by asking, "What do you feel right now?" to integrate the past with the present. They may also guide you through role-playing, guided fantasy, dream work or bodywork to help better tap into these emotions. To read more about gestalt therapy, read here[37].

Art Therapy

Art therapy has been proven by research[38] to be effective for victims suffering from PTSD, as trauma tends to shut down the part of the brain related to language (Broca's area) which renders us speechless. Art provides a medium through which we can still begin a dialogue with our trauma by reconnecting us to the somatic and limbic aspects of the brain where trauma is encoded. Whether you use a sketchpad or a canvas doesn't matter. Pottery, sculpture, painting, sketching – it all counts. Get your painting tools, your colored markers or pencils and create something new. If you currently reside in the U.S., you can find art therapists in your area on the American Art Therapy Association website[39].

Hypnotherapy

Hypnotherapy is a form of therapy which uses hypnosis as a way to help individuals make behavioral and emotional changes. Hypnosis is an altered state of consciousness, a trance-like state in which we are more susceptible to suggestion. Hypnosis can be helpful and effective for ailments like phobias, addictions, chronic pain, and traumatic memories associated with PTSD. Since adult children of narcissists are programmed at an early age with destructive, subconscious belief systems, hypnosis can access those beliefs, memories, and wounds which may not otherwise come to conscious awareness.

- Kelly Jo Holly has an excellent meditation on this called How to Heal Abuse Hypnosis[40], to begin to envisage your abuser as someone comical and childish.
- Joseph Clough has a self-hypnosis channel[41] to alleviate any fears or anxieties you're facing here.
- Michael Sealey also has a terrific self-hypnosis channel[42] that helps to raise confidence, improve sleep and mood.

To find a hypnotherapist in your area, click here[43].

Assertiveness Therapy

Assertiveness therapy is a behavior therapy that guides individuals to stand up for themselves. Adult children of narcissists often struggle with maintaining boundaries, being who they authentically are, and calling out abusive behavior. Assertiveness training can help with the resulting depression, social anxiety and repressed anger which often occurs due to childhood abuse, as it gives tools to survivors to effectively stand up for themselves.

You can also read more about assertiveness in the books *Your Perfect Right* by Alberti and Emmons and *The Assertive Woman* by Phelps and Austin.

Neuro-Linguistic Programming (NLP)

Neuro-linguistic programming (NLP) is a form of psychotherapy and communication created by Richard Bandler and John Grinder in the 1970's. It combines the knowledge of neurology, linguistics and programming (the internal models of the world that we develop) to help us become more effective in various facets of our lives. NLP is all about learning the language of the brain and learning to hijack the subconscious programming that might be running the show.

For adult children of narcissists, the NLP technique of *anchoring* can be especially helpful to rework our subconscious patterns and early childhood traumas. Anchoring is the process in which an internal response becomes associated with an external or internal trigger. This method allows for that response to be accessed automatically whenever that trigger is present. Similar to conditioning, anchoring is a way for your brain to automatically access certain memories and emotional states in your psyche to evoke a certain response from you.

The anchors can be anything such as specific gestures, a certain tone of voice, a scent, a physical movement or touch on a specific part of your body, a certain location, a song, a word – anything you can think of is fair game. The most effective anchors are ones that are unique (so that they aren't indiscriminately triggered), repeated to be associated with a specific emotional state, and are conditioned during times of peak emotional intensity.

The Rewind Technique or Reconsolidation of Trauma (RTM) Technique

First originating in Neuro-linguistic Programming (NLP), the Rewind Technique has been adapted by NLP practitioners to gradually desensitize clients to the original traumas of the past. Known formally as the "Kinesthetic Dissociation" technique, Dr. David Muss dubbed it the Rewind Technique. The client is placed into a state of deep relaxation, asked to bring up their anxiety, and told to visualize a safe space. They are then led to imagine that they are watching a film of the original trauma while floating outside of their own bodies. Then they are asked to re-inhabit their bodies while watching the film and go backwards from scene to scene of the film. They then watch the same images as if they were fast forwarding the scene. This process is repeated until the trauma no longer induces such an emotional response from the client.

Rewind Therapist Mike Tyrell writes in his article[44] for GoodTherapy, "{Rewind therapy} is a natural and painless way of lifting trauma. It uses relaxation and dissociation powerfully and comfortably, to allow the brain to reprocess memories from being contained within the 'fight or flight' part to the higher cortical centers where it can be reviewed without strong emotion and where, like many other memories, it will start to fade in time."

John Bradshaw offers multiple anchoring techniques to help you learn to re-associate your childhood traumas with feelings of strength and empowerment in his book, *Homecoming*, a book I highly recommend for all survivors.

You may also want to read this fascinating article on seven experts of NLP sharing their techniques here[45].

Group Therapy

Group therapy led by a mental health professional can be a safe space to talk about your struggles, fears, and traumas while witnessing others doing the same. Research groups which focus on domestic violence, trauma, and/or any other areas you may be struggling with at this time. CBT or DBT therapy groups can be excellent places to practice your new skills and engage in constructive roleplaying with others. Expressing our emotions with others allows us to gain the validation and support we never gained in childhood, enabling us to access relational healing. It also increases social accountability for maintaining progress and self-care. Search for a therapy group here[46].

Support Groups

If you struggle with dysfunctional, abusive relationships and have trouble setting boundaries with others, there are support groups with other survivors w http://coda.org/ho can help to validate you and cheerlead your recovery journey. Many survivors have benefited from attending CoDA[47] (Codependents Anonymous) meetings, Narcissistic Abuse Survivor Meetup[48] groups in their local area and 12-Step programs[49].

Nontraditional Supplementary Healing Modalities

Yoga

As children, we had no control over how our narcissistic parents micromanaged or exerted control over our bodies. They may have inflicted physical or sexual violence. They may have tried to control our sexuality and sexual agency. They may have instilled in us unhealthy beliefs about our body image, leading to eating disorders. Their emotional, verbal and psychological abuse undoubtedly created many physiological states of helplessness and a sense of perpetual trapped horror.

According to research from the Trauma Center[50], yoga has been proven as an effective complementary treatment for those with PTSD. Increasing a sense of mindful awareness, it enables individuals to experience "safety and mastery" over their bodies, giving them the resources to productively interpret intense physiological states of re-experiencing the trauma. This is especially helpful to survivors of physical and/or sexual abuse, but can also be deeply healing to those recovering from emotional states of terror which have paralyzed their bodies.

According to studies, yoga has helped survivors ease dissociative symptoms, affective dysregulation and reduce tension throughout the body. I personally love hatha yoga and hot vinyasa flow yoga. If you're a beginner to yoga, I recommend you take a beginner's class before moving onto more advanced classes. Or, if you struggle with physical injuries, it may be worth looking into restorative yoga.

Meditation

If you recall, in the essay *The Invisible War Zone*, I talked about how early childhood trauma creates specific changes in the brain, often shutting down communication between the more emotional parts of our brain and the frontal lobes which control executive functioning, our ability to organize, plan, think and make decisions.

Trauma can shrink the hippocampus and the amygdala, which affects emotion, memory, and learning. Good news: the very areas of the brain that were once affected by trauma can now be rewired by meditation. Research[51] by Harvard neuroscientist Sara Lazar showed that a regular meditation practice for eight weeks can literally change our brain, shrinking the amygdala which controls the "Fight or Flight" response and thickening the hippocampus which helps with emotional regulation and memory formation. Meditation not only thickens the auditory and sensory parts of our brain, but also increases grey matter in the frontal lobes, regardless of how old you are.

A forty-minute meditation practice every day can change the way you approach your emotions, your relationships and your overall sense of happiness and contentment. Meditation is free and can be done anywhere at any time. Contrary to popular myths, it does not require shutting off your thoughts but rather acknowledging them, accepting them, observing them and letting them come and go. All you need is a willingness to focus on your breath and a space where you can sit quietly and reflectively.

Here are some podcasts and channels I follow, some of which are meditation channels and others that are specifically about healing narcissistic abuse:

Meditation Oasis by Mary and Richard Maddux[52] (This is my favorite meditation resource and the one that began my journey. Wonderful for beginners and experts alike).

The Meditation Society of Australia[53] (free mp3 meditations on their website).

YellowBrickCinema – Relaxing Music[54]

Lucy Rising – Meditations for Narcissistic Abuse[55]

Self-Therapy for Narcissistic Abuse Trauma/EMDR Sound Therapy[56]

Joseph Clough – Self-Hypnosis Meditations[57]

Michael Seeley – Self-Hypnosis Guided Meditations[58]

Reiki

Reiki is a Japanese, spiritual non-invasive healing and stress-reduction technique which involves a Reiki practitioner using his or her hands to "heal" your body, based on the energetic blockages that may be present within your body. "Rei" means universal and "ki" means life energy.

Adult children of narcissists can develop chronic health conditions or pain as a result of the toxic stress they endured in childhood. Reiki operates under the idea that negative feelings and thoughts are not just stored in your mind, but also in your body, your aura and your energy field – which often results in illness. When our life-force energy is disrupted by emotions like depression, anxiety, anger - this results in us being sick. Energy flows through the practitioner's hands to where it is most needed during a Reiki healing session, restoring balance and harmony physically, emotionally and spiritually.

You can find reiki practitioners in your area here on the International Association of Reiki Professionals website[59] and you may also wish to search on Yelp, Groupon and LivingSocial for centers and practitioners that offer Reiki.

You can also learn how to use Reiki healing on yourself using the numerous resources available online. Watch this video on Reiki Healing here[60].

Nature

Scientific research proves nature's ability to lower cortisol levels, relieve stress, improve our ability to concentrate and improve our mood (Berman, Jonides, & Kaplan, 2008; Mayer et al., 2009). Even the act of walking barefoot[61] on the earth during warmer months can improve overall wellbeing and sleep while reducing pain and stress levels; the theory of the benefits of "earthing" suggests that walking barefoot connects us to the earth's electrons. You can also do this through gardening, which is a very therapeutic and mindful activity that allows you to see the growth you want within, manifest externally.

Some ideas for enjoying the daily benefits of nature may be: scheduling a morning or afternoon walk every day, taking a trip to a location with a beautiful natural landscape, taking a walk by a river, going to the beach, hiking outdoors, taking a jog in a park or the woods, taking your lunch break outdoors or picnicking frequently. If the weather is not warm, "access" nature in alternative ways: go camping and make sure to start up a fire; sit near a fireplace if indoors; open the window in the morning to let the sunlight in and hear the chirping of the birds; watch the snow fall or hear the rain. Listen to meditation music that incorporates the sounds of rainfall, a waterfall or the waves of an ocean.

Massage Therapy

Research shows that massage therapy can help lower cortisol levels and boost serotonin and dopamine levels, elevating mood. This effect is especially potent among populations of need such as depressed pregnant mothers, those suffering from cancer, as well as those with migraine headaches; given this, it's possible massage therapy can also potentially help with the somatic side effects of trauma (Field, 2005). Massage therapy can also decrease depression, anxiety, irritability and other trauma-related symptoms (Collinge, Kahn, & Soltysik, 2012). Get creative! Invest in a monthly or even weekly massage which incorporates hot stones or aromatherapy oils. Not only will it relieve tension throughout your body, it has many benefits for your mind as well.

Not all adult children of narcissists are comfortable with the idea of being touched by a stranger, even if it's a professional. Always take into account your own personal comfort levels and triggers when experimenting with different healing modalities. What works for one survivor may not be right for another.

Journaling and Writing

Trauma shuts down the Broca's area of the brain, the part of our brain responsible for communication and speech. Trauma literally can leave us speechless. Many traumas become "frozen" in the nonverbal parts of our brain. Journaling can be a way to start to re-communicate, engaging both the left and right sides of the brain as we begin creating a more cohesive narrative about the traumas experienced. Research[62] has shown that expressive writing can improve mood and post-traumatic growth among those with PTSD.

Writing unsent letters to your narcissistic parents, using the "how dare you" template I mention in the Connecting with Rage exercise can be helpful. You can also use journaling as an effective way to communicate with your Inner Parts or Inner Child.

Affirmations

Using positive affirmations to rewrite existing negative narratives is a technique we've already mentioned numerous times throughout the book. Affirmations are a vital part of many of the diverse healing techniques described, and using them is an important way to start healing subconscious wounds by reprogramming how we think about ourselves, our potential and the world around us. Affirmations are phrases that help us interrupt our normal thought patterns by instilling positive messages about ourselves and the world around us. Research confirms that positive self-affirmations can help improve problem-solving under stress (Creswell et al., 2013) and psychologists suggest that positive affirmations also help us preserve our self-integrity in the face of threat, enabling our "psychological immune system" to defend itself (Sherman, 2006).

A common criticism of positive affirmations is that they cannot work for people with low self-esteem, but I beg to differ; they certainly won't work for everyone, but they can work. Given everything I went through in my childhood and adulthood, how much I've been able to overcome strikes me as miraculous. Positive affirmations and reverse discourse have been essential in my journey to becoming my best self and accomplishing what I set out to achieve, despite the traumas and doubts that have threatened to deter me.

As discussed in this section on re-parenting the inner child, adult children of narcissists may benefit from using affirmations using "you" to direct the type of nurturing language towards themselves that they never received as children as a form of re-parenting.

For those struggling with low self-esteem, PTSD or Complex PTSD, positive affirmations may have to be customized in order to prevent triggers. Or perhaps they need to be said in a way that gently and incrementally approaches the aspects of yourself that are being reworked, much like in reverse discourse. As Daniel Perskawiec, a Certified Hypnotherapist and NLP Trainer from the NeuroIntelligence Institute suggests, you may have to say things like, "I choose to be happy" rather than "I am happy" if you have severe doubts about yourself.

Exercise

Those who exercise regularly have been shown to be less likely to suffer from anxiety and depression (Carek, Laibstain, & Carek, 2011). Being biochemically addicted to the chaos and crazymaking of our childhood can be counteracted by healthier alternatives which work with our reward systems and lower our cortisol (stress hormone) levels. When we release endorphins through exercise on a consistent basis, we can habituate our bodies to become accustomed to the "drama" of sweating on the treadmill rather than the toxicity of our toxic parents or bullying peers.

Creating a weekly or even daily exercise regimen can be so helpful for adult children of narcissists. Not only is it a natural mood-lifter, research has shown that exercise can potentially improve PTSD symptoms and even curb suicidal ideation among those who are bullied (Fetzner & Asmundson, 2014; Sibold, Edwards, Murray-Close, & Hudziak, 2015). Exercise can also help with overall well-being and coping strategies, giving victims a renewed sense of hope and determination, a heightened positive self-image and an improved quality of life (Caddick & Smith, 2017).

Exercise can also be a healthy outlet for channeling intense emotions. According to trauma experts, trauma lives in our bodies as well as our minds. It's important that we find at least one form of physical outlet for the intense emotions of grief, rage, and hurt we're bound to feel in the aftermath of abuse and trauma, in order to combat the paralysis that accompanies trauma, leaving us feeling numb and frozen.

I personally love kickboxing, yoga, dance, cardio and running while listening to empowering music or listening to positive affirmations. Do something you're passionate about and love to do. Don't force your body into activities that you're not comfortable with, and do not exhaust yourself. Even a daily ten-minute walk in nature can be more helpful than staying sedentary, so do the best you can. Using physical exercise as an outlet should be an act of self-care, not self-destruction or negative self-talk.

Laughter Therapy

Laughter lowers cortisol levels, eases pain, relieves stress, and enhances overall well-being. Adult children of narcissists and those who've experienced trauma may benefit from dark humor, as it has a way of still validating the pain they've experienced while still providing a portal for lightheartedness. Some research has explored how dark humor or "gallows humor" can be a coping mechanism for those who've been traumatized or work in situations where they are likely to encounter secondary trauma (Craun & Bourke, 2014).

If you're not a fan of dark humor, you should still take advantage of the healing benefits of laughter. Laughter yoga, for example, incorporates the use of voluntary laughter to reap the same benefits. Take time each day to make yourself laugh. You could watch a comedy stand-up on Netflix, browse through comedic Instagram meme accounts, attend a comedy show, remember funny memories, watch funny Youtube videos, read funny books or stories, watch amusing movies – the possibilities are limitless! Stick to what makes *you* laugh – everyone's sense of humor and personal preferences are different, so find something that uniquely tickles your funny bone.

Aromatherapy

Aromatherapy is an alternative healing method where the individual uses scents and essential oils as a way to help with emotions and health. Individuals can choose to inhale the fragrance or apply the oils directly on their skin. According to Suzanne Bovenizer, CMT, CST[63], our sense of smell is connected to the limbic system in our brain, where emotions and memories are stored. Scents stimulate that part of the brain, releasing chemicals that cause us to become calmer and more relaxed. Aromatherapy can help a great deal with anxiety, which can be a key component of the distress victims of narcissistic abuse experience.

You can buy essential oils and an essential oil diffuser for your home so that aromatherapy is always accessible to you. You may also seek aromatherapy in alternative ways: some yoga centers offer yoga with an aromatherapy component, and many massages can also incorporate elements of aromatherapy in a session.

I recommend both essential oils and incense. Here are some links to purchase products for aromatherapy:

PRODUCTS FOR HEALING

Artizen Aromatherapy Top 14 Essential Oil Set
URPOWER Essential Oil Diffuser
Aromatherapy Incense Sticks: Certified Organic and All Natural
Essential Oils

The Complete Book of Essential Oils and Aromatherapy by Valerie Ann Worwood

You can find these above products on Amazon and other online retailers.

Acupuncture

> STRAIGHT FROM THE HEALER'S MOUTH: "People may recognize there are unresolved issues in their lives: "ghosts" from their past. But most are unclear how to go about resolving them. Many go to talk therapy. However, according to Chinese Medical theory, trauma lives in our bodies. It becomes stuck in our blood and bones where it incubates, causing various physical and mental symptoms. To fully resolve trauma, the body needs to be released. There needs to be a physical detox." – Acupuncturist Nicholas Sieben, M.S., L.Ac, *Stories of Healing Emotional Trauma in My Acupuncture Clinic*[64]

Acupuncture is an ancient Chinese healing technique involving the use of needles at specific points of the body to heal a wide variety of physical and psychological ailments. There are 12 primary and eight secondary invisible lines of energy flow in the body known as "meridians." An acupuncturist targets specific points of the body to help resolve the physical and/or emotional ailment plaguing the patient. To learn more about acupuncture, visit NIH's page on acupuncture here[65]. You can also search for an acupuncturist if you live in the United States here[66].

Animal Assisted Intervention (AII)

Perhaps our parents couldn't give us unconditional love, but animals are quite different. Researchers O'Haire, Guerin, and Kirkham (2015)[67] did a systematic review of research on Animal Assisted Intervention and how it helps survivors of child abuse as well as military veterans. They found that the use of AII as a complementary treatment for trauma was effective for reducing depression, PTSD symptoms, and anxiety. This will come as no surprise to any survivor who's engaged in a little bit of pet therapy – whether it be dogs, horses, cats, bunnies or birds. Animals also change our biochemical state: you can produce oxytocin by cuddling a cute animal; research shows that cuddling with a dog actually increases the oxytocin levels of both the dog and its owner (Odendaal and Meintjes, 2003).

STRAIGHT FROM THE RESEARCHER'S MOUTH: "With respect to intrusion, the presence of an animal is purported to act as a comforting reminder that danger is no longer present and to act as a secure base for mindful experiences in the present. Individuals with PTSD often experience emotional numbing, yet the presence of an animal has been reported to elicit positive emotions and warmth. Animals have also been demonstrated as social facilitators that can connect and reduce loneliness, which may assist individuals with PTSD to break out of isolation and connect to the humans around them. One of the most challenging aspects of PTSD tends to be hyperarousal. The presence of an animal has been linked to secretion of oxytocin and reductions in anxious arousal, which may be a particularly salient feature for individuals who have experienced trauma." – Animal Assisted Intervention for Trauma: A Systematic Literature Review by O'Haire, Guerin, and Kirkham (2015)

Music Therapy

Music helps us to regulate our mood, reconnect with our authentic emotions, reduce our heart rate and blood pressure, lower cortisol levels which cause stress and manage our anxiety levels. It's no wonder that music can even be used in a therapeutic relationship[68] to help an addict in his or her recovery, can help improve social functioning in patients with schizophrenia, and can reduce the side effects of cancer treatment.

Survivor Journey: "I have done a huge amount of healing especially in the last 10 years. It has been a long journey but I've come so far. Honestly, I feel music, singing, and songwriting have saved me. They have been amazing therapeutic outlets. I have the freedom to express myself and being able to perform for people is soothing. It's an amazing experience when I connect with an audience via a song. It helps me transcend the pain and maybe momentarily the listener is transported too. It feels like a spiritual experience. I feel the dark cloud of shame from my past is finally lifting. I am setting healthier boundaries for myself and nurturing better relationships with friends. I am considering doing some CBT to continue my journey of healing." – E. Fox

For adult children of narcissists, music can help us get in touch with emotions we've been suppressing, channel and release some of those emotions in a safe space of healing, and connect with someone else (the artist) through the lyrics, the beat of the music and/or the theme of the song. Music can also help lift a survivor from a mood of despair and powerlessness, gently guiding that survivor to feel happier and empowered while simultaneously giving their immune system a boost! Now that's what I call healing on the level of the mind, body and spirit.

You can choose to listen to the music you find most healing, or you can even seek out a certified music therapist at the American Music Therapy Association[69].

Here are some links to interesting studies on the effects of music.
CNN: This is your brain on music[70]
PsychologyToday: Does Music Have Healing Powers?[71]
Harvard Health Publications: Healing Through Music[72]

A Note About Hybrid Healing Modalities

You can mix and match healing modalities to make them extra powerful. It's what I like to call the Dual Mind and Body Method. For example, combining positive affirmations with movement (such as physical exercise) can also help to further reinforce them into your belief system and anchor them more deeply in your psyche. Record your positive affirmations on your phone or tape recorder and listen to them while you go for a jog or watch daily. This enables you to access multiple parts of your brain and reprogram both your mind and your body. It conditions you to associate your affirmations with movement, energy and vitality.

I love doing "hybrid" activities where I combine techniques. For example, I once attended a candlelit hot yoga class with music playing – it appealed to all of my senses and targeted multiple areas of my brain, allowing me to self-soothe and heal both mind and body at once. There are plenty of ways to combine healing methods and make it fun! This might mean activities such as the following:

- Relaxing in a scented bath with an audio of positive affirmations playing in the background.
- Listening to positive affirmations you record yourself (or, as Louise Hay recommends, a loving caregiver or friend recorded for you) as you walk on the treadmill or go for a run.
- When doing yoga poses, repeat powerful mantras such as, "I love myself," "I am safe," "I am balanced" during each pose aloud or in your mind.
- While getting a massage, meditate or pray silently, allowing your thoughts to simply flow.
- Taking a walk on the beach while meditating to the sound of the waves.
- Viewing empowering videos like "Mind Movies" that help you visualize the situations you want while listening to soothing music or a meditation with binaural beats.
- Using a scented oil diffuser or incense while writing/journaling.

Other Supplementary Healing Modalities (Survivor Experiences)

In the survey, survivors mentioned many alternative supplemental healing methods they used on their journey. They included things as diverse as crystal healing, yoga kundalini, martial arts, brain wave therapy music, ASMR, kinesiology, seeing a chiropractor, mountain biking, shadow work, and CrossFit. I mention these because by no means are the healing modalities discussed in this chapter the only ones available. Each healing journey is unique to the survivor and may include many alternative remedies in addition to the traditional or nontraditional research-based healing modalities discussed. What works for one survivor may not work for another. It's important to create a customized healing package that works for you, and to work with a trauma-informed counselor to ensure that the modalities you use are helping to ease the symptoms of trauma rather than heightening them.

References

Bergland, C. (2013, January 22). Cortisol: Why "The Stress Hormone" Is Public Enemy No. 1. Retrieved from https://www.psychologytoday.com/blog/the-athletes-way/201301/cortisol-why-the-stress-hormone-is-public-enemy-no-1

Berman, M. G., Jonides, J. & Kaplan, S. (2008). The cognitive benefits of interacting with nature. *Psychological Science, 19,* 1207-1212.

Bradshaw, J. (1990). *Homecoming: Reclaiming and championing your inner child.* London: Piatkus.

Caddick, N., & Smith, B. (2017). Combat Surfers: A Narrative Study Of Veterans, Surfing, And War Trauma. *Movimento (ESEFID/UFRGS), 23*(1), 35. doi:10.22456/1982-8918.71264

Carek, P. J., Laibstain, S. E., & Carek, S. M. (2011). Exercise for the Treatment of Depression and Anxiety. *The International Journal of Psychiatry in Medicine, 41*(1), 15-28. doi:10.2190/pm.41.1.c

Choi, J., Jeong, B., Rohan, M. L., Polcari, A. M., & Teicher, M. H. (2009). Preliminary Evidence for White Matter Tract Abnormalities in Young Adults Exposed to Parental Verbal Abuse. *Biological Psychiatry, 65*(3), 227-234. doi:10.1016/j.biopsych.2008.06.022

Collinge, W., Kahn, J., & Soltysik, R. (2012). Promoting Reintegration of National Guard Veterans and Their Partners Using a Self-Directed Program of Integrative Therapies: A Pilot Study. *Military Medicine, 177*(12), 1477-1485. doi:10.7205/milmed-d-12-00121

Craun, S. W., & Bourke, M. L. (2014). The Use of Humor to Cope with Secondary Traumatic Stress. *Journal of Child Sexual Abuse, 23*(7), 840-852. doi:10.1080/10538712.2014.949395

Crowell, S. E., Beauchaine, T. P., & Linehan, M. M. (2009). A Biosocial Developmental Model of Borderline Personality: Elaborating and

Extending Linehan's Theory. Retrieved from http://www.ncbi.nlm.nih.gov/pmc/articles/PMC2696274/

Creswell, J. D., Dutcher, J. M., Klein, W. M., Harris, P. R., & Levine, J. M. (2013). Self-Affirmation Improves Problem-Solving under Stress. *PLoS ONE, 8*(5). doi:10.1371/journal.pone.0062593

Fetzner, M. G., & Asmundson, G. J. (2014). Aerobic Exercise Reduces Symptoms of Posttraumatic Stress Disorder: A Randomized Controlled Trial. *Cognitive Behaviour Therapy, 44*(4), 301-313. doi:10.1080/16506073.2014.916745

Field, T., Hernandez-Reif, M., Diego, M., Schanberg, S., & Kuhn, C. (2005). Cortisol Decreases And Serotonin And Dopamine Increase Following Massage Therapy. *International Journal of Neuroscience, 115*(10), 1397-1413. doi:10.1080/00207450590956459

Foucault, M., & Hurley, R. (1988). *The history of sexuality.* New York: Vintage Books.

Klein, S. (2013, April 19). Adrenaline, Cortisol, Norepinephrine: The Three Major Stress Hormones, Explained. Retrieved from http://www.huffingtonpost.com/2013/04/19/adrenaline-cortisol-stress-hormones_n_3112800.html

Mayer, F.S., Frantz, C. M. P., Bruehlman-Senecal, E., & Doliver, K. (2009). Why is nature beneficial? The role of connectedness in nature. *Environment and Behavior, 41*, 607-643.

Linehan, M., Comtois, K. A., Murray, A. M., Brown, M. Z., Gallop, R. J., Heard, H. L., & Korslund, K. E. (2006, July 1). Two-year randomized controlled trial and follow-up of dialectical behavior therapy vs therapy by experts for suicidal behaviors and borderline personality disorder. *JAMA Psychiatry, 63*(7), 757-766. doi:10.1001/archpsyc.63.7.757.

McKay, M., Wood, J. C., & Brantley, J. (2010). *The dialectical behavior therapy skills workbook: Practical DBT exercises for learning mindfulness, interpersonal effectiveness, Emotion regulation & distress tolerance.* Oakland, CA: New Harbinger Publications.

Odendaal, J., & Meintjes, R. (2003). Neurophysiological Correlates of Affiliative Behavior between Humans and Dogs. *The Veterinary Journal, 165*(3), 296-301. doi:10.1016/s1090-0233(02)00237-x

O'Haire, M. E., Guérin, N. A., & Kirkham, A. C. (2015). Animal-Assisted Intervention for trauma: A systematic literature review. *Frontiers in Psychology, 6.* doi:10.3389/fpsyg.2015.01121

Palgi, S., Klein, E., & Shamay-Tsoory, S. G. (2016). Oxytocin improves compassion toward women among patients with PTSD.*Psychoneuroendocrinology,* *64,* 143-149. doi:10.1016/j.psyneuen.2015.11.008

Rowe, A., & Regehr, C. (2010). Whatever Gets You Through Today: An Examination of Cynical Humor Among Emergency Service Professionals. *Journal of Loss and Trauma, 15*(5), 448-464. doi:10.1080/15325024.2010.507661

Schwartz, R. C. (1995). *Internal family systems therapy.* New York: Guilford Press.

Sibold, J., Edwards, E., Murray-Close, D., & Hudziak, J. J. (2015). Physical Activity, Sadness, and Suicidality in Bullied US Adolescents. *Journal of the American Academy of Child & Adolescent Psychiatry,* *54*(10), 808-815. doi:10.1016/j.jaac.2015.06.019

Exercises for Adult Children of Narcissists

Practical exercises to help adult children of
narcissists put their newfound knowledge to
use. Best used with a journal and the help of a
trauma-informed therapist.

Naming Your Inner Parts

Many of us develop inner parts as a result of the traumas we endured in childhood. Some of these parts carry our childhood wounds; others carry defense mechanisms for survival. These parts often speak in certain voices and have their own miniature identities.

Do you notice parts of yourself that appear "out of character" with your true self? Even if you don't have a connection to your true self, yet, you can probably sense certain "alter-egos" that have surfaced throughout your life which sometimes seem to control your automatic reactions and behavior. Identifying these parts and beginning a dialogue with them (with the help of a trauma-informed therapist) can be so helpful to begin to integrate these parts in a healthy way in your psyche.

Below are some ideas for how to connect with an inner part. Ideally, you'll want to adapt these tips as you work with a therapist who is familiar with the Internal Family Systems model.

Tips for Accessing Your Inner Part

1) Write down the characteristics of your inner part. You may even choose to create a drawing of the part, to help you visualize what it would look like.

2) Based on those characteristics, you may want to give the inner part a name. Naming it allows you to look at it as an entity that stemmed from the trauma, rather than as part of your authentic self. It also allows you to identify it more readily in discussions with your therapist or when you're journaling about the inner part.

3) Notice where in your body you "sense" the part, if any. Visualize what that part would look like – in what kind of voice does it speak in? What facial expressions does it have? What gestures does this inner part exhibit? How does this part conduct himself or herself? Is there a certain aura, color, or energy you feel with that part?

4) Think about how that part has come out in the past throughout your life. When does it tend to "steal the show"? Perhaps you have an inner part that seems to come out during times of intense pressure or anxiety, and another inner part that comes out when you are being bullied.

5) What beliefs does this inner part hold about the world, herself/himself, and others? Brainstorm what protective function that part it may have played in your life. You can ask the part questions like, "What are you trying to get?" "What are you trying to protect me from?" "What has to happen to make you feel safe?" "What do you want me to do?"

6) List both the weaknesses and strengths of that part. What does that part allow you to do, that you might not otherwise do? For example, you might have an inner part that stands up for you – albeit, aggressively. Yet it allows you to assert yourself in situations you might otherwise feel powerless. On the other hand, that part might also become preemptively aggressive towards people who may not deserve it, thus isolating you from healthy friendships. How does it hold you back from achieving your goals?

7) Thank the inner part for its "service." Let it know that you know it was just trying to help, but that you can take it from here. Or, alternatively, offer a compromise or solution that allows your inner part to still get some of its needs met without compromising your values. Notice any resistance that comes up.

For example, some of my "parts" have included the following – maybe you can relate to these:

The CEO – This inner part would probably be best be described by Internal Family Systems founder Dr. Schwartz as a "manager." It is overachieving and perfectionistic – a quintessential "boss lady." The CEO kept people from getting too close to her by ensuring that her focus was on work. So long as she was perpetually achieving things and criticizing herself or others, she had no time to slow down and actually connect with her authentic feelings or fears of intimacy. You can imagine my astonishment, when I realized that due to the promptings of the perfectionistic, overachieving CEO, I hadn't taken a proper "vacation" from anything since high school! I had always been working, going to school, writing books, working on projects, taking care of others, immersing myself in a relationship or the dating scene, or overly socializing while doing all of the above. I was doing this all while overcoming numerous traumas and healing the traumas of the past. *No wonder I was exhausted!*

Many of us have inner parts like this – parts that keep us "doing" in order to numb out the pain. This inner part also holds the central beliefs that, "*If I do enough, I will someday be enough. If I am perfect, I am loveable. If I achieve, I am worthy.*"

But you are already enough. You are already loveable. You are already worthy, just as you are.

The CEO can be healthily integrated into my psyche by acknowledging the valuable function she serves (achieving her goals) without getting swept away into perfectionistic ideals which detract from her relationships or healthy self-care. The CEO's strengths include her ability to be independent, her ability to be financially secure, and her determination to achieve her goals. Her vulnerabilities include her tendency to let her ambition get in the way of her relationships, her frequent excuses for why she can't let people get close, and her inability to give herself rest, connection and nourishment.

The Party Girl – This is a firefighter type. Firefighters work to "douse out" the fires of immediate triggers by engaging in behaviors which would allow us to escape or avoid the pain associated with these triggers. My "Party Girl" loved to get lost in fun, allowing her to dissociate from the intense pain of her traumas. In her early twenties, she might have done this by drinking whenever socially anxious, going on hundreds of dates, becoming overly affectionate with strangers, and being the charismatic "life of the party." Now, in moderation and with healthy self-care, some aspects of The Party Girl might actually be a useful inner part to access in social situations, but in excess, she can self-harm by dissociating from her pain rather than confronting it.

The Party Girl also tended to date bad boys and emotionally unavailable men, allowing her to keep an emotional distance from men who might actually be healthy relationship partners. For her, life was a neverending celebration and party – one that would hopefully keep her safe from the darkness she had experienced in childhood and adolescence. But because The Party Girl preferred to act out rather than to take care of herself and soothe her traumatized parts, all these activities only compounded her traumas and never truly brought a resolution.

The party girl's central beliefs revolve around the idea that in order to be worthy, she must be approved of by others. Her function was to not only escape from her traumas, but also to attempt to retrieve the lost childhood and adolescence that I never got to experience as a sheltered teenager living with controlling parents. Since my true self is more introverted and reserved, The Party Girl's strengths include her ability to be extroverted and get along with *just about everybody*.

Her vulnerabilities include her indiscriminate choice of partners and friends, her tendency to drink when anxious rather than to confront her anxiety head-on, and her emotional unavailability. The party girl's cheerful façade hides a deep pain and sorrow. When healthily integrated in my mid-to-late twenties, this inner part helped me to relax and have fun (perhaps even convince the CEO to let me have a break) without succumbing to unhealthy choices.

The Fawner – This is an "exile" type, a traumatized inner part which developed people-pleasing habits in order to survive. "The Fawner" allowed me to survive my childhood by walking on eggshells around the adults who had the power to control and abuse me. In adulthood, however, The Fawner has come out maladaptively in situations with toxic people who trigger my regression back to childhood states of powerlessness. Rather than assertively standing up for myself, The Fawner might emerge to beg, plead, or attempt to please anyone who is toxic or dangerous in some way or to avoid abandonment. In order for me to healthily integrate the Fawner, I had to thank it for its valuable service in doing what it thought would keep me safe. Then, I had to gently tell The Fawner that, "I can also keep myself safe in other ways, like asserting myself."

Role-Self, Role Reversal,

and True Self

There are many roles we play throughout our lives which do not authentically represent or honor who we really are. Some of us play a fixed role in childhood, like "the rebel" or "the scapegoat," while others rotate and shift roles depending on changing circumstances in dysfunctional family dynamics. We can also simultaneously inhabit multiple roles. For example, the rebel child can also become an overachiever if that achievement is tied to "proving" the toxic parent wrong in some way.

According to trauma therapists, the role-self is a role we inhabited to provide structure to the chaos and the toxic shame we felt. To protect it from intense pain, our role-self buried our vulnerable authentic true self, maintained the family dysfunction, and helped us to survive our toxic childhood. Explore some roles you still play and whether or not they're helpful to you in your adult life.

For example, you might inhabit a role such as The Caretaker because you grew up catering to one or more parents who suffered from an addiction or an illness. Perhaps you remember having to become a parent to your parent and you've carried that same role with you to adulthood. You may have strived to gain your parent's approval through this excessive caretaking. You might subconsciously seek out partners or friends you can take care of in some way because this role made you feel needed and important.

Now, imagine what it would be like to embody the opposite characteristics of this role. Rather than being conscientious and overly helpful, always thinking about someone else's needs, imagine yourself as selfish, self-centered, always looking out for *numero uno*, deeply engrossed in your own desires and needs. How would *that* person act? What actions would that person take on a daily basis?

The key is not to actually become selfish, but to find a balance. Often, we have to experience the other side of the pendulum in order to successfully vacillate towards a middle ground. What characteristics of the "selfish" person could you use in moderation to have healthier boundaries with yourself and others?

DEFINING THE ROLE

Write down a role you've carried with you from childhood to adulthood. Write down the functions that role served in childhood. Now think about what you get from that role in adulthood. There is usually some sort of perceived payoff. Then, think about the consequences of playing that role – there are usually many. Imagine what the opposite identity of that role would look like and act like. You may even choose to "play" that opposite role for a day and write down your thoughts, feelings, and experiences as you play that opposite role. Think about what characteristics you could incorporate from that opposite role which have a beneficial effect.

Example: As The Caretaker, I always think about other people. Even when I am making decisions that would have the most impact on me, I am considering how it would affect someone close to me. If I was the opposite of The Caretaker, I would prioritize my own needs and let myself be selfish. I would think about what would benefit me first, always.

The function that the caretaker served in childhood is that it allowed me to be seen by my parents in childhood. So long as I was taking care of them, they remembered I was there. I felt needed and important. Otherwise, I was neglected and abused. The function that the caretaker serves in adulthood is that I can always come to the rescue for my friends and my partner. When anyone needs something, they know who to call: me.

PERCEIVED PAYOFFS

I feel needed and important. My friends, family, and partner know they can depend on me and rely on me. I feel "seen" as a charitable, generous person.

EXPERIENCED CONSEQUENCES

I don't get my own needs met. I feel shy about asking for something because I play the role of the provider, always. It's difficult for me to speak out about something that I want, or to put my own needs first above someone else's. I also get taken advantage of frequently.

OPPOSITE ROLE CHARACTERISTICS

Self-centered, prioritizes self, takes self into account first, does what he or she desires.

EXPERIENCE: PLAYING THE OPPOSITE ROLE

Today I played the opposite role. I thought about what I would personally want and took into account my own feelings whenever someone asked me to do something. When my friend asked me to come pick her up from work to drive her to her boyfriend's house, I told her I couldn't today because I was finishing up a project. She seemed upset and taken aback, because she is used to me always catering to whatever she wants me to do.

When she tried to pressure me to change my mind and work on my project later, I repeated that I could not because my project is very important. I felt uncomfortable about doing this, but each time I repeated myself, I felt stronger. I suggested to her the name of another friend who had a car as well as a nearby train she could take as alternatives before we hung up. I felt proud of myself. I realized that if she stops contacting me after this, she wasn't a real friend after all. This friend is a bit of a "user" so maybe it's high time that I kicked her to the curb anyway.

Then, on his way home, my boyfriend called and asked me what was for dinner. Rather than asking him what he'd like me to cook and spending hours on creating a lavish meal, I suggested we try something different tonight and he get takeout. Like my friend, my boyfriend seemed surprised at this suggestion, but reluctantly agreed. I told him that he should do some planning and find a restaurant that we would both like. Rather than doing the planning, I got off the phone earlier than I usually do and used the extra time to do some self-care: I soaked in a warm lavender salt bath, lit some candles, listened to soothing music, and journaled about my goals. Usually I don't allow myself so much time during the day to tend to myself, but it felt really nice!

Later that night, after eating some delicious Chinese takeout from a restaurant my boyfriend knew was my favorite, I relished in the feeling of finally feeling taken care of for once rather than always doing the caretaking. When my toxic mother called me on the phone to complain as she usually does about where my life was going, I texted her letting her know I was getting some sleep and couldn't talk at the moment. She still tried to call me, but I didn't pick up. It felt so great! Rather than engaging with her about all the things she thought was wrong with me or comforting her fears, I turned off my phone completely rather than having to deal with her usual nightly call. For the first time in years, I had my deepest, most soothing sleep.

The hypothetical scenario above represents an ideal situation. Of course, you'll want to take baby steps if you feel you cannot do certain things just yet. You may feel far more discomfort and experience unforeseen consequences when you take even baby steps, because people are used to using you and taking advantage of you if you've always played the caretaker.

And by no means were any of the examples truly "selfish" – they may have just appeared that way for you because you're so used to thinking about others before you think about yourself. However, what you may have learned from this exercise is that it's okay to think of yourself, take time for self-care, and say "no."

Combat People-Pleasing

An overwhelming majority of adult children of narcissists surveyed said they struggled with people-pleasing tendencies. When you grow up in a toxic household, you walk on eggshells and please your abusive parent in order to survive. In adulthood, however, people-pleasing can bury our authentic outrage, our true needs and wants, and it can enable people to violate our boundaries just to get what they want.

If you're a people-pleaser, it's important to understand where this habit stemmed from, the situations where your tendencies tend to come out the most, and start to play with healthier alternatives which challenge your people-pleasing tendencies.

CONNECTING WITH YOUR TRUE FEELINGS

As people-pleasers, we tend to mask our true feelings about something because we were taught as children that our feelings did not matter. Our emotions were usually ignored or invalidated altogether. A part of reconnecting with our authentic self requires that we connect with how we actually feel about things, rather than presenting ourselves as something or someone other than who we truly are to please people.

When we are operating from our "false self" or "role-self," we are usually doing things and saying things we know other people would approve of – presenting ourselves as who we are "supposed" to be rather than who we really are.

Pick a recent situation where you felt you had mixed feelings or hidden feelings that were not "allowed" to come to the surface. For example, maybe you had a couple of dates with someone who didn't really stimulate you intellectually or connect with your specific sense of humor. They wanted to have another date with you, but despite an initial attraction, you didn't feel emotionally connected to them. When they text you again asking when you'll be free next, you struggled with your response because you wanted to like this person who appears good on paper but isn't truly compatible with who you really are.

IDENTIFY THE MIXED EMOTIONS.

Do you feel flattered that this person is interested in you? Validate that. It's okay to feel flattered. We all like having someone interested in us. Do you also feel a sense of being threatened or fearful because you're afraid of how this person would react to how you really feel? Validate that as well. You might even feel a small sense of hope that maybe if you keep on dating this person, you will somehow manufacture compatibility. If that's there too, it's important to acknowledge it. All of these feelings are valid, but that doesn't mean you have to act on any of them.

SIT WITH YOUR DISCOMFORT.

A lot of us who struggle with people-pleasing try to avoid the discomfort of our true feelings and acquiesce to whatever the other person wants. Instead of escaping from your discomfort, become curious about it. Where do you feel the discomfort? Is it a tightening in your chest? Maybe you feel back pain or an overwhelming feeling of guilt. Where is that guilt coming from? When did you first feel it in childhood?

EXAMPLE

Sandy feels an overwhelming sense of guilt thinking about letting the guy she's dating down, especially since he paid for the first couple of dates. Whenever she thinks of telling him they're not compatible, her heart races, her palms sweat, she feels stabbing pains in her lower back, and she becomes overwhelmed by the fear of retaliation if she rejects him. The first time she felt this kind of overwhelming guilt, it was after she stood up to her narcissistic father. Whenever Sandy used to say "no" to her abusive father in childhood, she would get hit on her lower back with a belt. Later, she had some abusive relationships. Her abusers would retaliate whenever she would refuse their sexual advances or refused to do something she felt uncomfortable with.

EVALUATE PAST CONSEQUENCES OF PEOPLE-PLEASING.

Think about any times in the past where you ignored your instincts and gave into your people-pleasing tendencies. Evaluating your history of people-pleasing and its consequences can help you to halt giving into your initial discomfort. There are usually perceived temporary 'payoffs' to our people-pleasing tendencies. For example, we might be able to avoid confrontation and temporarily avoid the reactions of whoever we're saying "no" to. Yet there are usually plenty of long-term consequences which come with people-pleasing that do not justify the payoffs.

EXAMPLE

For years, whenever Carrie would feel an urge to say no to something, she would automatically think about the terrible things that might happen if she asserted herself. She was overwhelmed by mixed feelings and would eventually give in to whatever someone else wanted her to do. This led her into some dangerous and unsafe situations. For example, she would go further sexually with someone she was dating than she was comfortable with because she feared their reaction if she did otherwise. She didn't want them to abandon her. Afterward, she would feel used and degraded because she made these choices out of her fear of abandonment, rather than her authentic desires. It didn't help that these same dating partners rarely called or followed up afterward.

Carrie had the temporary payoff of avoiding abandonment temporarily – but as she soon discovered, she was still abandoned even though she gave into the requests of her dating partners. She abandoned herself, too, by not doing what she wanted to do. Long-term, this led to a diminished sense of worthiness and self-esteem.

IDENTIFY YOUR AUTHENTIC DESIRES

What would you prefer to do? Whenever I find my people-pleasing tendencies come up, I think of the iconic literary figure Bartleby, who constantly says, "I prefer not to." What do you prefer *not* to do? Take it further. Who would you prefer not to see? How would you prefer not to spend your time? What would you prefer not to say?

Example: Carrie would prefer not to have any sexual intimacy with anyone she is dating until she is ready. Sandy would prefer not to go out with that guy again.

Write down a list of things you prefer not to do. Be as uncensored and honest as possible. No one will see the list, so you are free to speak your truth.

Then, underneath, brainstorm and write down some realistic ways you could meet some of your needs and give yourself some options on how to honor that desire. Notice I said "options." That means you can have a variety of different ways you could assert yourself. This will ease your anxiety as you don't necessarily have to start with the boldest action until you're ready. Below, I've included a sample list to help you make your own.

SAMPLE LIST

I prefer not to answer harassing texts from my toxic father.

Honoring this would look like:
- ✓ Blocking my father on my phone whenever he texts me.
- ✓ Letting my father know not to text me insulting messages again.

✓ Not responding to any of his texts.

I prefer not to hang out with that toxic mutual friend.

Honoring this might look like:
✓ Turning down invitations to events where I know the friend will be there.
✓ Asking my friends ahead of time who will be at the events they invite me to.
✓ Letting one of my trustworthy friends know I have an issue with the mutual friend so she can serve as moral support.

I prefer not to go out with that creepy guy from work.

Honoring this might look like:
✓ Letting the co-worker know that I am not interested.
✓ Actively avoiding the co-worker whenever he approaches me.
✓ Turning to Human Resources if he doesn't stop harassing me.

I prefer not to pick up my toxic mother every weekend to drive her places.

Honoring this might look like:
✓ Asking my sister to drive her on some weekends so I can catch a break.
✓ Letting my mother know that I will no longer be available on weekends.
✓ Compromising and letting my mom know I will only be able to pick her up on certain weekends and that she'll have to make other arrangements for the other weekends I am not available.

I prefer not to be friends with my toxic cousins who have enabled my abusive parent.

Honoring this would look like:
✓ Deciding not to go to the family reunion and keeping face-to-face contact only for emergencies.

- ✓ Slowly but surely cutting off contact without explaining myself.
- ✓ Unfriending my cousins on Facebook or hiding their stories from my newsfeed to get a break.

TAKE BABY STEPS. FOLLOW THROUGH WITH YOUR DESIRES.

Start small. What is one thing you can do right now that is true to you, rather than what everyone else expects of you? Maybe you've been wanting to wear a certain shade of lipstick but you're anxious about how you would be perceived. Try it out for a day. Then, as you ease into these baby steps, you can experiment with larger "conquests." Unfriending that annoying friend on Facebook that keeps harassing you, or shutting down that guy at work who keeps hitting on you, is far easier when you've learned to overcome your fear of social disapproval with the "little things."

Battling Imposter Syndrome

Due to the verbal and emotional abuse of our narcissistic parents, it's common for many adult children of narcissists to deal with Imposter Syndrome. Whenever we get praise, recognition, a raise, or a deserved promotion, for example, we may get a sense that we are somehow unworthy or that we're a fraud, regardless of how hard we've worked, the credentials we have, or how talented we may be.

Many adult children of narcissists on the survey noted that they never felt quite "good enough" regardless of what they accomplished. Imposter Syndrome isn't rooted in reality, but rather the traumas we experienced as helpless children. Our parents taught us that no matter what we did, we would never be good enough. If we were also bullied by our peers in addition to being abused by our parents, we may have internalized the horrific taunts and name-calling of our childhood as well. These deeply rooted beliefs can come up whenever we've accomplished something or are being recognized for it. Some adult children of narcissists may actually feel guilty about achieving a high level of success, even when they've rightfully earned it. This stems from the trauma of being taught that they were not deserving, that they were "bad" or "defective" in some way. Our toxic parents likely shamed us into believing that if we did outshine them or did anything to establish independence, we deserved to be punished.

Think about something you have Imposter Syndrome about. It could be your career, your friendships, your romantic relationships, your personality – anything that makes you heavily doubt yourself and feel like a fraud. Now write down your responses to the following questions:

What would other supportive people aside from my narcissistic parent say I've accomplished? (Ex. My best friend would say I am a Renaissance woman! She gushes to others all the time about how I am a professor and how I have a law degree, and how I am also artistic and have won some contests that have placed my artwork in galleries. She's really proud of me.)

_____

_____

_____

How do I feel when I receive healthy praise for what I've achieved? (Ex. When my non-narcissistic sibling congratulates me on a project I've finished, I still feel a sense of dread of whether or not the project will be well received.)

_____

_____

_____

Are there other people who may not have worked as hard, or do not have as many credentials who have accomplished similar successes or goals that you have? (Ex. If your goal is a happy relationship, you might remember your friend who has a really loving wife. They have such a happy relationship! But maybe your friend didn't have to go to extensive therapy to work on himself, or read relationship books, or do hours of assertiveness training or spend months on dating sites to find this happy relationship. He simply met his wife when the time was right).

As you go through these, realize that there may be a clear discrepancy between how others perceive what you've accomplished and what you deserve versus how *you* perceive yourself and your accomplishments. Many adult children of narcissists become overachievers to fill up the void of their childhoods. That's why they perpetually struggle with the sense that they will never be quite enough. When you see yourself through the supportive eyes of others, you realize that you are indeed worthy of far more recognition than you've given yourself credit for.

Evaluating what you feel when you receive healthy praise can be a barometer for how high your Imposter Syndrome is. If, whenever you hear praise, you feel an immense amount of discomfort, sit with that discomfort. Breathe through it and begin a gentle, curious dialogue with it. Ask it why it feels fear, shame, guilt, anxiety, surprise, disgust – whatever emotions come up. Behind that discomfort is often an unwillingness to accept our own gifts and talents because we've been taught to bury them or minimize them in childhood. And work on giving that kind of healthy praise to yourself.

As for the last question, it is not meant to compare yourself in an unhealthy way to anyone, but simply to remind you that you don't have to be perfect to be successful – there are many people who simply have faith in themselves and feel worthy of accomplishing as much as you, without necessarily working overtime for it. These people do not experience Imposter Syndrome as often and already feel "enough" and deserving.

Observing these people can be helpful because it reminds you that you are already worthy. There are plenty of people kicking ass in their careers and having happy relationships who may not have done anything exceptional or special. Or maybe they have, and they're just fully owning it. Whatever the case may be, haven't you done just as much, if not *more* than these people? So why would you deserve any less than them?

Hell, even the most emotionally deranged among us – psychopaths – find loving, doting partners even though they themselves are anything but. In a twisted way, they feel "deserving" and entitled to such a partner despite being callous, cruel and unempathetic themselves. Psychopaths actually deserve to have Imposter Syndrome, and rightfully so, because they *are* imposters. But they lack any emotional capacity to have that kind of guilt. Yet *you've* probably worked very hard for what you've accomplished and you don't deserve that kind of self-scrutiny at all. Funny how the world works!

So anytime you – an empathic, beautiful, hardworking, loving spirit - feels "undeserving" of anything in life, remind yourself of people who did not have to bend over backwards attempting to obtain their desires. The truth is, you do deserve it, you've probably worked harder for it than most people, and yes, you are indeed worthy of the rewards. You are not a fraud or an imposter. You're the real deal. You deserve infinite abundance in all areas of your life.

Tapping Into Your Inner Child

Apart from our inner parts, many of us have an Inner Child which has been wounded. Once we have worked to neutralize the intense defense mechanisms of our inner parts, we can begin to access the Inner Child and re-parent it (read the chapter on Re-parenting the Inner Child for more tips and strategies). Even if it is wounded, know that your Inner Child has access to the joy, spontaneity, innocence and playfulness that you came into the world with.

In John Bradshaw's book *Homecoming*, he recommends that we have a daily practice of communicating with our inner child, whether through writing or visualization. I also like to "speak aloud" to my inner child. Do whatever feels comfortable for you.

Here are some questions you can ask your Inner Child to get you started.

How old are you?

This answer may change from day to day. It helps you to visualize the Inner Child more accurately and assess its needs. For example, if your Inner Child presents itself as a two-year-old, it will have far different needs than if it presented itself as a ten-year-old.

What are you feeling right now?

This allows you to check in with the emotions of your Inner Child in real time. If your Inner Child feels sad, confused, or exhausted, you can give it some love, clarity, encouraging words, and attention. This can help you to go back to your adult responsibilities with more confidence and ease, because you know you've taken the time to nurture the child within.

What do you need more of right now?

For example, your inner child might respond by asking for more rest and relaxation. Even if you're in the middle of a project, you can always compromise by taking a short nap, meditating, or doing a mindless activity for a bit. Maybe your Inner Child just wants to cry for a bit. If so, let him or her cry. Hug yourself as if you were rocking your Inner Child and soothing them. It may seem silly, but it can be so healing when you comfort your Inner Child as an adult in this way.

How would you like to play today?

Play is such an underrated recovery tool, yet it is essential for the Inner Child to regain a sense of their lost childhood. Many of us became adults before we ever got to be children, so Inner Child play is crucial if we want to feel connected with this part of ourselves we never got to fully experience. You owe this to yourself. Maybe your inner child wants to scroll through funny Instagram memes, or play in the pool, or draw pictures, or giggle at funny videos. Carve out some time in the day to let your inner child "play."

Who do you most like spending time with?

This will help you to assess who makes your Inner Child feel really good, and potentially spend more time with people who are similar. Maybe your Inner Child loves seeing your best friend from California who visits every month or so. What qualities does that friend have? Are there similar people you can spend time with?

What is your favorite part of the day?

It may surprise you what your Inner Child perceives to be their most favorite part of the day. Maybe your adult self enjoys winding down with a glass of wine at the end of the evening, but your Inner Child loves that restorative yoga class where they get to feel cradled in blankets at the end of the class during Savasana. Maybe your Inner Child loves bubble baths and rubber ducks. Indulge your Inner Child in their favorite activities every day and give them that carefree childhood they lost out on.

Even just spending twenty minutes each day on your Inner Child's favorite activity can make a huge difference in your overall well-being. And for the overachievers out there feeling anxious about taking this time out for their Inner Child, this break can actually help you with your productivity. Believe it or not, when you take the time please your Inner Child, you get a lot of cooperation from them when returning to "adult" responsibilities!

What made you angry or sad today?

Connecting with what makes the Inner Child angry or sad can help you to better anticipate those emotions and triggers in everyday life. For example, if you find that your Inner Child becomes especially incensed when someone criticizes you at work, perhaps doing some self-soothing before the work day begins or reducing the amount of interactions you have with that particular co-worker throughout the day could help.

What do you love most about our life together?

This helps you to connect with what your Inner Child finds "cool" about your adult life. It is helpful to create a mutual appreciation about the magical things in your adult life, because your Inner Child did not get to experience much magic in their childhood. For example, my Inner Child would marvel at the apartment I live in and the city I get to explore every day. What would your Inner Child be astonished by? This exercise can also help you to cultivate a sense of gratitude and gaze through your life through the lens of childlike wonder.

Connecting with Rage

Many adult children of narcissists are divorced from their rage. They may have been taught in childhood that rage is "bad" and shamed for ever expressing their anger. Women especially are socialized by society to bury their anger because it is "unladylike."

I like to think of rage as the inner child crying out, defending itself, and saying, "No, I will not let you do that to me again." The valid anger you experienced at the injustice you endured should not be buried or repressed, because it is likely to come out in maladaptive ways.

You might find yourself expressing your rage by:

- Lashing out at others.
- Self-sabotaging.
- Criticizing yourself excessively.
- Being passive-aggressive.
- Turning inward in self-hatred.
- Cutting or using drugs.
- Feeling helpless and crying any time something goes wrong.

To connect with your anger, ask yourself the following questions:

When I get angry, where do I feel it in my body? (ex. I feel my stomach tightening up into knots, I feel my hands shake.)

_____

_____

_____

How do I usually react in situations where I should be angry or am taken advantage of? (ex. I go into "fight" mode – I am ready to take down whoever has violated me or, I feel so paralyzed by fear and helplessness that I go numb and silent. The other person never gets to know how I really felt.)

_____

_____

_____

What are the injustices I've suffered, that are making me angry? (ex. In my childhood, I was chronically bullied by my parents and peers to feel less than. Any time someone tries to bully me now, I become incredibly enraged.)

_____

_____

_____

What boundaries have been crossed? Or, alternatively, what need is not being met? (ex. Someone raised their voice at me and is talking down to me. This is the boundary that has been crossed. Or, my boyfriend is not validating my emotions when I tell him how hurt I felt when he said something rude. This isn't meeting my emotional need to be seen and heard).

_____

_____

_____

What healthy ways can I release some of my anger now and honor it? (ex. I can vent to my therapist, I can go for a run, I can enroll in a kickboxing course, I can write in my journal, I can write an unsent letter, etc.)

_____

_____

_____

Know that:

You have a right to be angry when someone mistreats you.

Anger is an emotion, it doesn't have to be "right" or "wrong."

There are ways to express and channel your anger that doesn't involve violence or "being bad," whatever your inner critic might tell you.

Anger is often a sign that some need is not being met or that a right or boundary has been violated. If you can figure out which one it is, you can then brainstorm ways to meet that need, request what you need, or reinforce the boundary that has been crossed.

You can channel your rage constructively by:

Writing an unsent letter to your narcissistic parent, outlining all uncensored thoughts and feelings you have regarding how they treated you. Therapist Lindsay Gibson suggests using the frame of, "How dare you" when expressing your anger about the narcissistic parent, to adequately connect to the outrage that you could not as a helpless child.

Start by writing or speaking into a tape recorder using "How dare you do this…" as a frame. List each and every injustice. Feel outraged on behalf of the helpless child you once were, and recognize that as an adult, you don't have to put up with it any longer. If you feel incredibly triggered by this exercise, enlist the help of your therapist or a supportive, loving witness.

Finding a physical outlet. Whether it's kickboxing, frenzied dancing, or running, finding a physical outlet for the anger you're experiencing can be life-saving. This is especially important for those of us who have a tendency to become paralyzed by our rage or dissociate from it.

For example, I always thought that I was *never* someone who was divorced from my rage – in fact, I was far more divorced from my grief. Anger was where it was at! I loved using my anger as an incentive to achieve my goals. I found that it gave me a sense of power and I have always been able to channel my rage into so many productive outlets.

However, after years of writing in this field, I realized that each time I experienced a cyberbully and troll, I would quietly bury the anger in my heart and move on with my day. When my sister got me a punching bag for Christmas, that all shifted. I finally had an outlet other than rage running for whenever my "fight, flight or freeze" response kicked in as a response to a horrific online psychopath – rather than burying the anger, I "punched" it out - *and* I got to have a healthy workout, each and every time.

Get creative! There are many ways to release your rage that won't leave you having a shame spiral afterwards.

Creative outlets. Writing has been a major creative outlet for me to constructively channel my anger. What creative outlets would help you to connect with your emotions? It could be art, music, graphic design, blogging, making videos – find ways to channel your anger into something that could potentially speak to the world.

If you want to solidify your commitment to connecting with your rage, write a letter to your angry Inner Child or Anger as an emotion in general, apologizing to it for not acknowledging it sooner. Then, make a pledge to honor it from now on. I've written a sample letter below:

Dear Anger:

I've run from you for a long time. I didn't want to believe I could ever be an angry person. It seemed "unspiritual" and unforgiving to hold a grudge. Bitter, even. But the truth is, what I am feeling right now has every right to be there. I know I experienced a lot of injustice that I never deserved. I know that the people who terrorized me did very bad things and were horrible humans. They behaved in deplorable ways, and it's okay for me to see the reality of that instead of pretending they weren't. It wasn't fair, and I didn't deserve it. I have a right to feel angry. I have a right to find a healthy way to express my anger and to release it or channel it. I have a right to use my anger constructively to set boundaries and to know when I am being violated. I know now it is okay to be angry, and that I have rights too. I don't have to violate the rights of others to express my anger. I plan to do it in a way that is safe, and if at any time it gets too overwhelming, I promise I'll consult a professional. I promise that from now on, when I feel anger, I won't try to numb it out, escape from it, or ignore it. You're there for a reason. I just need to figure out what it is, and use you in a way that benefits me.

Thank you for standing up for me.

Love,
Survivor

Connecting with Grief and Loss

On the flip side of anger is grief. Those of us who are perpetually angry but rarely grieve need to reconnect with the part of ourselves which carries the deep sadness of our lost childhood. Whenever that deep sadness, grief, or heartache comes up, adult children of narcissists tend to find ways to shut down or make themselves numb to the pain. They may dissociate by engaging in daydreaming or fantasy (especially retaliation fantasies which allow them to avenge their perpetrators). They may bury their grief in alcohol, compulsive shopping, gambling, sex, overeating. There are many ways in which we try to avoid the excruciating pain of our childhood wounds.

As Dr. Susan Forward writes in her book, *Mothers Who Can't Love*, "All those years of humiliation and pain don't magically vanish. The wounded child is an energy that's still alive inside, and that child is still afraid of being hurt...People often defend themselves against feelings of deep vulnerability with explosive anger." Our anger certainly has its place, but so does our grief.

Both grief and anger need to be expressed in order for us to heal.
Another way we attempt to bury our grief is by spiritually bypassing it. We may attend spiritual workshops where gurus tell us

secret mantras to magically morph our grief into transcendence. We may "numb" ourselves with our faith and belief systems, believing it was all for the greater good, so there is no need to confront the pain. But here is what some spiritual gurus get wrong about trauma: trauma cannot be spiritually bypassed. It must be processed within a safe space. Spirituality is a beautiful thing, but we don't need to negate the pain in order to believe in a greater meaning. We can pray even while acknowledging our wounds. We can give thanks and feel immense gratitude for what we have, even while honoring the injustices we went through.

What if I told you that the only way out of the sadness is through it? Connecting with the pain of a lost childhood, a parent that may have never loved us the way we deserved to be loved, and all of the traumatic effects of that abuse, can actually help us to heal. When the pain is felt, we can then slowly unburden ourselves, grieving our losses. No matter how long it takes to do so, grieving is an essential part of our healing journey. Take your time and be gentle with yourself. The more we avoid the pain, the more we compound the trauma. Finding healthy ways to grieve is essential.

Ask yourself the following questions and write your responses in a journal:

What does the grief feel like? If I could draw a picture of it, what would it look like? (ex. It feels heavy and overwhelming, or, it feels like I am numb. It's like the grief is frozen inside of me and I can't reach it. If I drew a picture of it, it would look like heavy black tar weighing down on my chest, or a huge set of bricks blocking me from seeing past it.)

_____

_____

_____

Where do I feel the grief in my body? (ex. I feel a void in my heart, I feel stabbing pains in my chest.)

_____

_____

_____

When does the grief usually come up? What do I do when it does?
(ex. I feel a terrible sense of loss when I look at children with loving parents on the street. But rather than acknowledging my deep sadness, I try to dissociate and tell myself that I don't need anyone, anyways).

_____

_____

_____

How can I make my grief work for me, rather than against me?
(ex. I can use my grief to finally address some core wounds that need healing. I can channel my grief to create something that helps others suffering like I am. I can use my grief as an incentive to show greater compassion for myself).

_____

_____

_____

As you work through your grief with a trauma-informed counselor, here are some ways you can grieve outside of the therapy space:

Let your Inner Child (and any active Inner Parts) know that whatever you are feeling is okay. Whenever you find yourself confronting intense emotions, speak to them in a gentle voice and tell them, "It's okay to feel sad. I won't judge you. Whatever you feel right now is okay. If you want to cry, cry. I'll be here for you every step of the way."

Physically cradle yourself. Wrap yourself in a warm blanket, or give yourself a tight hug, as you say these soothing words or whenever you are crying. Place your hand over your heart or cheek as if you were speaking to someone you truly adored and loved. Caress your own hair as if you were a mother caressing her child's head and soothing her to sleep. If you are unable to cry, simply be there with that numbness and mindfully breathe through it. Honor the numb feeling and know that it's trying to protect you, and let it know that you'll be there for it for whenever it's ready to uncover the real emotions bottled within.

Connect with your grief through art. Art therapy can be a great way to express buried emotions. Draw what you think your wounded Inner Child looks like. Doodle on a sketchpad or paint on an entire canvas. Use colors to connect with different emotions. Draw words in big letters which represent the wounded child and express what you went through. Words like, "Hurting," "Deprived," "Neglected" are accurate descriptors for adult children of narcissists. Then, draw empowering and self-soothing messages in big letters for yourself. "I love you." "I'll protect you." "I am here for you." "I will save you. "I am my own savior." Messages like these remind you that you are your own knight in shining armor.

Practice self-compassion. Tara Brach has an excellent acronym, RAIN, to help you do so. You can find it on her website at www.tarabrach.com. When you find yourself speaking to yourself with negative self-talk, judgment, or the same type of contempt that your parents spoke to you with, stop and pause. Remind yourself that you are a child of God or the universe. You are divine. You do not deserve to be spoken to in that way. Tell yourself, "You are doing the best that you can. That's all anyone can ask for. You were just a child when you were abused. There was nothing you could've done to stop the abuse. You deserved so much better. The abuse ends now. You won't continue the cycle. Be gentle with yourself. I love you."

Find emotional anchors to connect with buried emotions. Some therapists recommend "exaggerating" any emotions that come up by physically expressing those emotions (for example, scrunching up your face and pretending to sob) so you can tap into these emotions. You might listen to a sad song, reminisce nostalgically over a memory or watch a sad movie if you really want to tap into the grief. However, I would always recommend consulting with a therapist first before doing this if you feel this would be too overwhelming for you.

Know that:

It's okay to feel sad, depressed, lonely, or scared.

It's okay to not be okay.

It's okay to take your time to grieve your losses.

It's okay to go back to the grief when you're ready to feel it.

It's okay to reach out for help.

It's okay to "mother" yourself as you cry.

It's okay to be held by others as you cry.

If you can't cry, that's okay too.

You don't always have to be society's image of "strong." There is immense strength that lies in your vulnerability, in your ability to feel and the ability to allow yourself to feel what you feel.

The grief will come and go. You may feel you've released all of it, only for it to come back. The truth is, you are experiencing the intense pain that has been buried for decades bit by bit. It may come in pieces. It will take time. Be gentle with yourself. You are worthy of your own compassion.

Write a letter to yourself and the abused child you once were with the utmost compassion and tenderness. Read it to yourself whenever you feel overwhelmed by grief or record it on a tape-recorder, so you can listen to it whenever you need to. I've included a sample letter below.

Dear Little One,

I am so sorry you were abandoned. You didn't deserve to be called names and put down so often. You didn't deserve any of the abuse or the bullying you went through. The ones who should have protected you violated you. It was never your fault. You must know – it was never your fault. You were innocent. You did nothing wrong. You deserved to be cherished and seen for the beautiful treasure you are. You are so smart, lovely, and kind. You are so beautiful, inside and out. I am so glad you were born and brought into this world. You have so much to offer. You are so strong. Everything you feel right now is okay. It's okay to cry. You deserved so much better. I will never leave you. I am always here if you need me. You are never alone.

Love,
Survivor

Communication Skills

for Dealing with Difficult Parents

There are a variety of techniques you can use when you're forced to deal with a toxic parent. If you have a physically violent parent, I recommend staying away from them altogether and avoiding any face-to-face communication. However, if you are in contact with a non-violent (at least physically) parent, I list some of the methods you might find helpful below. See which technique works best for you. You should also speak with a therapist if you have any doubts about using a certain method to communicate with your parent.

Broken Record Technique

Repeat your "no" or boundary if they continue pestering you. For example, if your narcissistic parent tells you that you must come home for the holidays and you are unable to, you would exercise this technique by continually saying, "No, I won't be able to make it."

Assert and Exit

Asserting yourself and exiting means that not only do you set a boundary, you follow through with the consequences by enforcing that boundary. For example:

"If you don't stop yelling, I am going to hang up the phone." You then hang up the phone if they continue to yell.

"If you call me at work again, I'll have to block your number." The next time they do call you while you're at work, you block them on your phone.

Third Party Support

Bring a third party "witness" with you if you are required to attend an event with the narcissistic parent. This witness should know about the abusive nature of the narcissistic parent and be well aware of how these types can turn on the charm around strangers. Many parents will either tone down their abusive tactics around third parties or, if they do bring out the abuse, you will at least have someone to give you moral support.

Non-defensive Response

The non-defensive response can help to deescalate the drama if the narcissistic parent is attempting to emotionally bait you with an insulting remark, passive-aggressive comment or guilt trip. In order to respond non-defensively, you keep a neutral tone, try not to emotionally react, and simply say one of the following:

"Interesting that you would see it that way."
"I see."
"I don't agree, but okay."
"Funny you would say that."
"I see it quite differently."

The Handy Excuse

Keep a list of excuses handy if you have a narcissistic parent who is overbearing and enmeshed, constantly checking up on you or hovering over you whenever you visit. You can pull out these excuses to cut an intense conversation short without letting them in on the fact that you don't wish to talk to them – which is something that can feed into the drama as they lash out at you for not being the dutiful daughter or son.

The handy excuse could sound like the following:

"Hate to get off the phone, but I have to eat dinner now. Talk to you another time."

"Mom? Someone's at the door. I'll have to call you later."

"I am feeling ill. Let me visit another time."

"I have to pick up the kids early, seems like the babysitter's unavailable. I'll visit you another time!"

"Dad? I am actually in the middle of cooking a meal. I'll talk to you another time."

The Redirect

Narcissistic parents are notorious for baiting their adult children into conversations which belittle them. The redirect method depends on the fact that they can become distracted if you ask about something that's important to them, their self-image and reputation. It feeds their ego rather than feeding into their need to demean you. For example, a narcissistic mother might ask, "You know, your cousin Nancy just got engaged to a doctor. When do you think you'll get engaged, Carol?"

You then redirect by saying something like, "Interesting! Hey mom, didn't you tell me that you had that Tupperware party last week? How did that go?"

Redirect to a topic you know they can't resist. If your parent is a gossiper, for example, you might redirect to a rumor you heard in the neighborhood. If your parent hates their boss, redirect the conversation to how their work is treating them these days. The possibilities are endless. Narcissistic parents simply can't resist a topic that gives them the reins to feed their own toxicity. Once you set this "trap," it's very difficult for a narcissistic parent to continue baiting you unless they are very determined, because they are quite self-centered people.

Stick to the Facts

Since it is common for narcissistic parents to gaslight their adult children, it's important to stick to the facts whenever you're met with a gaslighting attempt.

For example, if your narcissistic father claims something outrageous like, "You and your sister never visit us anymore! You're such ungrateful children!" you might respond with:

"Actually, dad, we visited last week. Let's not make up stories."

Your toxic parent may still continue to try to gaslight you, but let it fall on deaf ears. Keep repeating the facts and then exit if they refuse to acknowledge them.

Dating With Detachment

Many adult children of narcissists struggle with the idea of dating, even after they've done a substantial amount of inner work and healing. For those who have insecure attachment styles, it's important to experiment with **_healthy detachment._** This state of neutrality is empowering because it allows you to become an observer, rather than actively participating in trying to please someone.

What's important to remember is that dating is not about commitment. It's important to distinguish between the two. People could date for a variety of reasons that may not lead to commitment.

When you are healthily detached, you no longer depend on the other person to be anything other than who they really are. Think of it this way: you're just coming to witness their true character unfold. Sure, you might enjoy their company and learn a lot about one another in the beginning, but the true aim of dating is to assess compatibility and not to make assumptions about them being a good match _unless_ they've proven that to you. From there, you will decide whether this is a person you want to continue seeing or not.

Read the two rulebooks below. The first one is likely very much the subconscious script you've been going by when you've been dating someone. The second rulebook is what you will try to practice from now on to experiment with healthy detachment.

The Old Ways of Dating, According To Your Formerly Anxious and Insecure Attachment Style

RULE #1: The next person I date *has* to be the one. They just have to! Even if they aren't, I am going to put my blinders on and pretend they are, ignoring all of the red flags and incompatibility issues.

RULE #2: This person has to complete me and save me from myself.

RULE #3: I am going to force myself to trust this person blindly and assume he or she is being honest. After all, I can't be insecure or mistrusting if I want a great partner, right?

RULE #4: I can't displease this person or they'll abandon me! The horror!

RULE #5: I have to prove that I am worthy.

The New Rules of Dating, According to Your New Healthy Detachment

RULE #1: This person may or may not be compatible for me. That's what I am trying to find out by going on dates with them.

RULE #2: I am already whole and complete. I would like someone who adds joy and support to my life, but they won't be the center of my existence. We can depend on each other in healthy ways without becoming consumed by each other.

RULE #3: Trust has to be earned. I barely know this person. I can be cautiously optimistic, but I won't turn a blind eye to any red flags or dealbreakers.

RULE #4: If this person abandons me because I set a boundary or stick to my core values, so be it! That means we were never compatible to begin with. Anyone who is willing to abandon me for being myself is not someone who would be a good relationship partner in the long-term.

RULE #5: I am already worthy. But is this person right for *me*? Do *I* like this person? How do *I* authentically feel about this person?

Many of us go into dating anxious about the outcome. We treat dating as a game to prove our worthiness, when we are already worthy. A part of our subconscious programming tells us that we must find a savior, a tribe, a partner, a family – we just must! It just has to work out! And if it doesn't, we attribute it to our lack of self-worth, or some defect. Something about "us" must have led the person to abandon us, right? Or so we think. Rarely do we realize that the actions of others often have nothing to do with us, and that someone else's personal preferences has very little bearing on our actual self-worth.

> Imagine what it would be like to date with the expectation that it will not work out. What would that feel like? What if the knight in shining armor never came? Or, better yet, what if the knight in shining armor did come – but it was us, all along?

Adult children of narcissists who have ambivalent attachment styles might have one foot in, one foot out the door as soon as they begin to have a connection with someone. Those with anxious-preoccupied attachment styles may become obsessed with a partner right away without even getting to know them and their true character. Adult children of narcissists may also find themselves sabotaging themselves and becoming entrapped in another vicious cycle with yet another narcissist or sociopath. That's why, as I wrote about in my essay on healing while being single, it's important to take a substantial amount of time out for ourselves – alone – to heal.

After you've done that and gotten back into the dating game, you have to approach it differently than you've ever done before. You have to enter it with no expectation for a set outcome – at least, not with the specific person you just met. This fact may make perfectionistic and idealistic adult children of narcissists incredibly anxious. Wait, you may be asking. *Are you telling me I have to be uncertain about where this is going and I still have to impress another person? What fresh hell is this?*

Well, you do have to embrace the uncertainty that is dating. But forget so much about impressing the other person – yes, you may do a little of that on a first date, as everyone loves to make a good first impression. You're here to see if the other person is actually compatible or not. That means that if you discover, at any point, that they have emotionally unavailable traits, narcissistic tendencies, or an addiction that's taking over their lives – press pause, now. You cannot fix them. You cannot heal them. They need a therapist, not your love and empathy. And it's better you learned that sooner than later.

It's important to have a life outside of any significant partner that may enter it. That means that you have a healthy support network, a career, passion or mission that you're pursuing or actively engaged in, your unique hobbies and interests, and that you have a healthy sense of self. If one of these areas is lacking, you might still be tempted to fill the void with a boyfriend or girlfriend. Do yourself a favor and work on those first *prior* to committing to a long-term relationship.

This is also *not* about being guarded all the time or expecting perfection. You can be optimistic, yet cautious, about anyone who enters your life. You can remain neutral *until* you see red flag behaviors or consistent signs that this person may truly be a healthy and compatible partner for you.

If you're used to becoming attached to a dating partner too quickly, now is the perfect time to start practicing this healthy detachment.

Remember, you are now your own savior and knight in shining armor. You are the one you've been waiting for. You are the one who will now be looking out for your own best interests. You are the only one who can give yourself unconditional love and support. So, in order to practice healthy detachment, you might try the following things:

Rather than texting or calling that person immediately when you start dating, you wait a bit. It's very exciting to be in contact with the person you desire, I know. But, *unless* you're in a long-term committed relationship, slowing down the pace, speed and frequency of the contact will help you discover more about the person. It will help you discover whether they respect your boundaries or lash out when they feel that you're practicing healthy detachment.

Do they continue to repeatedly text you for a response even though you've only gone a few minutes without talking? This is a huge red flag of controlling behavior. Even just waiting an hour more than you usually do to respond and doing something productive – soaking in a bubble bath, going for a run at the gym, or working on a project, can really help to put in focus the person who is most important: you.

A Note About Sexual Boundaries

It's important that any dating partner who enters your life understands how far you are willing to go with them sexually. Rushing intimacy can cloud perceptions and many survivors actually end up dating narcissistic people due to the fast-forwarding nature of the relationship. If you don't feel comfortable having sex with someone in the first few dates, you can express that. If you don't want to really get physical aside from kissing at all within the first week, stick to that. If they leave, they were going to anyway.

Trust your instincts – and your body. If you sense something is "off" about a potential dating partner, trust yourself. It is those "tiny terrors" which inevitably escalate to terrible acts of psychological violence later on. "Small" red flags like off-color jokes, a weird sarcastic comment, a covert put-down, or an amused smirk after a taunt can all be tip-offs that you may be dealing with someone sadistic. You can read more about the signs of psychopathic dating partners on my Psych Central blog, *Recovering From A Narcissist*.

Your body also knows before you do whether or not you're in the presence of someone toxic. If you have unpleasant visceral reactions to someone, there may be a reason. For example, I remember when I began dating one particularly manipulative person, I got the intense feeling of sharp pain in my lower back, almost like knives were cutting into me. This happened after a strange conversation we had. He "seemed" so nice in the beginning, so this physical reaction seemed quite out of place. It turned out he had quite a few sociopathic traits and had no problem treating me and others with cruelty and brutal indifference. With another dating partner, I literally would get the sensation of wanting to throw up in my mouth after we would talk. I would *actually gag*. It turned out that he had a significant other he had been hiding from me and a few other girls. His double life and pathological lying were beyond anything I had ever experienced before, which explained why I had such an intense physical reaction to him that I've never had with anyone else.

Yet on the surface and at the onset, both men appeared normal, sensitive, handsome, caring, successful, and desirable. My body just sensed something about their true callous nature before I consciously confirmed it. If you're an empathic, highly sensitive person, you're more likely to get these bodily sensations and visceral reactions to predators earlier and more intensely than most people. Pay attention and heed the alarm.

Schedule dates on a timetable that seem comfortable to you. You don't have to see someone five times in a week to get to know them. Take things slowly and assess your own comfort levels. Seeing a dating partner once a week might be the most appropriate level of investment early on. See how your dating partner reacts to you slowing down: if they pressure you in any way or disappear altogether, then you know that they most likely had an agenda in mind. When people truly want to get to know you, they know there's no rush. They move at a steady pace because they want to get to know you organically.

Have basic and personal boundaries in place *before* **you start dating.** Basic boundaries are all about respecting your basic rights as a human being – such as the right to not be abused, the right to be respected, the right to privacy. As I've mentioned before, you can brush up on your basic rights by reading Pete Walker's Human Bill of Rights.

Personal boundaries, on the other hand, are the custom physical, emotional and interpersonal boundaries which are unique to you.

A great way to think about what your personal boundaries would be is to evaluate toxic experiences you've had with partners in the past. What did you provide for these partners that you rarely received back? Are there healthy relationships you've observed as an outsider you can use as "models"? Perhaps your friends have relationship partners who have qualities you would like in a partner and you know *those* partners would never do certain things to hurt you. What are those behaviors which disturb you and ultimately feel violating to you? What are behaviors which ultimately uplift you and make you feel supported and loved?

I have a personal boundary where, if someone doesn't seem interested in my work or goes so far as to minimize or undercut it in any way, I immediately detach from them. Why? Because I am interested in my partner's career and support his goals. I expect the same kind of respect. That is a personal boundary – not everyone needs someone who will show interest in their career. Not everyone makes work a priority. However, it's probably a boundary many of us *should* have because that kind of pathological envy is a huge red flag of a toxic partner. How someone acts towards your success and passion in life can tell you a lot about their character.

This is a boundary I developed after I encountered an abuser who was envious of my career and would actively try to sabotage me. Mind you, I did everything I could to support him. I had also encountered a few dating partners who showed signs of jealousy or feeling emasculated when they realized that I was financially independent, lived alone in my own apartment, and had a career of my own. Sadly, this is more of a common experience for women than we would assume.

The next step, after you've decided on a boundary, is to actively follow through with it. I no longer tolerate that double standard and believe that a healthy partnership requires both partners being each other's biggest cheerleaders. Otherwise, what is the point? If a dating partner doesn't ask follow-up questions about my passion in this life, I am not interested in them. It doesn't matter if they're a 6'2 Adonis with a Ph.D, chiseled jaw and rare signs of emotional availability. I require that a future partner supports my mission on this earth, just as I will do for them. Because I know I am emotionally generous and conscientious about encouraging my partner, I know I am deserving of the same.

This is the tricky part. We can sometimes get sidetracked by how good a dating partner looks on paper. But if this is a non-negotiable personal boundary, it's there to protect you from something which would cause you harm in the long-term. If you would be personally unhappy staying with someone who engages in certain harmful behavior, honor that. It will help you cut out incompatible and potentially abusive people from your life earlier on.

Another personal boundary could be not tolerating anyone who is excessively sarcastic and condescending. While I do think this type of behavior *can* be abusive, I know that other people enjoy a sarcastic sense of humor, so this is still a personal boundary and not necessarily universal. Someone else might actually enjoy constant sarcastic remarks because they have a similar sense of humor. As a highly sensitive person, I simply do not, and I've learned to no longer make apologies for that. There is no need for me to bury my discomfort every time a potential partner makes a remark like this – guaranteed, they wouldn't do the same for me – so we are both better off finding someone more compatible.

Make your own personal boundaries list of at least ten non-negotiables and how you will follow through with the boundary in cases where it is not respected.

A sample personal boundary list might look like the following:
I will not allow anyone to talk down to me. If someone talks down to me, I will call it out. If they refuse to apologize and change their behavior, I will cut ties with them.

If someone is excessively sarcastic and condescending, I will let them know I don't appreciate that kind of behavior. If they refuse to tone it down, I am out.

If someone tries to make me jealous, I won't tolerate it. I will either detach or call them out if I feel comfortable doing so.

Someone I date should respect and take an active interest in my career and passions. They will encourage me. If they discourage me or become envious at any point, I will no longer continue to see them.

I will take things slow sexually. If a partner pressures me to fast-forward intimacy, I will opt out of dating them.

I will be spoken to respectfully. That means no put-downs, no backhanded comments, no minimizing my success or positive attributes. If I experience any of these, I will leave. Nobody gets to make me feel small, especially not my intimate partner.

Overcoming Self-Isolation

A number of adult children of narcissists struggle with self-isolation due to fear and mistrust – and understandably so. Even before you attempt to overcome self-isolation, it's important to first learn how to enjoy your own company. Make a habit of taking yourself out on "dates" – treat yourself to your favorite meal, a funny movie, a daytime stroll in the park, a trip to a cabin in the woods. Sit with the discomfort of being alone until you become accustomed to it as a place of safety, clarity and calm. Learn how to ease your Inner Critic. Work with your counselor to lessen your hypervigilance. These will all help you as you break out of your cocoon.

Solitude can be a necessary component of the healing journey, but relational healing includes a safe community and trusted allies. Therapists, life coaches, friends, family members, supportive co-workers – can all be helpful in overcoming a pattern of self-isolation. As you work through your trauma symptoms with a trusted, trauma-informed therapist, you can take baby steps in gradually dissolving the barrier of self-isolation.

One way I've done this on my healing journey is by incorporating daily "safe indirect community time" into my schedule. This means finding a community that doesn't require your active engagement. Let me explain. Many adult children of narcissists may shy away from activities that require them to interact with others directly. The threat of intimacy and exposure can be very anxiety-provoking for survivors who are still gun-shy from severe trauma and are simply looking for a sense of community without the need to expose themselves and be vulnerable in the early stages of healing.

Meditation workshops, gyms, and yoga classes are perfect "indirect" community safe spaces, and are ideal for the beginning of the healing journey. The main focus is on the activity, not on directly interacting with one another, which relieves the pressure of having to "perform" for others or to impress anyone. Instead, you're all joined by a shared activity and goal. You then have the option of organically meeting people by the virtue of having similar outlooks and core values, which is a lot less stressful than an event super focused on finding friends or a relationship partner. You can even go to cafes where all the baristas and customers are all familiar to each other, or a community center with sports.

Low-investment hobby and interest groups. Sitting down with a group of people who share your hobbies and interests can also be helpful in reaping all the benefits of community without pressures. What are low-investment communities you could join right now? Some ideas might be: joining a local church service, a book club, a knitting club, a running club (also great for fitness, so that's a plus!), a writing club, a fan club for a book series (Harry Potter, anyone?) or television series.

Get creative and explore your local Meetup groups! Meetups have the additional benefit of being very low-investment when it comes to special events as well. For example, you could attend a cool 90's dance party if you are feeling up to some fun with no commitment to ever seeing the people you meet there again. This is the perfect level of investment for a survivor in the early stages of the recovery journey who wants to start exploring what's out there without cultivating lifelong friendships with the first people they meet.

Online forums and pages. There are many online support groups for survivors of narcissists out there. Find one that speaks to you and has the level of privacy you're comfortable with. A simple google search, Facebook page search or search on Instagram for hashtags or profiles listed under "adult children of narcissists" "narcissistic abuse" and "narcissistic abuse survivors" can yield multiple groups which share inspirational memes and informative discussions about healing from this type of abuse. Try to find balanced accounts which address both information about the abuse experience along with empowering messages for the healing journey.

On the next level of community are support groups, which require more active engagement with others and more intimacy. Many adult children of narcissists reported being helped by groups such as CoDA (Co-Dependents Anonymous) and 12-Step programs such as AL-Anon. Once you've begun work to clear some of the trauma with a therapist of your choice, you may want to consider entering one of these programs.

A therapeutic alliance and relationship with your therapist are important because you do want to be able to do inner work even without the support group and these groups can provide much-needed relational healing. It is this type of healing that is so important for survivors of childhood trauma. It can be helpful to have a validating safe space where your stories are heard. Hearing the stories of others can also remind you that you're not alone. You can learn more about the power of support groups in the chapter "Healing Modalities for Adult Children of Narcissists."

Coping and Emotional Regulation

Skills for Adult Children of Narcissists

When we grow up in emotionally abusive households, our skill sets for emotional regulation can become quite dysfunctional. As we've learned throughout this book, adult children of narcissists can become quite prone to burying their emotions and resorting to self-destructive coping methods in times of distress. Learning valuable emotional regulation skills can be life-changing for when we encounter crisis in our lives. Ideally, practicing these skill sets and tools can help them to become hardwired, automatic behaviors so that they become the first course of action we take when we're confronted by conflict, chaos, or any form of emotional turmoil.

SKILL #1: Mindfulness

Mindfulness is the ability to bring yourself back to the present moment, and it is an essential life skill for adult children of narcissists to have. The capacity to attend back to yourself, your emotions, your breath, and your environment is extremely useful when you're plagued by emotional fatigue, overwhelm, or hijacked by a trigger that causes you to regress back into childhood states of hopelessness and fear.

5-minute meditation break: One popular way to practice mindfulness, and one we've already discussed extensively, is meditation. Even a five-minute breathing meditation like this can work wonders to bring us back to a state of calm. If you're looking for a laugh and don't mind strong language, I always love listening to this hilariously irreverent mediation which uses dark humor to snap you out of your negative thought processes and coax you into mindfully breathing through stress. Or, you may prefer this ten-minute guided imagery meditation.

However, you can also be mindful in other ways. Simply becoming aware of your breath can help you to slow down your breathing and practice what is known as deep breathing.

Practice deep breathing: An effective way to do this is by inhaling through your nose for a count of four, then exhaling through your nose for a count of six. Repeating this process several times has the effect of slowing your heart rate and giving your parasympathetic system a boost. While the sympathetic nervous system prepares our body for the fight or flight response, releasing stress hormones like cortisol and adrenaline, the parasympathetic nervous system helps us to recover from stress.

Mindfulness and grounding can also be accessed through "noticing" and "observing" through our five senses. You can notice the colors in your room, the smell of your coffee, the sound of cars outside, the feeling of your shirt's fabric against your skin, and the taste of your oatmeal. You can also observe your emotions, thoughts, and body from a detached, nonjudgmental perspective.

Ground yourself with this sensory awareness exercise: Name five things in your environment you can see, four things you can hear, three things you can touch, two things you can taste, and one thing that you smell.

Notice the tension in your body. Are your fists clenched? Is there tension in your jaw? Tightening in your stomach? Do you feel sadness? Or anger? Or shame? What kind of thoughts are running through your mind? What topic does your mind keep running towards? Just notice these thoughts – don't jump to categorize them as "bad" or "good." Just let them be, and observe how they float into various tangents. You may benefit from imagining your thoughts as leaves on a river floating downstream, or written on clouds passing by.

Do a body scan: From head to toe, notice the tension in each part of your body. You might exaggerate the tension before letting it go.

Mindfulness can also help you take actions that are most conducive to your well-being. If you find that you are overly anxious about something, you can notice any thoughts feeding into that anxiety and figure out whether there tends to be a pattern of thinking that evokes greater anxiety in you than usual. If you observe that there is immense tension in certain parts of your body, you can find ways to release that tension and address any trapped traumas that may be exacerbating that tension. If you notice your emotions during a heated conflict, you can mindfully address both your triggers and feelings without being reactive. This can also help you to manage your emotional flashbacks. Let's say a toxic co-worker is deliberately provoking you at work by criticizing a project that you did. Rather than automatically jumping to the conclusion, "This person is ruining my life," or, "I am so incompetent," mindfulness allows you to say, "I notice I am feeling judged and ashamed. I notice I am getting increasingly angry with each comment this co-worker is making. I am having an emotional flashback. This reminds me of something from childhood. It reminds me of the way my mother would criticize me."

Mindfulness helps us to "begin again." Since we are taking a pause before we react to something, we now have the option of acting differently than we would have if we had rushed into our emotions and launched into a defensive attack. Perhaps you choose to take some deep breaths before exiting the conversation with your co-worker politely, or you choose to assert yourself in a calmer, more confident manner than you usually would. Knowing that this person has similar narcissistic tendencies as your parent is helpful information. You know that this co-worker's criticism may have nothing to do with you or your competence; this has the effect of freeing you from self-judgment or self-blame. You now have the power to observe the toxic actions of others from a detached perspective. When we are allowed to observe the chaos from a place of calm observation, we can then better look for solutions rather than continuing to feed into the problem.

> *MINDFULNESS TIP* - Do a quick "self-care" check every day: Have you eaten today? Have you showered today? Did you drink a glass of water? Get some fresh air, sunlight, and exercise? Reach out to a friend? It's hard to be mindful or grounded when we haven't physically or emotionally given ourselves the basics.

SKILL #2: Distraction

Distraction can be a powerful coping method in times of distress. When we don't feel we have the ability to strategically address overwhelming emotions, it can be helpful to take a break and distract ourselves with a pleasurable activity, knowing that we can come back to the problem when we are in a better emotional state.

Some effective distraction activities can include things like the following:

Going out for a walk or a run. This will release endorphins which will help you enter into a more positive and empowered emotional state.

Coloring in an adult coloring book. Research shows that structured coloring exercises can reduce anxiety, increase perseverance and enhance mood. This is also a perfect way to soothe your Inner Child.

Play a video game like Tetris. There's been exciting research that suggests that playing a game of Tetris disrupts the formation of mental imagery involved in PTSD-induced flashbacks due to its visual-spatial demands on the brain.

> *Exercise:* Choose ten distraction activities you can do from the following list: **101 Distraction Techniques: Tools for Intrusive Trauma Symptoms**.

SKILL #3: Visualization

Visualization can be enormously helpful when coping with a stressful situation. We can visualize the best-case scenarios in times of crisis to soothe ourselves. We can visualize ourselves in a safe space when we feel anxious (more on how to do that here). We can visualize placing the problem in a box and temporarily shutting it out of our mind as we go on with our day – we know we can always return to it later when we are ready.

Fun fact: According to brain scans, our brains **actually can't tell the difference** between when we're vividly imagining something and when we're actually doing it. That's great news for those of us who have very vivid imaginations! So, today, practice imagining the best-case scenario or what you *want* to happen rather than what you don't want to happen. If you need help, look up images or videos which can serve as visual aids for what you want to manifest. You can also visualize a beautiful place in nature and create your safe place there whenever you have an anxious thought. The possibilities are truly endless.

SKILL #4: Cognitive Reframing

If you've ever attended Cognitive-Behavior Therapy, you've probably already benefited from an essential life skill known as *cognitive reframing.* As adult children of narcissists, we are prone to numerous cognitive distortions spawned by the negative belief systems and programming our toxic parents instilled in us. This includes **catastrophizing** (imagining the worst-case scenario and blowing it to epic proportions), **black-and-white thinking** (seeing things as only all good or all bad – we can also perceive ourselves that way), and **emotional reasoning** (which makes us feel like all the terrible shame, fear, and self-hatred we experience must have a basis and must be true).

Cognitive reframing places the power back to us. It allows us to see events from a broader perspective, so that we can brainstorm more empowering narratives, and view ourselves or our life circumstances through a more accurate lens.

So the next time you're...

Thinking that your narcissistic mother was right, you are a terrible person: Write down evidence of the times you've done good things for others and they appreciated it. Reminisce about the friends who love and care for you, and who express gratitude for having you in their lives. Repeat the affirmation, "I am a good person. I always was and always have been. My narcissistic mother was projecting onto me her own insecurities and shortcomings when she told me otherwise."

Catastrophizing about how you won't accomplish that project in time because your toxic father told you that you weren't capable: Remember all the times you completed projects successfully and met your goals. Think about all the achievements you've completed so far. Also, remind yourself that you don't have to perfect. It's okay to make mistakes, postpone things, or change around a deadline occasionally for the sake of your mental health or self-care.

If you're an overachiever, this reframing might cause you some great discomfort and pain initially. But, eventually, as you learn to become more self-compassionate, you also stop catastrophizing and you cut yourself some slack. Repeat the new cognitive reframing affirmation, "I've already been through so much. I don't need to continue to beat up on myself. What my toxic father told me wasn't correct. I am capable of accomplishing great things and I've done so in the past. I am capable of fulfilling my true potential, and I don't have to be perfect all the time to do so."

Believing life is over because someone criticized you: Realize you're likely having an emotional flashback to the all the times your narcissistic parents criticized you. Remember all the support you've gotten from other people *aside* from your toxic parents. Say to yourself, "This is just one person's opinion. A lot of other people support me and encourage me in what I am doing. I support *myself.* Life isn't over and the world won't end just because this one person doesn't see what I am capable of. If anything, this can make me even more motivated to become more confident within myself."

SKILL #5: Gratitude

Gratitude enhances social connectivity, lifts your mood, and reminds you to look at the larger picture. Gratitude is not about ignoring our pain or invalidating it. Our mind already has a tendency to think about negativity and danger more than the positive aspects of life because it's trying to protect us from any kind of threat. Gratitude simply allows us to balance that emotional seesaw by remembering the positive. Cultivating a daily habit of gratitude can do wonders for your overall mental well-being. You can practice gratitude in so many different ways. For example:

- *You can write a gratitude list that you refer to daily which reminds you of all the basic necessities you have as well as the amazing bonuses* (ex. I am grateful to have a roof over my head. I am grateful to have food to eat. I am grateful I can walk. I am grateful I can see. I am grateful for the fact that I love my career. I am grateful that I love the city where I live. I am grateful that I have such amazing friends, etc.).

- *Write in a gratitude journal to remember all the beautiful moments in life that you cherish day by day.* Keeping track of daily blessings can keep you grounded in all the miracles that enter your life that you may otherwise forget. It allows you to keep a record that you can refer to whenever things get tough (ex. Today I spent time with my wonderful puppy, Walter. I am so grateful for the nice weather today and the fact that I have such a lovely pet! I also went to my favorite meditation place, followed by a yoga class. So grateful for the sweet teachers there and the fact that I have the time to relax after a long day.)

- *Decorate and use a gratitude jar.* Decorate a jar with beautiful stickers, positive affirmation magnets and even glitter if you wish – whatever strikes your fancy. Each day or week, however frequently you'd like, write down a small note about something that you're grateful for. You can drop these love notes into a gratitude jar for an entire year or month – however long you want to keep the jar is perfectly okay. Then, at the end of each month or each year, unload the contents of the jar and re-read all the things you were grateful for. This is a fun activity your Inner Child will love, and it has the added bonus of celebrating each month or year that has passed.

- **You can create a bulletin board with images and words that represent what you won't take for granted** (ex. Pictures of you and your significant other, photos of vacations you had the privilege of going on, phrases like, "I am so lucky to have my family." "I am so grateful to be alive." "I have the privilege of doing what I most love." – anything that reminds you of how blessed you are). Alternatively, you can create a Pinterest board or keep a separate Instagram account which celebrates all the things you're grateful for.

- **Give thanks every morning you get up and every night before you go to sleep.** Whether it's in a prayer to God or a simple thank you to the Universe or your Higher Self, give thanks for being alive, for having survived the experiences that you did, for the best thing about your life in the present, and for all the blessings you anticipate receiving in in the future. Example: *Thank you God for keeping me alive. I am so grateful to have survived and thrived after my experiences. I am so grateful for all the infinite miracles and abundance coming my way.* This gratitude method helps you to tackle your past, present, and future in positive ways.

- **Give back.** Giving back to the less fortunate by helping out at your local community center, donating to a cause you care about, or helping out a friend who is struggling can also help *you* in cultivating a sense of gratitude. When we give back, we remember to appreciate all the things we have that other people are still praying for.

11 Self-Directed Activities

For Nourishing The True Self

When we are operating from our wounded inner parts, our true self does not get permission to come out. Once we've uncovered our true self, however, there are eleven self-directed activities we need to engage in order to keep our true self healthy. Adult children of narcissists need these eleven activities in their lives in order to sustain the true self and nourish the true self in their healing journey. These are:

Self-soothing

As children, we had parents who abandoned us when we most needed their compassion and comfort. They were, in fact, the cause of our discomfort. During difficult times, we were left to mend our own scars and wipe our own tears. We may have never learned to self-soothe and instead relied on our natural defense mechanisms – numbing to protect ourselves from the intense pain of abuse, dissociation to escape it, or overeating in an attempt to fill the void. As adults, learning how to self-soothe without blocking out our pain with some form of emotional analgesic is an essential skill. Speaking to ourselves with comforting words, giving ourselves a gentle hug, visualizing holding the wounded child that we have inside of us can all be a part of self-soothing. So can activities like taking a warm salt bath, meditating, breathing mindfully through intense emotions, listening to calming music, doing a body scan, or watching our favorite television show.

Self-praise.

When we are treated as extensions of our parents, we are seen as objects. We learn our roles and our functions, but we do not learn about our inherent self-worth. We learn how to perpetually please, even though to the parent it is never enough. We do not learn how to authentically congratulate ourselves on a job well done or how to give ourselves healthy praise. Learning self-praise is a tool that adult children of narcissists may feel a great deal of discomfort with at first. After all, they've been taught and conditioned to engage in a great deal of negative self-talk. They've been under the scrutiny of a hypercritical caretaker most of their lives and have internalized a lot of the negative messages about themselves. After we have grieved our losses and done some crucial healing work, new, positive, and empowered belief systems can finally become effectively integrated into the psyche. Self-praise can be practiced on a daily basis. Each time you do something well or something you're proud, let yourself feel that excitement. Beam and look upon that accomplishment, big or small, as if you were your own parent looking down at yourself as a young child. Do some mirror work and say to yourself, "I am so proud of you! You are so amazing!"

Self-care.

Abandonment in childhood leads to self-abandonment in adulthood. We don't learn at an early age that we are worthy of being taken care of. Even if our basic needs such as food, shelter, and clothing were met, our emotional needs were often disregarded, even violated. Self-care is all about learning how to get your emotional, psychological, and physical needs met. It's about replenishing yourself during times of distress. Self-care can look like reaching out for help when you feel you're at the end of your rope. It can look like decluttering your physical spaces. It can look like exercising on a day you feel particularly down, or getting some sunlight when you feel stuck in a rut. There are many ways to practice self-care that allow you to come back to yourself, renewed.

Self-compassion.

Adult children of narcissists often struggle with an immense amount of toxic shame and self-blame for the abuse they suffered, as well as any cycles of abuse that were repeated in adulthood. Self-compassion is needed to counteract this shame. Whatever you have been through, know that the abuse was not your fault. When you find yourself feeding into a narrative about how you were unworthy, flawed, or defective in some way, or latching onto a comparison your narcissistic parent tried to instill in you, return to self-compassion. See yourself as if you were your best friend or as the helpless, innocent child you were. No one deserves to be treated the way you were. You did not deserve it. You were not at fault. You deserved so much more than this pain. Give yourself the compassion, the love, and the respect you always deserved as a divine human being.

Self-love.

True self-love means loving all the parts of you that you were taught to disapprove of. It means integrating your fragmented inner parts and coming to love your wholeness, just as you are. Self-love isn't just repeating affirmations to yourself all day, though that can be a part of your self-love regimen. A lot of the things we do to protect ourselves are actions grounded in self-love. When we leave a toxic relationship, this is an act of self-love. When we detach from a verbally abusive friend, this is self-love. There are many ways to practice self-love in order to reinforce the belief system that you are worthy of being treated well.

Self-sufficiency.

It is common for adult children of narcissists to search for a rescuer and a savior. After all, in childhood, no one came to rescue them. No one stood up for them or protected them the way they deserved to be protected and cared for. Self-sufficiency means that we learn to be our own protectors and saviors. Standing on our own two feet and meeting our own needs means we work on sitting with our feelings and meeting our emotional needs without overly depending on other people. It can also include meeting goals like gaining financial independence, having a place of our own, pursuing a career that fulfills us, being able to "take ourselves" out and date ourselves for a while, and learning to enjoy life even without the presence of a significant other. There are multiple ways to achieve self-sufficiency that do not have to involve our toxic parents or any other abusive person.

Self-esteem.

Being able to recognize our worth and value as a human being regardless of external circumstances is an essential skill to have when navigating the healing journey. Self-esteem allows us to stand firmly in our worth regardless of what others say about us or any rejection or disappointment we might encounter along the way. Regaining self-esteem can be challenging for adult children of narcissists who've been trained since childhood to always please others and care about their opinions. However, once we've grieved some of our core wounds, a space for healthy self-regard and self-esteem can be created. We can then react from that place of self-esteem, rather than neediness.

Self-actualization.

Reaching our full potential in multiple facets of our lives is the pinnacle of self-actualization. We achieve self-actualization as we incrementally work on our goals – these can include things like educational goals, financial goals, career goals, relationship and friendship goals, and self-care goals. That doesn't mean we give into perfectionism or overachieving from a place of "need" but rather a soul-directed sense of fulfillment whenever we meet those goals. Becoming the person we were meant to be and fulfilling all we were meant to achieve is valuable for adult children of narcissists who are taught that their only value lies in what they can do for others. It's up to us to also do things for ourselves, and to build a life that reflects a high sense of self-worth.

Self-validation.

In the trauma repetition cycle, adult children of narcissists become accustomed to seeking the validation of others, and to avoid abandonment. Because they did not receive the unconditional positive regard they deserved in childhood, they try to get it from others in the form of validation that they are indeed beautiful, successful, worthy, and loveable. External validation, while sometimes necessary and part of relational healing, however, cannot always satisfy us. We need self-validation: an inner knowing that we truly are worthy and loveable, just as we are. We have to slowly build that confidence from within, so that when we encounter people and situations that tell us otherwise, we are able to dismiss them far more readily.

Self-forgiveness.

Forgiving ourselves for things we shouldn't even have to forgive ourselves for. That is what I think of when I think of self-forgiveness. A lot of adult children of narcissists are struggling with self-blame and toxic shame over the abuse they suffered, or the trauma reenactment they went through with toxic partners in adulthood. It's important to forgive yourself – you were not to blame for the abuse you suffered. Another person's disordered behavior is not your fault. If you were a target of toxic people, it's because you threatened them in some way. You are more powerful than you know.

Self-respect.

Honoring our divine worth as human beings is important. Every day, remind yourself that you are a child of God (or the Universe, whatever you prefer). You deserve the same rights as anyone else. You deserve love and respect. You deserve to be happy and successful. You deserve to be free of mistreatment and abuse. Truly respect the survivor and warrior you've become, even after being victimized so much. You, of all people, deserve your own recognition. You really are that worthy.

Survey Says:

Adult Children of Narcissists On What They Recommend On the Healing Journey

"Be patient, kind, and compassionate with yourself on this healing journey. It takes as much time as it takes, do not judge your process and do what feels right for you. Learning to give yourself the same love and understanding you would give to others is key. I practice the RAIN of self-compassion I learned from Tara Brach when I find myself in critical thoughts. Be honest with yourself and learn to trust yourself. Keep seeking and you will find what you need to heal." — **Leia**

"Seek support. Don't do this alone. If you second guess your gut or intuition, seek outside support. Make sure you are working with someone who leaves you feeling empowered. If you feel confused, you are being tricked." — **Marsha**

"Remember that people SHOW you who they are. Take words at face value. Nurture your inner child with your adult self. Be your own best friend. Understand the abuse is not personal and that narcissists CANNOT love ANYONE. Cry, get angry. Let it out. Don't deny yourself any of the range of human emotions that you experience in relation to the abuse and loneliness you have endured. Do not allow yourself or anyone to shame you for being authentic with your feelings or for speaking the truth... even if it means standing alone! Avoid enablers. Zero bullshit tolerance. Laugh. What hasn't killed me has given me the biggest sense of humor. It has saved me many times. I still suffer, I cry, I feel lonely, I get scared, but I'm not ashamed of any of it." — **Clare, UK**

"Be patient with yourself. It's likely that your growth as a person was slowed down severely because of the abuse you endured. Find different ways to take your power back, meditation and being in nature works for me. Always remember you have the right to exist as a human just like everyone else in this world, and it's your right to feel however you feel. I would highly recommend finding a way to express yourself creatively, either through music, photography, painting, drawing etc. You can look at those expressions as being something which cannot ever be taken away from you." — **Tegan, Australia**

"Trust your body and gut feeling. Sometimes it can feel like you can't trust your own feelings and thoughts because of how screwed up you are from the years of abuse, but when you look at the hard facts, the way you and your body react to their presence, you will learn a lot! Don't feel selfish or guilty for leaving and putting up a boundary. You deserve to do good and healthy things for yourself!" — **Elise, Texas**

"Find good people to validate your reality. It's been the most important part of the healing process for me. Having someone else that I trust tell me that I'm not crazy." — **Lee, Tennessee**

"Go no contact sooner rather than later. The effect they have on you is cumulative. Learn to spot the signs of narcissism early in new relationships and avoid getting involved with such people." — **Anonymous**

"See yourself as the baby that you started out as. None of the abuse is your fault, and none of the recovery is your responsibility to suffer through alone. Keep looking for someone who can hear you and give you their undivided attention in listening to you. Validation is key. And we need a lot of it... over and over again. Peer counseling has proved to be invaluable." — **Nadine**

"You are not your abuser. You are not an extension of your abuser. You are not a narcissist because you've inherited some of their traits, and you're not a narcissist because you have prioritized self-sustainability. The fact that you've recognized an issue in someone else and applied the possibility of it to yourself - is proof in itself that you are not a narcissist. You do not have to be a statistic. You have a choice. You can redefine yourself, outside of your abuser(s), any way that you want. You will meet people who love and respect you. You will meet people who see you as more than a burden, that genuinely want to be around you for everything wonderful you can bring to their life. Someone is always willing to see beyond the collateral damage you have. You won't always feel this alone. And you will find people who are willing to put in the work to deal with your mistrust or anger issues." — **Nicholle, Calgary, AB**

"Do everything you can afford monetarily to heal: books, yoga, reiki, massage, therapy, meditation, etc. Decide that the most important goal of your life is to heal and free yourself from the invisible toxic tethers of pain inside, and start the journey. Your answers will appear." — **Pippin**

"3 things are needed to heal from the abuse: Talk, tears and time. You need to talk about what happened with a therapist, get the emotions out that have been trapped (tears) and allow yourself time to heal and grow. The abuse happened over a long time, so it will take a while to heal." — **Zosia, Tennessee**

"You aren't crazy! The fact that you are questioning this is the key to your sanity! No contact is crucial to healing, even though ten years in, I am far from healed. It takes so much time to acclimate to a non-toxic life. EMDR has been the biggest factor in my improvement, and I am still using it. Just know you aren't alone. When I finally realized I wasn't the only one with a sadistic mother that was actually hell-bent on destroying my life, I felt such immense relief. Stick with therapy, stick with continuing to weed toxic people out of your life, stick with putting your health and needs first and you will get better. It's a painfully slow process, but there is peace on the other side - at least there has been for me. I don't regret a moment of No Contact." — **Amanda, Texas**

"Learn as much as you can about Cluster B disorders through books & Youtube videos. Practice self-care without guilt: eat healthy, nutritious foods you enjoy, get the sleep you need, do yoga and some form of exercise; join a gym if your finances allow it. Vow to love and protect your inner child at all costs and work at replacing the messages of toxic shame in your head with positive, loving self-talk. Watch stand-up comedy, listen to music you love, draw/paint/write and be in nature and around animals as much as you can. Surround yourself with everything good." — **Imu**

"1. Go no or low contact with parents, and don't blame yourself for not feeling love towards your parents. 2. Have close people, who love and respect you, and don't behave the same way as your parents. Understand that you deserve to have what you want in this life and you don't have to please other people so that they would "allow" you do what you like. 3. Most importantly, always remember that you don't have to please anyone or abandon your point of view." — **Alyona, Moscow, Russia**

"Leave. Do better for yourself. Get help and talk to someone. People think therapy is a little bizarre or they feel uncomfortable but bouncing your mental thoughts (verbally/externally) with an unbiased third party is SO good for the soul! Also, make your own family. Family doesn't mean anything other than the people you pick to surround yourself with, so don't subject yourself to continued abuse from people who think their blood relation to you ought to keep you in their toxic line of fire." — **Devin Cotton, Texas**

"I would like survivors to know that just because they are your parent does not give them the right to remain in your life if they are toxic. ANY toxic person has the right to be eliminated from your life." — **Chastity, MS**

"I believe things happen for a reason. I believe we are all on a journey. Things always get better. Look to God - He IS there! If you don't mesh with your therapist, keep looking! Yes, you can afford therapy - some services go by your income. Last but not least, the gifts you receive when you come out the other side are immense! There is beauty, there is love, there is YOU. Be kind to yourself." — **Cindy, Evansville, Indiana**

"Learn to love yourself. You are enough. You can do this. Dig deep and find those pieces of yourself you hid away because of the criticism. I rediscovered my art." — **Phoenix Warrior**

"Remember that the NPD parent is not normal. You didn't deserve that treatment at all. Get all the information you can on NPD and find a therapist that deals with childhood abuse and CPTSD. You are not defective and deserve to be happy. Find what makes you happy. Do everything you can to erase the bad programming and replace it with loving, nurturing thoughts. Meditation helps, so does prayer for those so inclined. Medication has helped me through some rough times. Whatever it takes to make you thrive." —**Cealie, Queens, NY**

"No one can be your rescuer or substitute parent, stop searching and people-pleasing, you will be taken advantage of and thrown away." — **Carla, Minneapolis, MN**

"Support groups, therapy, bodywork, surrounding yourself with loving people that have empathy, staying away from toxic relationships, self-care, reading articles and books about narcissism, reading books about trauma bonding, staying away from bullies and abusive work environments." —**Nancy, Los Angeles, CA**

"As our society has *finally* acknowledged this disease, understand that none of it is your fault. Get into therapy as soon as possible to break the abuse cycle. Fix the damage the parent(s) have caused you before you get married and have children. I did this, and I am a much better wife and mother for it. Of course, I believed in mental health issues long ago and embraced stopping the cycle. So did my brother. We both are proud to say we did not become narcissistic by choice and hard work. But we do still deal with some PTSD." — **Denise, Iowa**

"Once I realized that my inner critic wasn't healthy, I was then able to identify whose voice it was and where it came from. My narcissistic parent took over my entire mind and wanted to destroy me from the inside out. Once I learned whose voice was in my head, I knew that the only way I was going to get better was to find myself, my own voice. I have to learn how to be the parent for myself that I needed and never had. It's the hardest thing I've ever done in my life. It's something I have to practice each day." — **Angie Powers**

"What really helped me was your book, Shahida. When I realized that my family knew what they were doing, were doing it deliberately, and were never going to stop, I was done with them. Until then, for 58 years, I kept trying to have compassion for them and tried to help. Until then, I could not conceive the fact that there are people who deliberately are like that. Even now it's impossible to understand, but I know I want to live, and it means never having a relationship with them." — **Kim**

"If at all possible, become your own best friend. Get away from rescuers and people or relationships which just keep you from being alone. I do not know of any other way to get to the root of the personal and individual needs that you are unaware of. There must be a place for abused people to find this out for themselves. No books or opinions (even of highly educated helpers) will find this out for YOU. It must be yours alone. I hope, wish, and pray for this for every survivor." — **Wejoly, Southern California**

"I am sorry you had a narcissistic parent. It's not your fault. You're not crazy. Educate yourself by reading books, blogs and watching YouTube videos about narcissism. Find a counselor familiar with narcissism and narcissistic abuse so you can be validated. Be a gray rock if you have to be around your narcissist. Don't react, keep things on the surface, go low or no contact to preserve your sanity." — **Lynn, Chicago**

"Seek Gestalt Therapists. Seek education regarding the tactics used by narcissists. Do core therapeutic work to identify shame, gain self-compassion, and strengthen your personal boundaries. Seek compassionate relationships and those who can gently hold you accountable for mistakes in relationships to build corrective emotional experiences and decrease shame." — **JoyTree5, California**

"I would tell them before you diagnose yourself with depression, anxiety, a mood disorder, or a personality disorder, make sure you are not surrounded by a narcissist." — **Nancy, Colorado**

"Move away from the familiar. Learn to be your own best friend and be as independent as you can be. Find strength in your independence, take it one day at a time (healing isn't linear), remember it's not your fault, accept that most people will never understand what you have been through, allow yourself to thrive. You are more than the voice(s) in your head, you are allowed to take up space and to be heard. Lastly, not everyone is worthy of knowing the real you and your real story— you don't have to share it with anyone you don't want to. Be your best self." — **Nikki, Orlando FL**

"Talk to a professional immediately, specifically someone who is informed and educated on this type of abuse. Do not be afraid to tell your story—but only tell it to someone that is safe. Take care of yourself. Do not ignore your intuition—if something or someone feels familiar (i.e., to past trauma), get out immediately. You do not have to relive the past. You and your inner child deserve to be nurtured and protected." — **Alex-Angela, Texas**

"A multi-pronged approach helps the most - that includes treatment of the mind, body, and spirit. I work extensively with clients with Complex PTSD from narcissistic families. Approaches which focus on empowerment are helpful to break the feelings of being stuck in the horror of this abuse. Very few people understand the enormity or pervasiveness of this abuse, so as a survivor you have to be careful who you share your experiences with. For both myself and the clients I work with, recognizing the deep impact of this abuse takes a long time to come to terms with." — **Suzy, South Africa**

"By all means go NO CONTACT if your circumstances allow. If you can afford it, find a therapist who has knowledge and experience in this area. The most important thing for me was that she validated me and my experiences and created a safe space for me to heal in. Read books, articles, blogs, YouTube videos that will help educate you on the language of narcissistic abuse and explain the emotions and cycles of healing that you will go through so you will be better equipped to handle the ups and downs and that teach you all the red flags to watch out for in future relationships. Practice self-care on a daily basis. Whether it is downtime to sit and read a book, getting a massage or luxuriating in a hot bubble bath or SLEEPING! Learn to how to get some peace of mind with meditation, yoga, spending time in nature, listening to music.

Surround yourself with safe loving people. Those people who love you know matter what. They will be your constants - the ruler to measure others by. Find a creative outlet for your pain, your memories and the HEALED version of yourself! Take photographs, paint, draw, write, sing. Find a community of support on social media or in group sessions. Try to get good consistent sleep because it's such a vital part of healing. Exercise. A good workout brings back into my body and out of my head space for a while. Practice yoga and deep breathing. Watch comedies or stand-up comedians. See if you can become a part of helping others in some way. This has been very empowering for me, because not only do I get to help, listen to and nurture another survivor, I get to solidify my own healing that much more deeply by practicing what I've learned. And above all else, be kind-hearted and ever so gentle with yourself. Take small steps and heal on your own timeline. There are no rules." — **Melissa, Florida**

"You can heal from this. There is a wonderful life waiting for you if you choose that path. Grab that inner child by the hand and say to him or her, "Hey it may be scary at first, but let's go on the journey of a lifetime… and don't worry, I will always protect you."
— **Layla, El Paso, Texas**

"Trust in your ability to rise above the childhood experience. As long as we breathe, we have the ability to choose. Good choices make us emotionally healthy. There is always a next time to improve things."
— **Sal, San Francisco**

"Figure out who you are at the core, soul level; your real self. Then honor your real self in all areas of life. Ask "does this honor my real self" before doing something." — **EvelynAura**

"Start with geographical separation before practicing emotional separation. Join a local community, adopt new hobbies, and reconnect with old hobbies from childhood. Experiment with different ways of expression (e.g. fashion, writing, interior design, tattoos, etc.) as a way to reconnect with the self. Practice yoga once per week and educate yourself on narcissism and/or high conflict people. Write down a list of things you won't tolerate from others and practice self-affirmations every day. Once established in a city, seek out a trauma-informed therapist and or trauma-informed support group. Augment therapy by keeping a feelings journal. Recommended book: *The Body Keeps the Score*. Remember, it gets easier every day." —**Moon, Houston, Texas**

"Realizing that they have the problem and it was not about me. Give that person the responsibility of the disorder instead of internalizing their negativity. Do not own what is not yours. We have a responsibility to get help to try to heal from this abuse. We also can learn to protect ourselves from future disordered people but this takes time, education and practice. It also takes a ton of self-compassion." — **Jessica**

"Work on yourself, practice self-love. Do what you need to do to heal yourself and your inner child. I cry when I speak to my inner child because I feel for her, but I let her know she's safe, she's loved and most of all that she's worthy!" — **Kelly, San Francisco, CA**

"Do everything you can to spend time alone and get to understand yourself, don't hide from the sadness, experience it. And just keep going. I'm not healed yet but I'm still working through a lifetime of abuse from my narcissistic parent and subsequently husband as I didn't look at myself or my situation before I replicated it. My greatest fear is it happening again. Educate yourself on these toxic relationships and then find a way to accept what happened to you and move on." — **Rosie, United Kingdom**

"Be gentle with yourself. Cry it out if you need to, but don't lay in self-pity for too long. Try to make the best out of this and maybe become a voice to help others deal with abuse. You are not alone. You are not to blame. You are loved. You matter." —**Jenny**

"Healing looks different for everyone but if you're willing to do the work it will come. Start with forgiving yourself for not knowing and not being able to control what happened. It's not your fault. Seek out a good counselor who is trained in trauma and C-PTSD. Join a trauma survivor/support group and learn how to make good friends and have good boundaries. Love yourself. It's ok to do that!" — **Jennifer, Michigan**

"It's time you put yourself first. Take a moment and ask yourself what you need, then do it. You are not alone." — **KC Hazel**

"Just because narcissism is a mental disorder does not mean that the offender(s) should be excused for their behavior. Forgiveness work should begin with you and in no way does it mean that you should forget. You are not a bad person for cutting off contact. You are, in fact, serving your highest good by choosing to care for yourself first and foremost. That is not narcissistic; it is self-loving." — **Dina**

"Identify which inner voice you hear. Is it the abuser or your gut? Each decision or emotion ask yourself why you feel this way. Who gave you this info to form this decision and what benefit would they have received by doing so? Understand it was nothing you did to deserve this treatment. They cannot change. There is no shame or guilt in cutting off unhealthy and toxic relationships regardless of who they are. Self-care is not negative. Not all family is blood. Not all family is healthy. Removing toxic energy opens the path for healing energy. Healing takes time. Be patient. Don't give up. Reward yourself at each new level. It's never too late to start over. Learn all you can about boundaries." — **MJ, Victoria, Australia**

"Give yourself time. Treat yourself well. Spend a lot of time by yourself. If you can learn to not be afraid of being by yourself, and even learn to enjoy it, that's over half the battle." — **Sue, San Diego**

"Don't give up. The fact that you think you might be crazy is a sign that you are not." — **Jessica Christina Weeks**

"My advice would be to find your passion and you'll find your voice. I feel following MY own path in life has lead me to the things I'm good at and, in turn, helped build my confidence. Once I had that everything else came easily until I became not 'the person I am today', but ME." — **Erin**

"My advice would be to move out of the city of your narcissistic parent so they cannot get to you. Also, practice acceptance. The child of a narcissist needs to accept they lost what was supposed to be a healthy loving and supportive parent. Once you accept that, then you are no longer trying to fight for their love. The fact is, they are incapable of giving love. Acceptance breaks the circle of their conditional love. I am going through this process now and it is extremely hard, but I know I am on the road to recovery. Realizing and accepting this fact, I believe, is the way." — **Leilani**

"Open your eyes to the abuse you suffered, take them off the pedestal. Read everything you can. Love your inner child - get a photo of you as a young child and speak kindly and lovingly to it daily. Learn unconditional love by getting a pet - my dogs give me purpose in my life." — **Lorna, West Sussex, UK**

"Find a safe person to talk to. The reactions of other people to my story affirmed that there was something wrong. Reflecting on educational material about narcissism and relating to everything that is being described helped me realize how big this is and how hard my parents worked at deception. No wonder it took me so long to identify what exactly the source of the problem was." — **George, Vineland, Ontario**

"Don't ignore your inner child that hasn't healed. Take the time to get to the root of your pain and begin your healing process through healing your inner child. Find a great therapist to help you through this painful journey and don't give up when it gets too hard. Lean on the people who love you unconditionally and care about you. Find groups of people who have been through the same thing. Learn about their lives and share your struggles with them. It's so enlightening to be able to share your life's journey with those who have been through similar struggles. Do things that make you happy and proud. Be the hero your inner child so desperately needed and love yourself for the person you are. Embrace your flaws and see how beautiful your flaws can be because they have made you the person you are. Don't chase perfection because "perfect" doesn't exist. Keep on learning and don't give up on your own happiness because it's out there for you to find. Fill your heart with love and respect for yourself." — **Anne, Massachusetts, USA**

"I found a therapist who specializes in survivors of narcissistic abuse. Her office is three hours from where I live, so we do our therapy over FaceTime. Having a specialist has been the biggest help." — **Lily, Bend, Oregon**

"The biggest lesson for me was that I'm not being disloyal by detaching from an abusive parent. I focus on facts and less on my emotions. I try to see the person for their actions more than for their words." — **Kelly, Ottawa, Ontario**

"It gets better. It takes time, but it will improve. It's okay to take care of yourself. It helps to remind yourself that the parent is disordered and it's not you or anything you have or haven't done. And despite what society says, you don't owe them anything just because they are your parents. You are entitled to take care of your mental and emotional health." — **Kara, New York**

Superpowers All Children

of Narcissists Have

Being the child of a narcissistic parent can make you feel like you're defective in some way. After all, this was not a normal, happy childhood – you went through psychological terrorism at a developmentally vulnerable stage. Yet the idea that you're somehow less than due to your adversity couldn't be further from the truth.

It's true that we have many obstacles on our path to healing and wholeness – but we *also* have some enhanced superpowers as a result of the traumas we've experienced. You are a fighter, a warrior and a survivor. Never forget that. You developed some mighty skill sets and a level of maturity that is unparalleled due to what you experienced. Here are just some of the amazing strengths and assets you likely developed on your journey:

SUPERPOWER #1
THE ABILITY TO ADAPT AND SURVIVE – PRETTY MUCH ANYTHING.

I have said this time and time again: children of narcissists are gifted with a resilience like no other. Their ability to "bounce back" from horrific incidents of abuse, something no child should ever have to do, can still serve them in positive ways too. This resilience gets used against us by predators, but what if we used that resilience to move forward and kick some serious ass every day of our lives? Metaphorically speaking, of course! We can use this resilience to remain determined even in the face of obstacles and continue to grow professionally, academically, socially and interpersonally as individuals. We can use this resilience to achieve our biggest goals and dreams.

SUPERPOWER #2
Our creativity, focus, and imagination.

Being a survivor means you learned how to overcome even the most brutal periods of your life and channeled them into something greater. As a teenager, my ability to focus on my teacher even in the most chaotic of classrooms was often remarked upon – and for good reason. I developed the ability to "tune out" noise and only focus on what I needed to as a result of the screaming matches I witnessed growing up. This survival mechanism in childhood has helped me in adulthood, too. I've been able to finish projects and meet my goals even in the worst of circumstances. I've been able to create in the midst of chaos and turbulence – and though I went through a childhood no child should ever be subjected to, I can't deny that some of my strength and ability to work well under pressure can be attributed to what happened to me as a child.

Often survivors of childhood abuse "escape" into themselves. They may dissociate and create fantasy lives to get a break from what is occurring to them. When we use this ability in unhealthy ways – like escaping from the reality of abuse in toxic relationships or shutting ourselves out from the world completely, we inevitably suffer. However, when we use this superpower in *productive* ways, we can tap into an infinite sense of imagination, concentration and creativity which is intense and vibrant. We can channel that creativity into the greater good and our highest good by creating art, writing, producing films, creating a photography project – the sky's the limit.

SUPERPOWER #3
An unparalleled ambition, resourcefulness, and drive.

The perfectionism demanded by the narcissistic parent did have *some* perks – it gave us the incentive to always "be the best," but it also provided the essential skill sets and resourcefulness on taking the initiative to do so. Children of narcissists learned how to move with shifting goal posts and cater to their parent's expectations of them constantly. They can use that same type of ambition, resourcefulness and drive towards their authentic goals too – the ones they *truly* desire to fulfill. Maybe you dream of creating your own business or going back to school. Maybe you fantasize about having a loving family one day. Your ambition doesn't have to be wasted. You can use it to create your best and most authentic life – professionally and personally. The trick is applying your need to "please" in the other direction – towards yourself. How would you make yourself happy? What would *you* truly be proud of accomplishing?

SUPERPOWER #4
The capacity for empathy and building strong bonds.

Having struggled through the horrors of a psychologically or even physically abusive childhood gives you acute empathy for others who have struggled too. Your ability to create long-lasting, deep and meaningful bonds is one superpower your toxic family members do not possess. Find creative and safe ways to use this empathy. You can use it to help other survivors, build friendships with nurturing people and use it to model empathy for those you care about (like your children if you have any).

SUPERPOWER #5

The ability to perform enormous amounts of emotional labor.

Your ability to "please" the narcissistic parent also gave you an added level of thoughtfulness and ability to tap into what other people need and desire. Use this power for the greater good by giving back to your local communities and to those who are actually capable of empathy and emotional reciprocity. You can be emotionally generous towards those who most need your compassion and will reciprocate it with respect – not abuse.

SUPERPOWER #6
A trained eye for discerning changes in their environment and detecting threats.

This is what I call "private investigator" mode. You were a detective, a cop, a psychologist and an FBI agent well before the age of eight. Remember that children who grow up in unpredictable or violent homes learn how to detect threats or changes in their environment early on in order to protect themselves. They can read nonverbal body language, notice microexpressions and catch changes in tone before someone's even said "Hello." You can use this superpower for discerning toxic people and detaching from them *before* you get involved.

SUPERPOWER #7
A sharp intuition.

You experienced a tumultuous childhood that came with plenty of emotional invalidation and gaslighting. Did you ever wonder why you were gaslighted so often? Well, it was because your actual instincts were powerful enough to expose the toxic person abusing you. Buried beneath the manufactured self-doubt was a sharp intuition about people and situations which your toxic parent tried to diminish and stifle. You "knew" things before you truly knew, which made you powerful and threatening to any abuser who attempted to manipulate you.

Practice honoring that intuition and you'll find yourself creating the life you always dreamed of. You will be able to spot toxic people and cut ties before you invest. You will be able to chase the opportunities that are actually meant for you. You will be able to say yes to that inner voice. You will find that you have not only survived your childhood, you can thrive after it.

Further Resources

BOOKS ON NARCISSISTIC PARENTS AND COMPLEX TRAUMA

Complex PTSD: From Surviving to Thriving by Pete Walker, M.A.

The Complex PTSD Workbook by Dr. Arielle Schwartz

Homecoming: Reclaiming and Healing Your Inner Child by Dr. John Bradshaw

Toxic Parents: Overcoming Their Hurtful Legacy and Reclaiming Your Life by Dr. Susan Forward

Mothers Who Can't Love: A Healing Guide for Daughters by Dr. Susan Forward

You're Not Crazy, It's Your Mother by Danu Morrigan

The Toxic Parents Survival Guide by Bryn Collins

Healing the Daughters of Narcissistic Mothers by Dr. Karyl McBride

Adult Children of Emotionally Immature Parents by Dr. Lindsay Gibson

The Drama of The Gifted Child by Alice Miller

Daughter Detox: Recovering from An Unloving Mother and Reclaiming Your Life by Peg Streep.

Healing the Child Within: Discovery and Recovery for Adult Children of Dysfunctional Families by Dr. Charles Whitfield

ARTICLES ON CHILDHOOD ABUSE, BULLYING AND COMPLEX TRAUMA

If you purchased the paperback directly through Amazon, you are eligible for the Kindle Matchbook program, and you can access the links below free of charge by reading the Kindle version of the book on Amazon. You can also google the titles of these resources to find them online.

The Complex Trauma Survivor Faces A Lifetime's Worth of Bullying
Grieving and Complex PTSD by Pete Walker
Daughters of Narcissistic Mothers by Darlene Lancer
PTSD and Complex PTSD: What Happens When You've Lived In A
    Psychological War Zone

VIDEOS AND INTERVIEWS

How Childhood Trauma Affects Health Across A Lifetime – TED Talk
    by Nadine Burke Harris
The Intersection of Complex Trauma in Childhood & Toxic
    Relationships in Adulthood – My Interview on the Savvy Shrink
Inner Critic vs. Healthy Internal Dialogue by Kris Godinez
6 Ways Narcissists Abuse Their Children by Lisa A. Romano
How Daughters of Narcissistic Mothers Can Survive & Thrive by Terri
    Cole

Links

[1] https://abcnews.go.com/US/40-years-jonestown-massacre-jim-jones-surviving-sons/story?id=57997006

[2] See my article, "50 Shades of Gaslighting" at www.thoughtcatalog.com/shahida-arabi/2017/11/50-shades-of-gaslighting-the-disturbing-signs-an-abuser-is-twisting-your-reality

[3] https://www.npr.org/sections/health-shots/2015/03/02/387007941/take-the-ace-quiz- and-learn-what-it-does-and-doesnt-mean

[4] https://thoughtcatalog.com/shahida-arabi/2018/03/ptsd-and-complex-ptsd-what-happens-when-youve-lived-in-a-psychological-war-zone/

[5] https://www.themeadows.com/blog/item/842-the-complex-trauma-survivor-faces-a-life- time-s-worth-of-bullying

[6] https://www.psychologytoday.com/us/blog/the-legacy-distorted-love/201302/will-i-ever- be-good-enough

[7] https://www.cdc.gov/violenceprevention/acestudy/index.html

[8] http://www.cirp.org/library/psych/vanderkolk/

[9] See "This Powerful Manipulation Method Keeps You Bonded To Your Abuser" on Thought Catalog: www.thoughtcatalog.com/shahida-arabi/2017/11/this-powerful-manipulation- method-keeps-you-bonded-to-your-abuser/

[10] See my article, "Your Brain on Love, Sex, and The Narcissist" on Self-Care Haven: www.selfcarehaven.wordpress.com/2015/04/27/your-brain-on-love-and-the-narcissist-the-addiction-to-bonding-with-our-abusers/

[11] www.pete-walker.com/shrinkingInnerCritic.htm

[12] www.sideeffectspublicmedia.org/post/childhood-trauma-leads-brains-wired-fear

[13] www.psychologytoday.com/us/therapists/allison-hutson-plano-tx/

[14] www.psychologytoday.com/us/therapists/lea-voigt-nashville-tn/384883

[15] www.brighteroutlookcounselling.com.au/about-us/

[16] www.psychologytoday.com/us/therapists/paul-s-brandt-sandy-ut/101649

[17] www.fernhill.com.sg/about-us/lilian-ing/

[18] www.psychologytoday.com/us/therapists/rebecca-johnson-cape-coral-fl/326342

[19] www.selfleadership.org

[20] www.tinyurl.com/IFSPart1

[21] www.tinyurl.com/IFSPart2

[22] www.tinyurl.com/IFSPart3

[23] www.tinyurl.com/IFSPart4

[24] www.beckinstitute.org

[25] http://www.getselfhelp.co.uk/freedownloads2.htm

[26] http://www.specialtybehavioralhealth.com/pdfs-cognitive-behavioral-therapy/

[27] http://www.martincbt.com/maladaptivecycle.html

[28] https://www.apa.org/ptsd-guideline/treatments/prolonged-exposure.aspx

[29] https://www.apa.org/ptsd-guideline/treatments/cognitive-processing-therapy.aspx

[30] http://www.emdria.org

[31] https://thoughtcatalog.com/shahida-arabi/2018/06/what-dialectical-behavior-therapy-is-and-how-it-can-save-your-life/

[32] http://www.traumahealing.org/

[33] https://www.psychologytoday.com/us/therapists/somatic

[34] https://selfcarehaven.wordpress.com/2016/11/04/breaking-the-codependency-myth-the-power-of-the-trauma-bond/

[35] http://coda.org/index.cfm/meeting-materials1/twelve-promises-of-recovery/

[36] https://www.intapt.com/

[37] https://www.goodtherapy.org/learn-about-therapy/types/gestalt-therapy

[38] http://psychcentral.com/news/2011/05/06/art-therapy-alleviates-ptsd-symptoms-in-veterans/25979.html

[39] http://arttherapy.org/

[40] http://www.verbalabusejournals.com/sound-files/detach-from-abuse.mp3

[41] https://www.youtube.com/user/josephcloughhypnosis

[42] https://www.youtube.com/user/MichaelSealey

[43] https://www.psychologytoday.com/us/therapists/hypnotherapy

[44] https://www.goodtherapy.org/blog/trauma-fear-phobias-elderly-0425137

[45] https://www.psychologytoday.com/us/blog/the-squeaky-wheel/201401/nlp-experts-speak-out

[46] https://groups.psychologytoday.com/rms/

[47] http://coda.org/

[48] http://www.meetup.com

[49] https://drugabuse.com/support-groups-12-step-programs/

[50] http://www.traumacenter.org/research/Yoga_Study.php

[51] https://www.washingtonpost.com/news/inspired-life/wp/2015/05/26/harvard-neuroscientist-meditation-not-only-reduces-stress-it-literally-changes-your-brain/

[52] http://www.meditationoasis.com/

[53] http://download.meditation.org.au/

[54] https://www.youtube.com/user/YellowBrickCinema

[55] http://www.tinyurl.com/LucyRising

[56] http://www.tinyurl.com/EMDRSoundTherapy

[57] https://www.youtube.com/user/josephcloughhypnosis/

[58] https://www.youtube.com/user/MichaelSealey

[59] http://iarp.org/find-reiki-practitioner-teacher/

[60] https://www.tinyurl.com/ReikiHealing

[61] http://www.ncbi.nlm.nih.gov/pmc/articles/PMC3265077/

[62] https://www.ncbi.nlm.nih.gov/pubmed/18230238

[63] http://www.suzannebovenizer.com/aromatherapy-essential-oils/the-limbic-system

[64] http://blog.nicholassieben.com/

[65] https://nccih.nih.gov/health/acupuncture/introduction

[66] http://aaaomonline.org/

[67] https://www.ncbi.nlm.nih.gov/pmc/articles/PMC4528099/

[68] http://alcoholrehab.com/addiction-recovery/music-therapy-in-addiction-recovery/

[69] https://www.musictherapy.org/

[70] http://www.cnn.com/2013/04/15/health/brain-music-research/

[71] https://www.psychologytoday.com/blog/brick-brick/201402/does-music-have-healing-powers

[72] http://www.health.harvard.edu/blog/healing-through-music-201511058556

Printed in Great Britain
by Amazon